# ENGLISH IN EDUCATION

# ENGLISH IN EDUCATION

*A selection of articles on the teaching of English at different levels from infant school to university*

*Edited by*
Brian Jackson
&
Denys Thompson

1962
CHATTO & WINDUS
LONDON

Published by
Chatto & Windus (Educational) Ltd
42 William IV Street
London, W.C.2
*
Clarke, Irwin & Co. Ltd
Toronto

*These essays were originally published in* The Use of English *under the editorship of Denys Thompson. The present selection, introduction, and commentary is by Brian Jackson.*



Printed in Great Britain by
T. and A. Constable, Ltd
Hopetoun Street, Edinburgh

# CONTENTS

# *Acknowledgements*

The authors and publishers make grateful acknowledgement to the following people for permission to include copyright material in this book: to Mrs W. B. Yeats and Messrs Macmillan & Co., Ltd., for W. B. Yeats' poem 'An Irish Airman Foresees his death' taken from *The Collected Poems of W. B. Yeats*; to Messrs J. M. Dent & Sons, Ltd., for extracts quoted from *The Shadow Line* and *Nostromo* by Joseph Conrad; to A. P. Rossiter's literary executor for an article entitled 'An Exercise in Applied Criticism' which first appeared in *English in Schools*.

I

# INTRODUCTION

THIS book is a selection of articles published in the last twenty-three years by the *Use of English* and its predecessor *English in Schools*. They take up problems of English teaching at many levels, through precise discussion of classroom conditions in this school and in that. To the practising teacher they offer a generous harvest of tips and reminders.

This is one way of putting it, and a very practical one. And yet the impulse behind these essays rises from deeper and more troubled concerns than this suggests. They establish a dialogue that reaches out, not merely to doubt this mode of teaching English or to affirm that, but to draw into question the very nature and quality and direction of our civilization itself. For all the contributors write from a common concern with the centrality of English studies in our time: a centrality which has to do on the one hand with transmitting a cultural heritage in a world ever less ready to receive it, and on the other with a training in the use of language which shall (despite environment) define and nourish growth in the young, rather than blur and obstruct it. This is why passages playing critically over matters of judgment, over the place of grammar and linguistics, over the very tools given for use in the classroom, pulsate with a more than ordinary urgency.

The first section gathers together pieces of children's writing that teachers have placed before other teachers in the *Use of English*. They are of different kinds and qualities, and from varying occasions: a much-pondered poem for the school magazine from a seventeen-year-old girl, a hot, scribbled intimacy from the diary of a seven-year-old boy: 'then my mummy held my hands together and said Good night, the Champion of this house'. They are drawn together not simply as an anthology, for they are not quite that – but as a gathering of voices, children at work in the schoolroom. Preceding a succession of essays from teachers, they record the child's presence, the direct human particular around which discussion will move.

Often they do more than this, and in very distinct ways open up themes that have troubled the journal's audience over these twenty-three years. It is encouraging to meet a small boy's sardonic response to daydream advertisement: 'if I ever met such a boy in real life I'd give him a punch on the nose'. And encouraging to read a young girl's prose as it feels its way into values of skill and labour: 'the master himself supervises the corners and takes a personal pride in making them clean and square'. For it was out of this concern for the workaday bases of culture in a civilized community that young people have been invited to reject the trivialities of the press, bookstall, screen, advertisement, and encounter the prose of, say, Sturt and Conrad. Such moments speak for reserves of strength in children and in teachers vital enough to resist an increasingly soft and erosive environment. As we read, it is worth noting how the writing has come about.

The strength, often enough, is nurtured by way of a training in which the quickened attention directs itself to delicate sensory notation, picking up, in the urgency of communication, the very rhythm and stress of the speaking voice. The voice of a young boy still growing into the formal skills of language: 'The three newts I caught, two were a bright orange on the belly with big black round spots all over, the other one was smaller and was a muddy colour and its belly was a bright orange with very small spots on it. I mean, the spots on this one were only on the belly, not all over.' Or of an older girl compelling further strength from just that formal mastery:

> Fallen raindrops cling to the lupin leaf
> In tiny, spherical balls, like drops of mercury.

At deeper levels still, probing into more elusive areas of desire and fear, techniques of free writing release verbal formations which record not so much a child struggling unrewardingly with formal syntax, as dragging back from consciousness language nearer the moment of birth, words moving towards each other in the initial act of definition: 'a cavern of death-to-be, so hot, so hot, a maze of gas with dragon's teeth . . .'. We might well read alongside such prose, work from that other boy who, in the sharpened moments when the doctor's needle pierces his arm, achieves a kind of impersonal correlative embodying release and barely controlled fear: 'I felt the fine needle enter my skin. In the next room, which appeared to be an office, there was a sudden outbreak of typing. I felt myself shiver. . . .'

Merely to glance over this informal collection of prose and verse, pondering the more compelling moments ('Words are our subtillest and delicatest outward creatures being composed of thought and breath') is a useful way to take our bearings, and to prepare entry for the general themes that, under the pressure of particular classroom discussion, are to be introduced.

II

# *'A GATHERING OF VOICES'*
# *CHILDREN AT WORK*

## *Diary*

Yesterday I ran in the school sports. First it was the shuttle, then it was the flat race. First it was me and I won, and then it was Charly and he lost because he kept looking round and I won the final. . . . When I got home I had some hot milk and some cornflakes. Then I got undressed and then I washed my face and cleaned my teeth and had my coff-micksture then my mummy held my hands together and said Good night, the Champion of this house. Then I went up the stairs and got into bed and said to my mummy night-night, and I went to sleep, and I had a hot and exciting night, but I got to sleep eventually and I had good dreams too.

*Andrew, aged 7*

## *The Onlooker*

As day dies, the air becomes drowsy
  With the sweet, irresistible perfume of the honeysuckle;
And foamy cones of double-white lilac
  Sway rhythmically in a barely-detectable breeze.
Fallen raindrops cling to the lupin leaf
  In tiny, spherical balls, like drops of mercury;
Even the upright iris shames the peony,
  Whose rich, cerise head droops into its encircling leaves.
  From the apple-tree only, Nature has taken
  And of blossom and fruit has left it forsaken.

*Girl, aged 16*

## *My Visit to the Hospital as an Out-Patient*

As I alighted from the trolley-bus I wondered by which gate of the hospital I should enter – the main or the back gate – for I did not know the hospital at all well from my last visit, having been rushed there in the middle of the night and having come home by taxi after my operation and recovery. All I knew was that the hospital grounds were very large.

I decided on the back entrance, for I seemed to remember that the Pathological Laboratory, which I was to attend, was nearer there. After checking on the numerous direction-boards I was able to find the place; it was situated quite near to my old ward, but was unlike the other buildings in being built of wood instead of brick. In fact it was not unlike a large hut. I knocked and entered.

Men and women dressed in white overalls sat busily testing test-tubes of blood. Bunsen burners were alight on the benches. As I entered, my card was taken and I was told to remove my raincoat and jacket and sit down. I looked around me: many bottles of chemicals were arranged on the shelves and I saw a large refrigerator in one corner with the notice – 'The nation urgently needs blood-donors. Why not you?' Much glass apparatus lay about the benches and the smell of ether was particularly apparent.

Finally the doctor (I called him this only I do not think it was his correct title) who had tested the B.S.R. of my blood before when I had been in hospital came up to me. He had my card. 'Ah, ex-Robin ward, eh?' I replied with a nod and he told me to roll up my sleeve.

Now before I had been in hospital I would have dreaded having the needle, but now after being made like a pin cushion for weeks I did not mind it. The doctor tied a thin piece of rubber-tubing lightly around my arm near the shoulder. I had the skin cleaned with some ether and then I clenched my hand as I had done before and looked away; I think it is always better to do this. I felt the fine needle enter my skin. In the next room, which appeared to be an office, there was a sudden outbreak of type-writing. I felt myself shiver, not through my blood test but through the bitter cold. I was told to open my hand. Quickly the needle, together with a sample of blood in the syringe, was withdrawn. For a few seconds there seemed to be a gap in my arm. The spot was cleansed and a small plaster stuck over it. I dressed, and meanwhile the doctor filled a small bottle with the dark red blood from the syringe.

That was all, and as I left the hut a man passed in. I walked over to my former ward and looked through the window. Tony, the little boy with the burnt hand, was the only one I knew.

*Boy, aged 14*

## *Free Writing*

A terrible earth, so beautiful, so beautiful, too beautiful to be, soared above me, a mighty mount with a mantle of descending air too cold to flow like mercury. Yet down below there was a cavern of death-to-be, so hot, so hot, a maze of gas with dragon's teeth like red-hot irons: such a fiery wall of death. Yet where I stand, a medium spot, not cold not hot, from this pleasant place I watch this terrible earth.

*Boy, aged 10*

## *Waterfall*

A shining arc curves majestically,
Thundering down on the glittering rocks below;
Little fountains rise from the commotion
As if, trying to escape the tumultuous water,
They take the air.
Droplets of water dance like may-flies
In the shimmering world.
A salmon leaps from the tumult,
And for one brief moment
Hangs stark in the sky.

*Geraint, aged 12*

## *Advertisements*

Everyone has seen the small boys in advertisements who catch crooks and then eat some food or other that they are advertising. I always read their adventures, and the more I read them the more I hate these boys, particularly one little chap named Tommy Chester. This yellow-haired brat goes about with two other silly idiots, and between them they manage to catch thugs, rescue children from under 'buses, save people from drowning, and do other noble deeds. Then at the end of every adventure someone pats Tommy on the back and says, 'You did a great job, my boy. What would you like for a reward?' And Tommy Chester answers, 'I want Chester's Choc Ices, because they keep me fit and strong.' Somehow they always have enough money to buy about ten ice creams a day. Pity they aren't sick. If I ever met such a boy in real life I'd give him a punch on the nose.

*Boy, aged 13*

## *Diary*

16 May.

I found an ants nest in our lawn and I dug it up an I saw that it was nearly 1″ down and I found the nest with some egg shaped thing in the middle and the ants were dragging them away they seemed to be mostly workers but there were some small black ones with wings and the workers were collecting the black ones and driving them into the ground with a large ant at there hed. I think that it must have been the Qeen.

17 May.

The ants nest I dug up yesterday is deserted exept for some remooval men clearing up their furniture. All the small black ants have gone and I think they are like the ones we had last year in our bathroom wall, they came in millions and covered the whole of a large shelf and what was werse was that they started flying and landing in my hair and in the wash basin. We sqerted flit at them and pored boiling water on them but they made an awfull mess afterwards.

*Campbell, aged 10*

## *Frost*

A cart has clawed a track and frost has cracked and cut
The clay which brittle grass
Will clutch, till sap is spent
By bites of wind, which whisk all warmth to cold and chill;
When spiky frost will
Prick and probe stone walls
And gull will pierce an icy air with shrieking calls.

*Girl, aged 17*

## *Milk*

Once I went on a visit to a dairy farm. I saw the cows being milked, they were milked by machines. There was a bucket under their tummies. Then the farmer took it to another machine to be cleaned. Then it had to be put into big milk churns. The cow has to be milked twice a day. It is useful when it is dead as well. We get beef from it and its skin is used for leather, and its horns are used for knife handles. It feeds on grass, it has four stomachs. He gets a lot down him, I will tell you why he does it. Because a long time ago, wild animals came and ate him up, that's why he still does it. He has still got a habit of that. The food goes down one stomach, that is called a paunch. Then when he gets into his barn he brings up a little at a time. He does not bring it up in a great pile. After he has had a lot to eat, he has to be milked. After, as I told you, it is cleaned and brought to the market place and sold to the dairy shops and some is delivered by milk-men and comes to houses. My mother has one pint a day. A good cow gives 600 gallons a year. Once I was helping the milk-man for a day. I saw him milk his own cow with his hand with a bucket underneath its body. Once he tried to milk it with a machine but it kicked and kicked so he could not milk it. He brought my mum one pint because she must not have over one pint a day.

*Boy*

## *Diary*

1st April. Rainy with sunny periods. After breakfast I went out to get some newts. I got a large jar, washed it and put a stone in it, then went to poplar pond with a stick and a tin.

It was cold and very windy. After about a hour I had caught one femail newt. I was frozzen. I could hardly feel my hands they were so cold. I half filled the jar with water and a few water weeds and put the newt in. In the afternoon I tride to get abother. I saw one just out of my reach. I waded out a bit and foregot that I had a hole in one of my wellington boots. The water just flowd in. I didn't catch any more newts, and went home with a boot full of water. I'm going to try and get some more to-morrow and I hope I have better luck.

2nd. Very rainy dull and wet. To-day I made a fishing net, not to catch fish but newts. I cought six. I picked out the ones I thought best. I kept three and let the others go. There were lots of newts in the pond to-day I daresay they like this kind of weather.

The three newts I caught, two were a bright orange on the belly with big black round spots all over, the other one was smaller and was a muddy colour and its belly was a bright orange with very small spots on it. I mean, the spots on this one were only on the belly, not all over. The one I got yesterday was a dark yellow ochre.

All afternoon I sat watching them, I think they are very interesting things.

*Boy, aged 10*

## *On Looking at a Picture*

I know the sort of person who lives in this house. He puts barbed wire on his gate and a notice saying 'Trespassers will be Prosecuted'. That'll be the day when I see a notice saying 'Trespassers will be forgiven'. Also he puts broken glass on the wall and stops up the holes in his hedge so it's no use trying to scrog his apples though he has more than he can eat and they lie on the lawn being eaten by wasps and buzzers. If he did catch you inside he'd probably empty both barrels of a shot gun into the seat of your pants or more likely pretend not to see you so that you would think you were getting on fine and then ring for the police. He is very kind to birds as you can see by the bird table and I expect he hangs up coconuts for the tits in the winter but he doesn't like human beings especially school boys and would probably kick a poor beggar down the steps. Mean old bastard.

*Trevor, aged 12*

## *Hay-making*

On a small farm one skilled worker directs the whole operation of hay-making; part of his effort goes into every load of hay and his word is law.

He comes into his own towards the end of June, when the hay has already been cut for a day and lies like a dull blanket on the fields. He confers with the sky and the wind and together they come to an agreement that rain will be withheld for four days, so now the blanket of hay will be turned. Quite nonchalantly he spears the hay with a fork, with a quick flick of the wrist he turns it in the air like a cook tossing a pancake and it settles down again with a rustle. Only when he has done the whole length of the field do we realise that the hay has formed up into very straight green rows.

The next day, after the sun has dried the dew, the hay-maker comes out to the fields armed with an evil-looking rake. He throws the rake away from him, like a sailor throwing a coil of rope, and drags the hay towards him and up into hay-cocks. He progresses down the rows, his brown arms flashing in the sun, and he never stops for rest, for his is the hardy strength of the countryman.

In the afternoon he loads the hay-cocks on to the waggon and he talks to no one, for the tractor has replaced the horse. With a fork he folds the hay over and over until he can lift the whole cock safely; then, his muscles rippling with the weight, he swings the enormous pile of hay onto the waggon. The expert knows just where to place each fork load so that the hay will be packed evenly and tightly, and survive the jolting of the waggon down rutted lanes to the farm.

Once back at the farm, the hay-maker starts his most difficult job, that of building the rick. The foundations are easy, it is the first and top floors that give trouble. The eager helper below on the waggon passes up a load of hay; they hay-maker, high on the rick, holds the load while the first fork is withdrawn, then with a tremendous heave, he flings the hay into the centre of the tick. Other workers spread it out and stamp it down, but the master himself supervises the corners and takes a personal pride in making them clean and square. The rick is gradually shaped inwards until there is only room for one on the top and we wonder however he will find place for the last waggon-load; but he manages it and by his smile of satisfaction we know that he had planned the size of the rick down to the last pound of hay.

Then he goes round the rick combing out the loose hay with a fork, rather like cleaning a coat with a clothes-brush, for the hay-maker is essentially a tidy man.

His task is now finished and the expert goes home and leaves his rick to sink before the thatcher gives it its straw sou'wester as protection from the winter weather.

*Girl, aged 15*

## *Hiroshima*

Noon, and a hazy heat;
A single silver sliver and a dull drone;
The gloved finger poised, pressed:
A second's silence, and
Oblivion.

*Boy, aged 15*

## III

# *NOURISHING THE CREATIVE SPIRIT*

In this section three teachers explore problems as they declare themselves in primary or secondary schools. It is a moment to turn over questions of 'sincerity' and 'imitation' in children's writing, and more importantly, a place to consider how and from what sources the creative spirit can be nourished now. Mrs Marshall begins with the inherited strengths of common idiom; Mr Holbrook with the ample reserves of folk-song and work-song – arts which, though of slender importance and range in our society, yet have a special place and continuation in the school. Mr Reeves draws in the poetry of the present; and all three move outwards towards music, drama or art in order to make that total address to the personality by which growth in these terms can be sought and celebrated.

# *English and Idiom in the Primary School*

SYBIL MARSHALL

NOWADAYS, whenever an educationalist opens his mouth to speak, a few words are bound to fall from his lips on the teaching of English: the importance of English as a basic subject; the necessity of giving it a prominent place on the time-table, and of making sure that the school-leaver possesses enough of it to be able to fill in forms at the labour exchange. Even if the educationalist does not emphasize these points, his audience, generally composed largely of teachers, understands that this is what is meant by 'the teaching of English'. It seldom occurs to anyone that the phrase might possibly be used to mean that children should be taught to love and respect their native tongue.

At the word 'English', the average primary school teacher is bound to conjure up in his mind's eye the printed sheets of 'intelligence', attainment (mechanical reading and comprehension), and secondary-school-selection-examination tests which for him are the criteria of primary school English. While the educationalist pauses for breath, Miss Jones mentally reviews the time-table of her junior school, and wonders if, by substituting another English lesson for IVA's one weekly art period, she could achieve better results in next year's comprehension tests. It might be, that with that much more practice, even young Smith would underline 'inhabit' instead of 'cohabit' in the context of natives and palm-fringed islands. Miss Jones leaves the meeting determined that it shall be so, and also that her next meagre requisition allowance shall be stretched to cover the cost of yet another set of the books of 'English Extracts' (with ten laboured questions on each one) that a colleague has recommended to her as being of 'real scholarship standard'.

The teachers cannot be blamed for this utilitarian attitude towards English; neither can the educationalist who dictates policy or suggests method to them in grammatically correct 'officialese'. The truth is that 'education for all' has proved to be a mixed blessing, for with a little knowledge of English has come an overwhelming degree of linguistic snobbery. To 'speak well', or to write 'good English', has come to mean to speak or to write within certain well-defined limits which are set by snobbery. The pseudo-educated peasant endeavours to speak and to write within these limits that his lowly origin be not suspected; the tenth baron in his open-to-the-public castle throws away his heritage of full-blooded English lest he be thought different from his half-a-crown visitors.

Education has ironed out the creases in the English language, and in doing so has also destroyed the texture of the material; or, to change the metaphor, the sophisticated beauty, the rosy country wench and the raw-boned fishwife are now all so coated with the make-up of convention that they now appear plain, uninteresting and indistinguishable. Is it a matter of wonder that no one bothers to give them a second glance, and that none arouses in any heart a grand passion or an abiding love?

The small child is the first to notice the out-of-the-ordinary, the first to be impressed by individuality or eccentricity, the most susceptible to the influence of robust vitality, in whatever form it appears and from whatever source it emanates. Observe the alacrity with which the aforementioned haphazard selection of 'extracts' is exchanged for the American type comic at play-time; listen to the toneless voice reading one of these meaningless extracts aloud, and then to the same voice, in the very next moment, as its owner greets a crony in the playground with a string of epithets learned from a gangster film, and hear the vitality flow back into it; to do that is to understand what has happened and is still happening to our own language. It is also to realize that small children have need of something more than the plain, bare bones of 'good' English they are offered as their continual diet in school. Robbed as they are today of their natural heritage of local dialect, and discouraged far too often from using that gift all small children have of inventing their own words and phrases to fit the experience of the moment, they turn instinctively to the nearest and most accessible form of linguistic vitality. The language of film-land has the same fascination for the child as the witch-like visage of the mad woman on the corner of the street. Though we should all discourage him from staring, most of us would hesitate to suggest that the proper object of his gaze should be the plain, honest face of his teacher. We should all have enough sense to know that if we want him to forget the witch we must attract his attention with something equally interesting. Text-book English is no substitute for American slang, and if we hope to encourage children to choose English buns instead of American candy, we must at least leaven the dough. If English as a living language and opposed to American is to be preserved for posterity, the last remnants of it must be seized and revived while yet they exist. It is in the schools that the ironing-out process must be arrested, and the revivifying of our native tongue begin.

The task before the teacher is no easy one. How can the socially conscious parent be made to realize that a good, solid English idiom is as acceptable from the lips of her eleven-year-old son as its modern equivalent coined yesterday in the streets of New York? Or a word retained from local dialect, perhaps with an earthy tang to it, but its roots in Anglo-Saxon, as suitable at drawing-room tea as a catch-phrase learned yesterday in the cinema?

Every village still contains a few folk who speak the tongue of their fathers unadulterated by too much 'education' or too many visits to the pictures. At their command is a language full of concrete imagery, pointed idiom, expressive words and phrases, and amusing metaphor, in which they can express themselves with clarity, subtlety, heavy sarcasm or delightful irony.

'I can't abide them fur-lined snowboots,' says an old countrywoman to her granddaughter, 'they make you look like *a feather-legged old hen.*'

'I started business without much capital,' says an old countryman. 'I went into business with Charlie when we were both about twenty. I had one gold sovereign, but Charlie were *as bare o' money as a pig is o' side pockets.*'

'How are your 'taters this year?' says one smallholder to another. 'Well,' replies the other slowly, with a wry smile, 'there's some as big as walnuts, and there's some as big as Basseloney nuts, but there's some very small.'

This is the kind of language we are giving up in our search for a false sense of respectability. There is still time to rediscover it, if we begin at once. The first positive thing to be done is to encourage in small children the ear for the word which will best fit the occasion, whether it be an age-old dialect word or one invented on the spur of the moment. The danger lies in continuing to impose a too-correct, flabby, devitalized and too respectable English.

Countless examples spring to mind. A four-year-old boy holds up a finger to his teacher and says 'Please will you cut my "jagger" off?'

His teacher, reaching for her own dainty manicure set, complies with the request, but replies, 'What a horrid word, Matthew. Next time, you must say "Please will you cut off my broken finger nail?" '

Now I have no doubt that in this instance the word 'jagger' was invented there and then, and I am not suggesting that it should henceforth be included in the Oxford Dictionary as a synonym for a broken nail; but to me it does express the peculiar discomfort that a broken finger nail occasions, and a child who can invent a word such as that has ears to hear.

A small girl born and brought up in the lonely depths of the fenland says wistfully to her teacher 'I wish when Christmas comes he'll bring me a sucker 'ug.'

'Rose! Rose!' comes the scandalized reply, 'Never let me hear you say that again! I suppose you mean "a sugar pig"? And you must say "hope", not "wish". Now say it all again, "I hope when Father Christmas comes he will bring me a sugar pig".'

But the child no longer cares, for what excitement is now left in the remark? The difference between the forward-reaching longing of 'wish' and the sedate reasonableness of 'hope', only deep desire can know. And what have the bony consonants of 'sugar pig' to do with the fondant succulence of the vowels in 'sucker 'ug'?

Again, I am not suggesting that I should deliberately encourage such expressions within range of the august ears of H.M.I.; but to forbid them without cause, and above all to make the child ashamed of having used them, is to make him distrust his own ear for the subtleties of his native language. After all, what is objectionable about the phrase Rose used? 'Hog' is a recognized synonym for 'pig', and the sound of 'o' and 'u' interchangeable in the most genteel circles. In the days of my fenland childhood, all 'sweets' were called 'suckers'. And in the name of heaven, why not? The word 'sweet' can mean almost anything nowadays, and can describe anything and stand for anything from a royal personage to cold sago pudding; as Feste says 'the word is overworn'. But 'sucker' conveys a suggestion of a movement of the body, and with Puritanism and respectability coalescing as they are at present, any word that does this is regarded as 'not quite nice'. So 'sucker' is now considered as vulgar as 'confection' or 'comfit' would be archaic. What remains—'Sweet' or 'candy'?

One last illustration: a mixed class in a tiny provincial grammar school had been set an essay on 'Horses'. The fourteen-year-old son of a smallholder had been stimulated by the subject and had excelled himself. He was invited by his English mistress to read his essay aloud to the rest of his form. After describing in vivid detail the process of grooming a horse, he read out 'When I have finished one side, I say "Cum uvver" and the horse stands over to let me get at his other side'.

The mistress intervened. 'Cum uvver?' she queried.

The boy eyed her with a look in which chagrin at this needless interruption was mixed only with pity for her ignorance. 'Well, Miss,' he explained, 'if I had said "Cam owvar", our horses wouldn't have understood it.'

Such fertile ground must be cultivated at all costs, even if a few tares grow together with the wheat; above all, the good farmer will sow good seed, and the teachers must follow his lead by making certain sure that the standard of English they set is such that will bring forth fruit an hundred-fold. I hope to be allowed to suggest, in another article, some ways of making English grow again, ways I have tried out and found to be workable, though once any teacher realizes the necessity for action, he can work out his own plan of campaign; for as my favourite country proverb says, 'There's more ways o' killing the cat than choking it wi' butter'!

## THE INFANT SCHOOL: APPROACH BY WAY OF ART

If we may now take for granted that the aim of the English lesson in the primary school is to enable children to speak, write, and in general, use and appreciate English which is straightforward, explicit, vigorous and exciting, we can proceed to discuss the means towards this end.

It is recognized that one of the first essentials of English teaching is to get the children to talk and to keep them talking, and for this reason infant class time-tables often show a period called 'News'. Many teachers must find this lesson valuable, or it would have died a natural death before now. I must confess that I cannot understand its value. To start with, I have never experienced any difficulty in getting children to talk – my problem is more often finding a way to stop them talking long enough for me to get a word in edgeways. Secondly, I do not flatter myself that they all want to talk to me, personally; nor, necessarily when the clock says 9.30 a.m.; least of all at my command. Thirdly, I do not expect them to be interested *at will* in other children's news. To a five-year-old child one person's news only is really important – his own. He wants to communicate his news to everyone, but in his own time, and his own way. In effect, he wants twenty private conversations instead of one general one organized by an adult. In this, surely, his instinct is right. Conversation is private and individual, and the level and style of the particular conversation depend on the people engaged in it. One has only to listen to an interview on radio or TV to realize how boring and embarrassing a 'guided' conversation can be.

So, right at the very beginning of school life is a significant pointer to the fact that English, of all the subjects in the curriculum, is of necessity the most individual. One simply cannot organize English teaching on the same lines as a hundred yards flat race. There is no definite starting-point, no set pace, no finishing tape. The best anyone can do is to see that every child runs in the right direction.

No two children start at the same place, because their temperaments, their pre-school environments, the impact of their teacher's personality and many other influences all bear upon their conversational abilities. They must want to talk, not to please the teacher, but to please themselves, and they must have something to talk about. The stimulating variety of creative apparatus in the modern infant school provides plenty of material for conversation, and the talkative, verbally well-equipped child is the best of all teachers for the slow and tongue-tied one. The role of the official teacher is to be there when wanted or needed, and to be so unobtrusively part of the class that she is included naturally in private conversations at all levels. She must be able to talk as easily to the shy, timid child who in a moment of excitement pulls at her skirt and utters 'Boy kick ball', his first sentence in her hearing, as to accept with sang-froid the reply of the sophisticated young gentlemen of five, who, when asked what he was looking at, replied, 'I was just considering what 'straordinary long eyelashes Mary has!' Both children have found words to use because they have something to say worth saying. The first inkling of the link between thought and word has been gained: the next step is to find means of strengthening the link.

I believe that even at this very early age the capacity of children for understanding the spoken word is greater than most adults realize. This is the age for rhymes and jingles, songs and folk-tales, well worn, straight-forward, repetitive; neither 'larded with words of foreign origin' to quote Lord Chesterfield, nor reduced to insanity by 'talking down'. The language and idiom of such stories as 'The Hobyahs', 'Tom-Tit-Tot' and 'The House that Jack Built' are the children's own, by inheritance. 'Little dog Turpie barks so loud I cannot *slumber nor sleep*' complains 'the little old man' in 'The Hobyahs'; '*Quick as a wink*', the little Red Hen flew up to a beam; while 'that little old black thing just sat there, *but lawk! how that twirled that's tail!*'

Though these expressions are only imperfectly comprehended, and could not be paraphrased in words, they are enjoyed and assimilated, and luckily, words are not the only means of expression available. To draw comes almost as naturally to a small child as to speak, and while vocabulary remains limited, the picture is the best stepping stone between thought and the written word.

The child's ability to draw a picture of anything recognizable by an adult matters not at all. A tiny boy projects the thought of a train on to a piece of paper by a few bold lines and squiggles executed in red paint. For the next few minutes he may be quite incapable of distinguishing a real train from his picture, or himself from either of them. His concept of a train includes them all, and he will perhaps pick up his picture, hold it in front of him, and rush, choo-choo-ing and whistling, round the room. If, by accident or design, he crosses his teacher's path, the chances are that he will begin to talk to her in words suggested directly by the movement, rhythm and colour of his momentary but intense experience; words, quite often, that many a professional writer would give his eyebrows to have at his command.

May I now become practical and describe my own method of using art as a means towards vigorous written English? (My school is only a tiny village one, and I am aware that in large classes the method could not, perhaps, be followed exactly; but that is a good thing, for the stamp of quality of any teacher is his ability to make the method fit the class, and thus give it the hall-mark of individuality. Nor do I attempt here to deal with any of the mechanics of reading or writing, but presuppose them to be proceeding normally all the time.)

When the infants have settled down in school, and have had a few weeks to experiment with the various media of art work, I make each one a simple sewn book of sugar paper and choose a rhyme or story well known to them, for instance, 'The House that Jack Built'. On the first page the children are invited to draw (in whatever medium they care to choose) a picture of the house. Opposite the picture I write the words, letting each child see me do his own book, and while doing it converse about the picture. The next bit concerning the malt may need explanation, but after that the rat, the cat, the dog and the cow are all well within the children's normal range of experience. Then the rhyme begins to expand, and with it the children's power to grasp and enjoy the extra information given in the words. 'The maiden all forlorn' is drawn with tears as big as turnips rolling down her cheeks, and all over the class impromptu dramatic portrayals of her are being given. 'The man all tattered and torn' can't wait till the next day to get into the story. While 'the priest all shaven and shorn' may need explanation, the farmer sowing his corn and the triumphant cock crowing on the last page combine folk art with folk idiom.

From this point onwards, thought, picture and word go together in the child's mind, and at a later stage, when the picture can be omitted, the absolutely essential principle of good written English has been established, that is, that thought must precede word.

The next step can be a set of books round a central idea, 'The Bus Station', for example. Each child draws a picture somehow or other connected with this theme, and tells me what he wants to say about it, so that now, though the theme is common, the subject-matter is individual. From that to the next step, which is that each child should contribute his own idea for a book, is easy, and before long the exciting climax is reached, when he can produce a story in pictures and words, unaided except for spelling.

Meanwhile, interest in the spoken word is never allowed to flag, and the instinctive search for the right words to describe a specific experience goes on all the time. Matthew, aged four and a half years, wanted to paint a witch – was dissatisfied with his effort, and painted another, and another and another. (As an incidental point of interest to those not used to small children's creative efforts, he painted every one upside down; that is to say, with the tip of the witch's pointed hat towards him, and her feet up in the air.) Finally, he produced a recognizable witch, and brought it proudly for me to see. 'Oh, Matthew,' I exclaimed, 'what a lovely witch.' His face fell, and he answered shortly, 'No, she's a horrid witch!' I realized my mistake and asked what made her so very horrid. By this time the rest of the school was interested, and suggestions came in 'as thick as hail'. 'She's ugly.' 'She's cruel.' 'She eats little boys.' 'She's a ragged witch.' 'She's a vicious witch.' 'Ugh!' said one of the older girls, shuddering dramatically, 'when you say "vicious witch", it makes shivers go up and down my back!'

To return to progress towards command of the written word, I would like now to illustrate it by reference to the work of one child. Jeffrey is, in our country parlance, 'a real old boy', which means that he is a healthy little tough of average intelligence. He came to school at four and a half, and took to it like a duck to water. His first book was unintelligible to anyone but himself: at five he had done 'The House that Jack Built', followed quickly by 'The Farm' and 'Jeff at School'. Then one day he came to me in great excitement and said 'I want to make a book about my donkey that ran away'. I knew he had never possessed a donkey, but that made no difference. The story of 'Jeff and the Runaway Donkey' was a great success, and had to be read and shown again and again to the other five-year-olds. By this time (about five and a half) he could read fluently, and while making this book Jeff grew very impatient at having to wait for my help, and made gallant attempts to write his own sentences. After the summer holidays a much more mature Jeffrey discarded my help altogether, and produced 'Jeff, the Brave Cowboy', only asking me for spelling and help with punctuation. The progress shown in this book was astounding. The story was complete, and adjectives began to appear. 'Jeff had a horse called Silver Star. It had a star on its face. Star could run very fast and jump very high.' Later in the story six Red Indians appeared. 'Jeff drew his sick shooter. Bang bang it said and they all fell on the ground.'

The success of 'The Brave Cowboy' inflamed Jeff (now about six years old) and almost before the paint was dry, he was away on 'The Dog Fight'. This was a new departure, because it was an attempt to describe accurately an incident he had seen on his way to school. His knowledge of grammar was not enough for this, and he enlisted my help. He wanted conversation in it. We talked it over and he understood. His mother appeared in a picture, carrying a pail of water to throw over the fighting dogs. 'How can I make it say what Mummy said?' Jeff asked. 'I told you the other day,' I answered. 'Have you forgotten?' 'No,' he replied. 'I know how to make it show that she was saying it, but not *how* she said it. She didn't just say "stop it" – (he struck a pose and mimed the throwing of a pail of water across the room) – she said "STOP IT!" '

During the winter Jeff joined the others in writing and illustrating his own version of the Christmas story, but after Christmas he turned author again, with 'Jeff and the Flying Bird'. This was the story of Jeff, the bold, bad pirate. I thought it time to drop a gentle hint that authors should know something of the subject-matter about which they choose to write. I supplied various books which Jeff read avidly, and for a spell 'The Spanish Main' came as glibly from his tongue as 'the village pond'. Again, the natural progression in the use of English showed. Opposite a picture of Jeff on the prow of his ship with the Jolly Roger flying above him, Jeffrey had written, quite spontaneously, 'Jeff held his tellscope up to his eye. What did he see?' The introduction of the rhetorical question here was the solution of his problem of expressing tension in words. (Another little girl did the same thing at almost the same moment, in describing our recent Christmas festivities. 'Did the people enjoy our plays? Yes they did.')

After 'The Flying Bird', came 'Jeff the Space Man' (the real Jeff now nearing his seventh birthday). After a morning's work he brought his new page for me to inspect. I read, aloud, 'Jeff pressed the button and the space ship swished up into the air and was gone'. The real Jeff was pressing an imaginary button on the side of my desk. Then he clutched the pit of his stomach with both hands, gazed upwards at the ceiling, and said, 'Coo! Can't you just hear it!'

All children have not Jeff's gift of imagination, though he is by no means an exception. Several others have produced as many, if not as exciting books as Jeff in the same time and at the same age. The process of thought before word is always evident. A girl of six, writing about a child called Jane, lost in a wood, brought to me a picture of the child being cared for by a friendly bear. In the background was a small house among the trees. I said, 'You've forgotten the chimneys.' Sarah said nothing, but went away. Later on, reading her morning's works, I read, 'The reason why the house has no chimneys is because bears have such warm fur that they do not need fires.'

In the same book was another amusing example of Sarah's capacity to think. On starting to write one day, this young authoress had the misfortune to get her book upside down. She had only written the word 'This' (in ink!) when she discovered her mistake. In distress she sought my advice. I suggested that she leave it and start the right way up, adding 'Perhaps when you get to the bottom of the page it will work in, somehow.'

The page described the bear's efforts to provide a bed for his guest, but at last a camp bed was borrowed, and Jane got in it. 'She was so tired that she turned over on to her stomach and went to sleep like "sıɥꞱ".'

There are, of course, the slower children, whose stories consist only of an unrecognizable picture and a few jumbled words. This kind of work is a pointer to the child's ability, and it is safe to say that the satisfaction derived from the actual doing of it is the best stimulus in the world towards better work, and that no other form of English instruction produces any better work from such children. Let me add here one technical point. This age has been dubbed 'The Eraser Age', and on such creative work the eraser may be permitted, but the red pencil, never!

Nevertheless, however successful this spontaneous writing may be, by the end of the infant-school stage, and in any case by the time the children are eight or nine years old, it is not enough by itself. Without reinforcement from other sources, it begins to deteriorate. Some children become self-satisfied, and go on producing books in which no progress is made; some become too ambitious, and bite off more than they can chew, defeating their own end, and their teacher's; some become too involved with the illustrations and subordinate words to picture; and some, worst of all, simply turn lazy and reproduce the trash of the ubiquitous comic.

The clever teacher will anticipate this inevitable end of the infant-school stage, and with her junior-school colleagues, prepare for the next. If she has faith in her methods, she may even be the one to light the fire into which the colourful bird she has tended so carefully is about to flutter. All that anyone can hope for, in its place, at least for a short space of time, will be a brood of ugly ducklings, of which quite a few may yet turn out to be swans: and it is always possible that one day there may even be a phoenix.

# *The Point of Making Things up: Composition Work in a Modern School*

DAVID HOLBROOK

THE first attempt I ever made in trying to stimulate imaginative composition was by reading with the children two poems (they had read similar poems in poetry lessons in various ways – dramatized or spoken in chorus, and in an 'A' stream they had been asked questions on them) – the sea shanty *A Yankee Ship*, and Arthur Waley's *At fifteen I went with the army*. I concentrated most on the pattern of *A Yankee Ship*, but threw in the other as a make-weight for those who might produce poetry without a regular form, or in a form they chose themselves.

> A Yankee ship came down the river;
> *Blow, boys, blow.*
> Her masts and yards they shone like silver,
> *Blow, my bully boys, blow.*

I described the shape of this – two chorus lines with their beats, which could be as nonsensical as one wished, and the two changing narrative lines which needed to have four 'beats' and to rhyme.

I touched, I think, on the child's relish for objective 'third ground' of nursery rhyme and folk-song where troubling things can be contemplated in phantasy. Some of the poems were conscious or unconscious reminiscences, but in so far as they are departures they represent individual explorations of experience within the same objective mode:

> Once there was a girl called Mary,
> Oh la, oh la,
> She milked the cows in the farmer's dairy.
> Oh Mary, la.
>
> Oh she was tall and slim and fair,
> Oh la, oh la,
> She combed her golden hair with care,
> Oh Mary, la.

But she is there no longer now,
Oh la, oh la,
For she looks after the one-eyed sow.
Oh Mary, la.

She hopes that she will wed one day,
Oh la, oh la,
The handsome farmer's son, in May,
Oh Mary, la.

*Girl, 2nd year, 'A' stream*

There was an old woman,
That old woman,
A very old woman was she,
That old woman.

She was as merry as she could be,
That old woman:
She danced and sang a riddle-de-de,
That old woman.

When she was tired,
That old woman,
She got in a bed that she had hired,
That old woman.

She was dead that next morning,
That old woman,
She died at the dawning,
That old woman.

*Girl, 1st year, 'B' stream*

Themes of love and death – intolerable and embarrassing to the child outside phantasy – are here dealt with directly, and have taken on their own simple level the timelessness and resignation of the folk-legend. The boys, on the whole, were technically more able, concerned less with the 'human situation' perhaps, and expressed their experience of life in technical virtuosity. This is a competent version:

A pirate ship once sailed the sea,
Heave, boys, heave,
She sailed into the pirates' quay,
Heave, lazy boys, heave.

She came in loaded up with gold,
Heave, boys, heave,
And also slaves to be sold,
Heave, lazy boys, heave.

Her terror filled the Spanish Main,
Heave, boys, heave,
And all that struggled, they were slain,
Heave, lazy boys, heave.

*A lazy boy, 2nd year, 'A' stream*

but these show interesting technical explorations in onomatopoeia:

The Bawdsey 'bus came down the Strand,
Honk! Honk! Honk!
Inside there was an army band,
Clang! Clang! Clang!

The conductor was a tall old man,
Click! Click! Click!
He was so hot he had a fan,
Swoosh! Swoosh! Swoosh!

The driver had a big moustache,
Twirl! Twirl! Twirl!
To look at him you'd think him posh,
La de da de da!

The 'bus looked like an old tin can,
Rattle! Rattle! Rattle!
Each seat was like a frying pan,
Frizzle! Frizzle! Frizzle!

The old 'bus reached its destination,
Screech! Screech! Screech!
They all got out and caused creation,
Clatter! Clatter! Clatter!

*Boy, 2nd year, 'A' stream*

and in end-rhymes:

A silly dog went to the dog show,
Ha, de, ha.
Although his owner did not know so,
Ha, de, ha, de ha!

But all the neighbour's dogs did know it,
Ha, de, ha,
And all the owner said was, 'Blow it!'
Ha, de, ha, de, ha!

And when that doggie made way homeward,
Ha, de, ha,
His owners said, 'That' dog's gone boneward',
Ha, de, ha, de ha!

*Boy, 2nd year, 'A' stream*

Both use their technical interest to explore a kind of nonsense-fantasy which has the slightly ironic commentary on life which the nursery rhyme has ('But all the neighbours' dogs did know it' reminds one of Pope's

I am his highness' dog at Kew:
Pray tell me, sir, whose dog are you?)

But some of the poems not written to the suggested pattern turned out to be the more personal in feeling, though maybe it was possible for them to be so written while the others were writing the more stylized poetry – the 'third ground' was assured. This, for example, by an orphan (that she was I only discovered later):

Jimmy Hast went out to play,
On a bright and sunny day:
Mary went out with him too,
Lost her doll's shoe that was new.

Mary was a naughty girl
To get the scissors and cut a curl:
Jimmy was a naughty boy,
Broke his car and brand new toy.

No one loves them, not at all,
Won't even let them play at ball:
So you see they're very sad,
Much the opposite to glad.

*1st year, 'B' stream*

And some of the 'free' poems turned out to be in the folk-song mode, too:

Spring is a season
All happy and gay;
Flowers have a reason
For blooming in May.

Flowers grow up
And buds come out,
Animals wake up
For the world wakes up.

*Boy, 2nd year, 'A' stream*

An owl flew into a barn;
The barn belonged to a dairy farm.
The farm was big,
As big as a pig.
The pig was fat,
As fat as a vat.
The vat was round,
As round as a mound.
The mound was ground.

*Boy, 2nd year, 'A' stream*

These poems weren't the result of any 'spontaneous creative' urge of the children: they were produced by the stimulus of my emphasis on a mode and a technique – that of the nursery rhyme and folk-song. Their creative activity was thus twofold – controlling their own experience in terms of mastering a technique. How successful they were appears at times when the speaking voice breaks through the scheme of the poem in its excitement:

No one loves them, not at all,
Won't even let them play at ball. . . .

Flowers grow up
And buds come out. . . .

And it seemed to me that the achievement of the 'know it' – 'Blow it'; 'homeward' – 'bone-ward' poem, and that 'barn-pig-vat' piece of nonsense, which has such an air of completeness, made a great difference to the two authors – neither very bright – in their attitude to language.

For one technical success which satisfies the child can provide a foothold for some advance in expression: but the teacher must know where he wishes to lead the pupil. I was discussing recently with some teachers a passage of strained film advertisement. While most condemned it, many said it represented a form of accomplishment ('If I could write stuff like that I shouldn't be teaching'). It is not commonly recognized how easy it is to write such stuff. One needs to learn only a few cliché modes: the hard task is to get the true rhythms of life. Some children acquire sophisticated conventional styles easily – and I was able to read my group of teachers this, by a boy in 1B, asked simply to 'write a short story':

> Suddenly a man came from behind a tree with two guns. He was not quick enough. Jesse's hand dropped to his holsters and in a flash his twin colts roared, and the Sheriff of Sante. Fe, his chest riddled with hot lead, collapsed in a heap on the trail.

He has the idiom and cadence of the Wild West perfectly, and to master a style like that suggests an interest in language which will bring dissatisfaction with its very limitations later. A more accomplished pastiche of the style is the following – however alien to these little boys the idiom seems the rhythm shows a real excitement in imagined incident (that the writer is aware that this is a pastiche is shown by his 'Wild Woolly West'):

> About seven years ago on the plains of the Wild Woolly West there was a wagon train travelling through Indian territory. The leader of the train was a scout named Rod Cameron. Rod, who had been scouting ahead of the train, suddenly came galloping back, shouting 'Indians on the warpath! Circle those wagons! Bill, you ride on to the fort and try and get some help!'
>
> 'Sure thing, Rod,' shouted Bill.
>
> 'What about the women and kids, Rod?' asked an old cowpuncher.
>
> 'Better get them under the wagon,' said Rod.
>
> 'Here they come,' shouted Jim Blake.
>
> The battle started. Men on both sides were killed. Twice the Indians retreated, but came on again bringing even more men each time. There were pitiful yells from each side, 'Ai! Ei! Ugh! They got me!'

The cowpunchers were rapidly getting less while they were still about a thousand Redskins left. The cowpunchers had hardly any ammunition left. Suddenly a wagon caught fire, then another, then another, until there were only seven wagons left out of the twenty-three. Suddenly Mike, a cowpuncher of about sixteen years of age, who had never taken part in a battle before, went outside the circle of wagons and was caught by some Indians who scalped him.

The Indians retreated again. While the Indians were away the cowpunchers were attending to the wounded people. The results were plumb bad. There were fifteen people dead and twenty-seven wounded, leaving only twelve men to carry on the battle.

'Well fellows, I guess this is the end,' said Rod.

'Hey, Joe! How many cartridges have you got left?' asked Rod.

'Fourteen,' answered Joe.

'Well, with my six cartridges that leaves us twenty altogether,' said Rod.

Suddenly the peace was shattered by a war cry. 'Here they come!' shouted Joe. The fight started again and after about fifteen minutes there were twenty more Indians dead. Then above the sound of battle came the sound of a bugle. The soldiers from Fort Worth had arrived. The Indians turned to face the soldiers and the fight commenced. The soldiers won and so ended the battle of Bitter Creek.

*Written and published by the one and only Ian Laidlow*, 1B

The writing is indeed superior to many stories in comics which I have read: it does not strain, the detail of the to-and-fro of events is rendered with great clarity (a numerical accuracy suggestive of Defoe's), and some of the rhythm is appropriate – 'Suddenly a wagon caught fire, then another, then another.'

For this reason it seems to me that the teacher who 'takes himself down' to what he considers to be the child's level (of the kind of text-book which condescends to children by using words like 'smashing') or who tries to teach by using comics in the classroom is betraying the child. The child has more interest in language than the writer of the comic, and knows it; the teacher need only wait for an opportunity to show this to him explicitly, and offer standards by which the advance can be made, away from the stultifying habits of language which the comic and comic strips aim to give him. They may even make something of their own from cheap journalistic modes.

Take these passages from two very dull boys in 1B. They combine an aggressive sophistication with a naïve childishness. But what is there in the way of observation and excitement gives a clue to the teacher where to lead:

Once upon a time there was a boy and he had a little pup called Toby. They went rabbitting and a gamekeeper said, 'Hi, you, get off this land or I'll kick you up the behind.' Toby and me never went rabbitting in his field. I only caught one little bunny that day.

It was on a Saturday afternoon when I was standing on the slope watching the speedway. There goes Denis Day, here comes Arthur Pilgrim, thundering round the track. Yes! and he's catching up on him, a-a-oh . . . and he's past him. 'One, two, three, four, what did we come for? W, I, T, C, H, E, S, Witches!' And here is the score: Arthur Pilgrim 3, Denis Day 2, Ray Wright 1, and if I count right Ipswich is the winner. The scractch race follows. Titch Read won nearly every race. Denis Day is only eighteen with no kids.

Even this latter disjointed, Joycean piece has a rhythm in places which betrays an excitement, and his reproduction of the chanting of the word and the manner of the loud-speaker commentator shows some observation. If the English teacher can direct that excitement and observation on to other themes he may take the writer's attention beyond the dirt-track.

These prose passages all come from an exercise with the one form 1B, at which, after several periods of making up stories orally they were asked simply to 'write a short story'. The only 'control' here was in the previous discussion by me of their oral stories which were in the nature of 'serials' – i.e. an episode was told by one child and continued by the next – though they had previously written poems on the above system (see the two poems from 1B above). Most of the children revealed a remarkable ability to tell stories. With about half, this may be traced to the influence of their mothers who read to them, or at least provide them.

## PEPPER AND SALT

It was a May morning when two little kittens were born. One was named Pepper, the other Salt. When they were old enough to play, Pepper said to Salt, 'I can climb higher than you.'

'No you cannot,' said Salt.

'Well, we will see who can climb the highest,' said Salt and Pepper both together. So off they went and found a tall fir tree. They went up and up the tree to the very top. When they got there they found they were both on the same branch. When they tried to get down they could not. They cried and they cried.

'It was all your fault,' said Pepper to Salt.

'It is not,' said Salt.

'It is,' said Pepper.

'It is not,' said Salt.

'Don't argue,' said Pepper.

Just then a bird flew by. Pepper shouted out, 'Will you help us?' but the bird took no notice and flew away with a 'cheep, cheep'.

Just then a they saw a pair of green eyes. They came up the tree very slow. When they were near a voice said, 'It is about time you were in bed,' At last they found out it was their mother, yes, their very own mother. She took the kittens one by one in her mouth down the tree. When they were down the tree they climbed in the kitchen window and went in their box and fell fast asleep.

Such children carry off the openings of their stories with a competent flourish:

It was early morning on a July day. The golden corn was waving in a field. The scene is Gladbrook Farm in Suffolk.

The farmer had just got up and was coming down into the kitchen, where his wife was cooking the breakfast.

'Good morning, George.'

'Morning, Martha. That smells good. What is it?'

'Egg omelette.'

But children, as I have learned later (and these paragraphs I am adding to this original article), have also an intuitive ability to use the imaginative story to explore life. Indeed, without such capacities for phantasy a child cannot properly grow up as a whole person at all: the phantasy is as vital to growth as physical adventure and recreation. This is not recognized fully enough in schools. But it means that the teacher who gives children the frequent experience of disciplined silent attention to written composition is providing a most valuable opportunity for the child to develop. If teachers are not convinced of this through their own experience of creativity, or the sustenance they have drawn from creative art, they may find the psychological reasons perfectly expressed by the great child psychoanalyst, the late Melanie Klein, in her short essay *Our Adult Society and Its Roots in Infancy*. There she discusses the means in child and adult of apprehending experience through phantasy and how this primary activity of the human mind is associated at the baby stage with the child's attachment to its mother. Because the mother is identified with everything that is good, the phantasy developing round her begins at once to go with moral discrimination. This is later an important means towards self-possession, to developing a high opinion of oneself, and towards the greater moral discriminations required of the adult. Thus phantasy goes with the development of character: and Melanie Klein's pamphlet thus vindicates phantasy activity, in private inward dreams, but also in imaginative activity associated with all that we call art, as a vital means towards personal integrity and stability, and towards social order. This psychiatrist, after her lifetime's work with children, virtually comes to emphasize as one of the most important influences in human life and society those activities which we may call poetic.

Her essay explains the powerful moral interest often to be found in children's work, its simple intuitive mysticism, and its rhythmical vitality. It helps us to make up our minds what to commend. Here are some examples, exactly as they are written by second year 'A' stream children, in another school:

### THE SEA DIVERS

Sam Faith and his girl friend lived by the sea, her name was lotte. Sams Father owned a small yacht he also had two sets of Frogmens out fits.

One summers day Sam and Lotte went diving in the Indian Ocean about twenty miles from where they lived.

They put on their gear, and loaded two spear guns because there were sharks about. They went down to one hundred and fifty feet. They held hands as they swam down.

They found a sunken ship which had been torpedoed by the Germans.

As they were examining the wreck lotte caught her foot in between two Iron bars as she was struggling to free herself, a shrk dived at her.

Sam fired the spear the shark wriggled and sank to the bottom. As he freed her he grabed her and took her by the neck, and pulled her to the service and into the boat.

When she came round, he asked her to marry him she said yes and flung her arms around him and she kissed him and they stood kissing for five minutes. Then he took care off her ankle, and they sat with their arms around each other. When they was on there way back, a storm arose and the sea was wild and open up and swollowed Sam and Lotte.

They were found hand in hand on the shore and the surf rolled over them.

From the strip cartoon on the cereal packet this boy makes, of himself, the myth – of Tristan and Isolde. It is not only that he is contemplating what it is like to be man to a woman as part of his growth to sexual maturity – but that his deeper levels of phantasy awareness perceive the nature of love – that there is, in the giving of oneself in love a kind of loss of self which is like death. This is the theme of many great myths, such as Tristan – 'O'ed und leer das meer' – which contemplate the ultimate significances of human relationship in time, and the mortality of men. It is a theme of Shakespeare's *Sonnets*, and of the writings of T. F. Powys. The theme of death in love may be seen in its sickest form in the poetry of Dylan Thomas, who could not come to terms with the loss of the self in love at all. But here we have a little boy experimenting with an unhappy, frustrated, ending, and, deeply, in his own intuitive way, with a great human theme. All the teacher has to do is to respect and secretly cherish such revelations and explorations.

At times the child's vision of the possible disasters to which flesh is heir is obviously part of a crucial stage in growing up: here a little girl imagines an earthquake, with the courage of the child who stands on the verge of the seismic changes in the self which adolescence brings:

## BURIED ALIVE

We had been walking down the High Street when the Earthquake had shaken the whole town, we had glanced up at the great mountain, fire and smoke was billowing out from the top of the crater. The air became hot and stifling and the sky a glowing red mass. For seven terrifying day's now the mountain had been threatening us, now its anger was beginning to descend on us. 'I say Jean we better hurry up and get home to mother, she won't be able to manage the twins and Jane as well, oh if only dad, wasn't at work.' Jean was my 10 year old sister and the twins were only 3 and almost everything frightened them and if a storm came they'd howl all the way through it, and this was no ordinary storm. Jane was only five as she wouldn't be able to help. So Jean and I ran for all we were worth to our house only built 6 months previously after our cottage had been completely destroyed by a fire resulting from an earthquake. The mountain gave another warning rumble as if to urge us on further. When we did get in sure enough the twins were causing havoc, and Jane and mummy and Jean some how, how I don't know, managed to pacify the twins. Then suddenly it came another fierce crash and a deep rumbling, peoples screams rent the air, children were crying for their mothers and fathers. The the house shook, slowly as if to torture us it seemed the walls of the house began to collapse, we had had it we would never be able to get back to the safety of the yard. Jane began to cry for the dogs as iff to make matters worse, then, thankfully I saw the dogs crouched in a corner where the kitchen door, had once stood, I pointed them out to her, and mercifully she at once became quiet.

This is a literate child: but the value of her work is that her moments of advanced expression are not here for display to the teacher, but indulged in for the purposes of dealing, coping, with a situation which tests her powers as an emerging adult: 'this was no ordinary storm', 'mercifully she at once' – she is experimenting with the language of the competent adult, mastering a catastrophe. In this she is striving towards greater self-possession, though the end reveals that she is still in the sheltered context of home:

Strangely enough when I did reach her all that was the matter was a badly cut and broken leg, and concussion. Mummy wept with relief. We remained like this for 36 hours when mercifully men came to our aid amongst them was Daddy. Everyone soon recovered after a week in hospital that is nearly everyone because Jean had to stay there for a month. But everyone said 'What a brave little girl she was.'

There always seems to me a great courage behind such writing, the courage of contemplating 'what men choose to forget'. Only a little while after this piece was written we were reading of children at Agadir suffering what Lesley here bravely considers as possible.

The greatest problem with children's imaginative work is for us to detect when they are thus engaged in explorations close to their deeper interests. We cannot, of course, expect this of them all the time, any more than we may expect it of an adult poet or novelist. But we may apply the same tests as we apply to adult writing: the chief test being that of rhythm. This it is almost impossible to convey without reading and discussion. But here are some examples of writing that seem to me to have the rhythms of that sincerity for which one must strive. They range from the captured rhythms of the football match commentator, to that of the wisdom of the small boy about marriage, who speaks aloud in written words, and the rhythms of spiritual apprehension in the child, restrained by a quiet, undemonstrative awe. These are by no means exceptional children, and it is this kind of writing one may obtain from any child, irrespective of streams and intelligence quotients – for it is the voice of the heart, in which all men are equal, to some degree.

## A CUP FINAL

Saturday May 7th Cup Final day at Wembly, 22 men will be hit with wembly nerves. 22 men will walk on to the wembly turf to the cheers of 100 thousand people. The teams line up for the kick off, the game is between Aston Villas and Manchester United. They kick of United had kick off. Violet pats it chalton who roles it back to crother who puts to Edwards who boots it down middle for violet to chase but is beaten by Villas centre half Dugdale who puts it to Crowe who centes it to McParland who heads for goal, it is a feeble header and goes straight in to woods hands but McParland chalanges wood and they both coilide into each other and the roles over the goal line for the first goal to VILLA. United kick of again but it is not long before Villa are attacking again and a centre by Lyne is headed againt the cross bar but McParland volleys in the rebound to put Villa two up. United kick off with 11 minetes left to play, Violet put the ball to Taylor who put it back to dawson who centreres for Taylor to head

United only goal. By winning the cup VILLA have made a new record by winning the cup seven times.

### SHOULD A WIFE OBEY?

Yes, because the husband goes out to work and earnes all the money. On Monday, most wives do the washing on Monday and the man comes home to dinner she still hanging out the washing and theres no dinner waiting for him he's got to fry him self some bacon and eggs for dinner and no man likes that and he gives her half of his wages and hardly gets a sqare meal once a week. On Tuesday most wives go to Cambidge to buy a new hat or a skirt while when he comes home he finds a note saying back 20-2 gone cambridge by new had dinner in the oven custured under grill. They only do house work and they have all the afternoon of because they have finshid by dinner time.

### A HYMN

God came from the Heaven above
And Jesus was his only son
Who was crucified by pontuis pilate

But he arose form the dead
And when his mother came to mourn for him.
He had rissen once more
And returned again unto his father

But he appeared again
To his disciples one day
Then he broke the bread
And blessed it
And then having showed
The nail mark to
Doughting Thomas he vanished

But he appeared to them again
On a mist covered hill
And talking to them for a little while
Was taken up for ever.

Once a teacher has a sense of what to find in children's work, and what to encourage, then the exercise of imaginative composition may take almost any form – the use of poetic models, or the making of plays, or composition stimulated by the reading aloud of short stories. Sometimes a good form will readily undertake to write a long story of exploration or some other substantial matter, progressing week after week, perhaps with illustrations, maps and all, helping to sustain the phantasy.

To return to my account of work with the children discussed at the beginning of this article: the stories were read out by me at various times – about once every three weeks, I suppose, each child could expect his story to be read aloud, and they had roughly two periods a week given to writing it. I marked errors regularly in light coloured pencil (simply using symbols: 'S' for spelling and '⊙' meaning 'you need to start a new sentence here') and they corrected them in the text. The adventure story of exploration was a conventional medium, like the folk-song mode, for their own dealings with experience. Many of the stories began with legacies which made the expeditions possible, but the stories on the whole weren't thin improbabilities – the children either used the unfamiliar scene to write about their own experience, or did realize their inventions vividly. Again the emphasis being on the finished product, on the technique whereby some thing was realized, and because feelings and fantasies were respected, nearly all the books contained what I sought after – the page or paragraph where the desire to express had over-ridden the labour of spelling, punctuation and 'construction', and the true rhythms could be heard.

Some children have a remarkable interest in rendering conversation. One boy's story revealed very early a desire to explore argumentative conversation (perhaps his mother was always on at him) for which his grammar and punctuation did not equip him. But a technical lesson, using his work with the whole class on the setting-out of conversation, enabled him to go on with a story whose realism came from its exchanges of conversation:

So Pete went down the hole.

'Have you got a match?' asked Dick.

'Why should I have a match?'

'Well, I thought you might have one because you are cook in camp.'

'I'll have a look.'

Pete felt in all his pockets and after a while he said, 'Yes, I've got one.'

Such care over a small matter (he forces the argumentative exchange on himself, despite the labour of extra punctuation marks involved by that 'why should I have a match?') is the product of the excitement of fantasy. This writer's need to explore argument wasn't severe: one or two children revealed the need to grapple with a severe personal problem. One, a girl, in a story of a trip to Switzerland, explored for many pages the idea of death:

The matron replied, saying that Mr. and Mrs. Crain could have no visitors because they were nearly dead. Joan said that they were their father and mother and it was very important that they should see them before they died . . . so they tip-toed along the corridor up the stairs and in the first door on the right. . . . Sheila went and looked at her mother and whispered to the nurse, 'Doesn't she look ill.' 'Yes,' said the nurse, 'but the doctor said that they would give her two hours to survive and if she didn't survive she was sure to die. . . .'

What use this may have been to her 'therapeutically' I've no idea: the theme brought us to a standstill – the next chapter. 'Waiting for Survival' was never finished, and I was so affected by the Kafka-like frustration of the corridors in the writer's hospital that I dared neither urge nor criticize the detail of the rendering. The writing to the above point was adequate enough, but obviously no idiom or technique of hers could carry her further: she had come too much out of that 'third ground' – half-serious, half-irresponsible, and was trying to grapple with a theme demanding more maturity. Maybe (I didn't, of course, enquire) she had to face the theme in real life while still so immature: the situation reveals at least that to teach English 'for the living' it won't do to be cynical, or to expect a young child to show a 'terrifying honesty'.

The last writer might have had more success if she had turned to the realization of a remoter fantasy, as others did. (That my reading aloud was in the children's minds when they wrote is shown by the fact that the writer of the following devised this for me to say – 'It was believed to be Pharoah Gilgusmustutugilgernustonusmen'):

They drew their gurkhas and charged but Jim produced something he had kept quiet all the trip: it was a machine-gun. He placed it on a hill of sand and small rocks. The Arabs came nearer. Jim fired. The Arabs fall like flies. The rest took cover behind their dead. The tommy guns had been taken by some villainous thief. The Arabs crouched as still as the rocks themselves. They stayed there until nightfall. . . .

A psychologist on Sir Herbert Read's principles might have seen in this an undertone of feeling about death if he had known as I did that the boy's brother had died shortly before he wrote it ('hill of sand and small rocks . . . fall like flies . . . dead (which he spelt 'died') . . . taken by some villainous thief . . . crouched as still as the rocks themselves'). But whatever the emotion it is depersonalized to such an extent in the tale that we have a description whose details and rhythm produce an effect remarkable for a not-very-literate boy. And such qualities can be pointed out to him and others: we are teaching English not as amateur psychologists, but as artists concerned with the art of the word.

Finally, I would like to try to indicate by two quotations from the same story what kind of 'technical' development there may be, once interest has been developed in the writing. This is near the beginning of the story of the bottom boy in the form.

The cliff we came to was so high we had to use ropes and pick axes. Halfway I saw Mickey disappear over a ledge, next Pete went over. But when I went over I heard a voice say: 'Keep walking.' And there (at least) in front of me were 8 or 9 black men. They (took) me to a mud hut were Mick and Pete were pushed on in and put a guard.

This a few pages later:

John after going to sleep in the trees with the others, woke up in the night after being disturbed (by) a monkey, which ran right acrossed him, felt very thirsty and he set out to find a stream which he could hear. He soon found it and had a good drink. Suddenly when he stood up he had a shock and felt the ground falling from under him. 'Bump.' Suddenly he stopped falling and found himself in a kind of tunnel.

The mistakes in the first spring from a lack of interest: the second flows more easily and the mistakes are those which come from the expression outstripping his acquaintance with 'the rules'. In the second the story has taken hold – teacher and pupil meet on that 'third ground' and we can endeavour to improve the English for the sake of the story.

This imaginative composition work is, of course, complementary to the reading of poetry and stories, and the practical training in English as a skill. That none can do without the others I feel sure – even the teaching of grammar, spelling and letter-writing cannot be successful without training in the other kind of use of English. Imaginative writing is often avoided because it is difficult to mark, and a teacher may be uncertain of his ground if criticized by 'authority'. It depends, a little, on the teacher having a delight in literature and being well-read in it; a teacher who has exposed himself to the discomfort of the increased awareness which a reading of, say, Blake's *Songs* or *King Lear* must bring, will be able to respect a child's fantasy. This is a problem for the training colleges and departments; for all the 'psychology' lectures they have in training, many teachers begin their work with insufficient training of the sensibility, and openly recognize it. How can they maintain their ground when they meet hostile authority?

But I hope I have sufficiently justified the need for imaginative training, and have shown that it is a training – a real discipline. By reading works of literature a child may be brought on to that 'third ground' – the traditional meeting place of minds where he can measure his own experience against the experience of 'the race' and its values. But if he can get on to that ground himself, using the modes whereby others have got there, and be, consciously or unconsciously, making his own thoughts and feelings public in an idiom which controls and judges them, then the exercise will be part and parcel of himself, and his growth.

# *Teaching Writing in the Grammar School*

## JAMES REEVES

THE teaching of writing is about the most important and exacting thing a teacher has to do, because writing in its widest sense is the most comprehensive of all human activities.[1] Language being the characteristic mark of developed man, and writing the refined and permanent form of language, it follows that there is a deficiency in any human experience which does not comprise some appreciation of the written word. Appreciation may come through writing or reading, which should be looked on as complementary. In a sense, all our early reading is, or should be, a preparation for writing: by which I mean no more than that fully active reading brings with it the urge to write – an urge which may be latent and lazy, or which may lead to immature imitation of what has just been read. The reader may, or may not, grow into a writer. In any case, it will be agreed that there is something decadent about a state of affairs in which we are content solely to read, to listen, to watch, never to take part.

I have a right to dogmatize, as the reader to dissent, but I have no right or wish to be pharisaical. The answer to my claim might well be, 'As a teacher of English you evidently have an inflated idea of the importance of your job. All that can be expected of you is to teach a boy to use his language effectively when he needs to: don't try to turn a likely civil servant into an ineffectual aesthete. A great many people go happily through life with what you would call defective experience.'

Self-realization is what matters. As a means of self-realization writing is unique. Those who have followed me in these contentions will already have an idea of the ways in which I think the teaching of writing could be improved. As a starting-point, let us say that self-assertion should be the keynote of a child's composition. Whatever is positive is good; whatever negative, bad. Most of what school-children turn out is negative.

[1] Some parts of this article have appeared in James Reeves' book *Teaching Poetry* (Hutchinson). We are grateful to the author and the publishers for permission to reproduce it here.

A piece of work which merely doesn't contain any considerable errors, digressions or departures from our laboriously inculcated rules and maxims, though it is often all we can expect by the time that School Certificate approaches, is a failure. It is a failure due, I think, to the current tendency to regard writing as a craft – that is, something you start at the beginning with and learn step by step, synthetically: first a word, then a sentence, then a paragraph. First a noun, then an epithet, then a better epithet. Synonym, antonym – nibble, nibble. Now an exercise on connections, now an exercise in correction. (Of all the perversions of the pedagogic mind, that of making boys systematically cold-bloodedly 'correct' wrong sentences deliberately invented by other people is the most futile and mischievous. Wilfully to introduce them to batches of five or ten plausible errors which they are expected to have the judgment to correct before they have the ingenuity to commit them is to waste and misdirect labour which might be usefully occupied in improving the innocent faults of their own composition.) No, writing should be thought of not as a craft, but as a gesture or an act of the imagination; something you learn from the end, not the beginning; something you bite off whole, not nibble at like a rabbit. I hear the voice of prudence: 'Don't teach them to run before they can walk.' It is the natural thing to run before you walk. It is only after the child has run its first tottering steps from its mother's knee to the sofa that it begins, so to speak, to take its act to pieces and do it again step by step. Of course, there are steps: you do not expect it to run a hundred yards straight off. But the separate steps should be learnt after the first excitement of the total act has been experienced. Let a child's first written compositions, though no doubt limited in length to one, or five, sentences, be in intention stories or descriptions rather than sentences or exercises. Let them be something capable of a 'total gesture' – I borrow this phrase, I forget from whom, to express the notion that when a child composes something, he should do so with the idea that he is finishing, not beginning something.

The speed of a child's composition presents a difficulty: even the shortest of stories or descriptions takes him so long to put down that all semblance of a gesture may be lost. Moreover, if he is thinking about spelling, punctuation and calligraphy, as well as content and vocabulary, as distinct problems, his speed of writing approaches that of a monumental mason. It is not too much to say that what some excessively conscientious teachers expect of the very young is not a composition but an inscription. One way to overcome the difficulty is to set a rigid time-limit. I recently read with some boys of eleven-plus a very short Chinese poem in Waley's translation, on the subject of home-coming; I gave them a quarter of an hour to write a free-verse composition of their own on the same subject. (I cannot briefly describe this procedure so as to make it sound less highbrow; in practice it was a modest experiment, tried only because the poem, which is beautifully simple in language and feeling, appealed to the class and seemed suitable for imitation.) The results as a whole were not startling, but some showed that their writers had 'got the idea'. One of them was:

> The boy came out of school
> When he came home
> The door was locked
> He asked the next door neighbour
> Where his mother was.
> She had gone out so he sat down and cried.
> After a long time his mother came home
> He ran with outstretched arms to meet her.

I quote this, not as being 'good', or even the best available, but as a successful effort by an 'average' boy, obviously not a prodigy, at completeness within definite time and space limits. One other point struck me: it seemed, in my judgment, to be rather good prose – at any rate, more promising prose than a boy of eleven usually achieves.

This has brought me to two important questions – verse composition, and imitation in general. The possibilities of verse composition are probably not sufficiently explored. Its value, apart from any artistic self-satisfaction, is twofold: it limits the writer's aim and scope, forcing him to be severely selective of his subject-matter, at the same time encouraging the achievement of a 'total gesture'; secondly, it concentrates his attention on the problem of style (choice and economy of words, imagery, rhythm). In other words, it creates the right difficulties. How many teachers, when reading a pile of prose compositions have shared with me the feeling that a great deal of what is written is mere flat verbiage, neither good nor very bad, and have wondered what to do about it? An occasional exercise in verse effects a surprising reduction in verbiage. After all, to write of memorable things in verse earlier than in prose accords with the history of man.

However, the mechanical difficulties of metre and rhyme are often found to be discouraging to boys who are not naturally 'bards'; so that what is called 'free verse' is often a better way of writing verse. Mechanical restrictions disappear, but economy of diction remains. The child thinks in groups of words instead of in the complete statements that constitute prose. He thinks in images; he tries to make each line telling. In short, he becomes a conscious artist. Above all, the apparently rigid barrier between metrical verse and ordinary prose disappears, so that the composition of free verse can have a direct and good influence on the writing of prose. It is true that the writer of free verse is apt not to put in most of the connectives of conventional prose; but this may be just as well, for on the whole I find that schoolboys tend in any case to write overlong and complex sentences. Perhaps another concrete example will be helpful, so I quote a poem by a talented boy of fourteen, written after reading a modern poem (I leave the reader to guess by whom): on this occasion there were no time or subject limits.

ROOKS

A black shape glides in front of the sun,
What is it?
A cloud.
What can it be?
There it is!
Hovering over that patch of scrub,
Could it be a hawk?
Another joins it. What are they?
Rooks!
I know them by their yellow beaks, like pointed hammers.
Their wings are like torn black sheets.
There's one, after a rabbit.
He's got it.
Murderer!

Ah! it's dusk now.
They swoop back to their rookeries,
A hundred feet above the ground,
Where nobody can get at them.
Rooks!

A poem like this seems to me to have at least a suggestion of everything that an imaginative composition by a boy of fourteen can have.

Except sincerity? I anticipate the sceptic's question in order to introduce my last dogma, that composition is learnt by imitation. You might conceivably teach a boy to write a good business letter by the nibbling system, but you will never teach him to write anything worth while. In a sense you cannot *teach* the act of writing; you can only implant the desire to write by inspiring a child with other writing and making him wish to emulate other writers. You can only make him want to write well, by showing him that writing is worth while, because it has the power of unique satisfactions. So that it is more important what you make him read than how you make him write. Most boys do not read widely enough or intensely enough; nor are they read to enough. Reading for pleasure is shut off in an air-tight compartment of out-of-school or leisure activity; writing is a stern task, for guidance in which the learner is directed to volumes of altogether unsuitable essays by Addison, Lamb, Macaulay and Robert Lynd – unsuitable because they cannot be appreciated without a reserve of literary, historical or social erudition and worldly wisdom far beyond the capacity of schoolboys. Boys should be encouraged to read much and widely, for pleasure – and to write in the manner of whomever they admire at the moment; not because imitation is intrinsically good, but because they want to write, and the manner of the writer they admire seems at the moment the only way of writing. Indeed, to admire rightly is to want to imitate. Are they never to be original? Certainly. But originality consists in being as like oneself as possible, not as unlike everybody else. Think of three such original writers as Blake, Wordsworth and James Joyce. Their early writings are almost slavishly traditional. But does not imitation encourage pretentious artificiality? Is not the 'Rooks' poem quoted earlier rather pretentious for a boy of fourteen?

Certainly; and I would say that some stylistic swagger in a boy of that age is a good thing. Let him respond to, and handle, as many of the tricks of rhetoric and bombast as he likes. Is there any adult now conscious of being able to write decently who cannot remember having in youth turned out some very turgid stuff for the school magazine or a private notebook? It may make one blush now, but that is no reason for being over-fastidious about one's pupil's excesses. Were not 'Venus and Adonis' and 'Love's Labour's Lost' just a little pretentious and artificial? It is irrelevant to object, 'Ah, but that was Shakespeare.'

IV

# *THE PLACE OF GRAMMAR, TOGETHER WITH A NOTE ON INTELLIGENCE*

THE English teacher at every level encourages the pupil to draw upon the common stuff of everyday experience, to keep diaries, make notes, write short pieces directly reporting the daily round. Beyond this he opens ways for prose to handle the more private and venturesome modes – even the personal fantasies and fears in which the pupil attains order and release – partly through the living connections of metaphor and image, long before his rational mind has learned to meet and analyse such experience. The growing boy or girl discovers that these other more elusive dimensions of living have each their proper right to prose, their special idiom and particular rhythm. Poetry, music, drama, art, the natural world, can all help to refine the young's in-drawing of life, and by extending the ranges of quick and imaginative sympathy, enlarge a sense of possible human situations.

But there is quite another, if secondary side, to English teaching. The pupil must master the formal aids to expression: punctuation, spelling, grammar. The teacher must pass on new and more sophisticated tools as the pressure of experience demands them in order to attain more accurate communication. Yet it is possible, especially under stress of the examinable, to overvalue this secondary side. Certainly many examinations from primary to university level seem to encourage this. The following section considers this other aspect of English teaching, and ponders the place of formal grammar. The whole subject needs clear and constant survey, for ill-used it can stifle and blank out so much that is vital in English teaching and, more subtly, can mislead our understanding of that 'intelligence' we wish to nurture, reducing the full, responsive self to no more than the quick-moving 'cognitive surface of the mind'.

# *Grammar, Language and Style*

## A. A. EVANS

Art thou lunatics? Hast thou no understandings for thy cases, and the numbers of the genders?

*The Merry Wives of Windsor, IV, i,* 61

FOR many years teachers of English have received complaints about the low standard of English attained by their pupils. Their History, Geography and Science colleagues grumble at the atrocious English in which their essays are written and their experiments are recorded, forgetting the platitude that 'every teacher is a teacher of English'. The Languages teachers complain that they have perforce to be teachers of English, and to instruct their classes in the principles and definitions of grammar neglected by the English teacher, before they can get on with their proper work. The complaints are continued by employers against the school-leaver, and by University teachers against the Sixth Formers who come up to them. A return to the teaching of English grammar is strongly advocated on all sides and in recent correspondence in *The Times Educational Supplement*,[1] well-known teachers of English publicly announced that they had decided to mend their ways in the hope that their pupils would learn to write as correctly as did pupils twenty and thirty years ago (the quality of whose English is obscured by the mellow patina of antiquity).

But the controversy of grammar-teaching is confused by ignorance, prejudice and contradictory opinions, and there are at least five pieces of evidence from the past which show that the nature of the controversy has not changed very much in the last forty years:

(i) The Report of the Joint Committee on Grammatical Terminology 1911. The movement to set up this Committee started in 1908.

(ii) *The Remarks on the Report* by J. C. Nesfield and the comments on them by Professor W. W. Skeat (1912) in the 1914 edition of Nesfield's *English Grammar Past and Present.*

[1] *The Times Educational Supplement*, 23rd January-2nd February 1953.

(iii) *English Grammar and Grammars* by Dr. R. B. McKerrow in *Essays and Studies*, Vol. VIII. English Association.

(iv) *The Teaching of English in England*. Board of Education. 1921.

(v) *The Problem of Grammar:* Pamphlet No. 56. English Association. The Report of a Conference held in 1922.

This last Report is disturbingly up to date, and if a conference were held this year we should hear pretty much the same arguments as were made then, for we are no less confused about aims, method and content in the teaching of grammar.

First, there is inconsistency of practice. Those of us who were at school in the twenties received a fairly thorough training in grammar. My text-book was the Nesfield mentioned above, which was reprinted fifteen times between 1900 and 1920, and his *Outline of Grammar* and *Uses of the Parts of Speech* were no less popular. I myself had to use the latter in my first three years of teaching (1928-1931). There was then a reaction, and again another swing of the pendulum. Today there is no consistent practice. Most grammar schools teach grammar, but the amount and the thoroughness depend largely on the personal conviction of the teachers as to its value. In the secondary modern schools the position of grammar is chaotic, but most of the newer text-books on English which are being published for these schools omit grammar.

Secondly, even when there is agreement that grammar should be taught, there is uncertainty as to *where* it should be taught. Many grammar-school teachers insist that the rudiments should be taught in the junior schools. In some junior schools there is no grammar-teaching: in most, a little: and I have been in a junior school where the 10-plus A stream is taken through clause-analysis. Some teachers think that the groundwork should be covered in the first two years at the grammar school: others that it should be spread over the first four years. As there are no compulsory grammar questions in the G.C.E. English paper and there are plenty of alternative questions, we can assume that where grammar-teaching is retained it is either because of inertia or because of a conviction of its educational value.

Thirdly, there are conflicting opinions even among teachers of English as to the value of grammar. It is maintained that training in grammar is helpful to colleagues teaching other languages: that it affords a sound discipline in logical thinking: that a sound knowledge of grammatical rules is essential, or, at the least, extremely helpful in training pupils to speak and write correctly. Others deny that there is any real link between knowledge of grammar and correct speech and writing, and that this has been clearly enough shown by the many pupils who have been 'good at grammar' and inept and inaccurate in writing, and by the considerable number of people who had no grammar-teaching at all at school and yet speak and write well. In any case, one of the best teachers of a correct use of language is the social and cultural background, and that is finding it difficult enough to maintain professional status. These conflicting opinions among teachers are illustrated by the text-books they choose for their classes. Some schools will select what is primarily and exclusively a text-book of grammar: others a book which is a conglomeration of vocabulary and style with an appendix summary of grammar. But that is insufficient evidence either way of the relation between knowledge of grammar and correctness in language, and research to that end would be an arduous and very lengthy project.

Fourthly, our discussion on the above points is considerably invalidated by the knowledge and conception of grammar of the teachers. Few of us examine at all critically the principles and concepts of the grammar we teach,[1] and modern English grammar is a fairly recent innovation in University Schools of English.[2] Most teachers of English, and especially the many who teach it as a subsidiary to their main subject, get the knowledge of the grammar they teach from what they remember of their own schooldays and from the text-books they have to use with their classes. One must sadly suspect that many of the grammar text-books which have been compiled in the last thirty years have had the same sources, judging from the repetition of methods and definitions. It would not be difficult to trace many of these back to pre-Nesfieldian days (and even Nesfield had the

[1] 'It is rare to hear a lesson in grammar in which the teacher does not make statements about the structure of the language which are, to say the least of it, open to question. Whence comes this lack of interest and this inaccuracy?' *The Teaching of English in England*, p. 282. Board of Education 1921.

[2] It is interesting to note that a school text-book is presented for study in some University Departments – Grattan and Gurrey's *Our Living Language*.

integrity to protest violently against the imposition by a Committee[1] composed chiefly of experts in foreign and dead languages of grammatical terms foreign to English) when the living growth of English was pruned and trained to a grammatical system based on Latin grammar, in order to give English grammar a similar disciplinary value to that of Latin. Indeed, I purchased at a publisher's exhibition at the 1951 Conference of Educational Associations a text-book which I was assured sold very well in which the verb *to love* was given in all its one hundred and sixty conjugations, finishing rather plaintively with the Third Person Plural Future Perfect Subjunctive Passive, *If they should have been loved.*

There is little space to examine the complete formal tradition of grammatical principles and concepts which are so baffling or seemingly useless to so many pupils, but we can perhaps exemplify with a few:

(a) *Case.* Case is the inflexion of the noun or pronoun which shows the syntactical relationship of the noun or pronoun with the other words in the phrase or sentence of which it forms a part. It is a valid concept in the grammar of highly inflected languages such as Old English and Latin. But in Modern English accidence has declined to insignificance: adjectives do not have to 'agree' with nouns inflexionally, and the syntax of the English sentence-structure is based, not on accidence, but on the law of proximity combined with context-recognition. All we need say of the syntax of a noun is that it is Subject, Object, Indirect Object or Possessive. Nesfield himself speaks of Nominative, Possessive and Objective Cases, which is simple and sensible enough in the light of his definition of Case as 'the *relation* in which a noun stands to some other word, or the *change of form* (if any) by which this relation is indicated.'[2] In the 1912 edition of his book he protests violently against the introduction of the terms *Vocative*, *Accusative*, *Genitive* and *Dative* recommended by the Joint Committee on Grammatical Terminology. But these terms entered our text-books and are still in them. One text-book actually says that these terms are retained for the sake of convenience, and only one, as far as I

[1] Joint Committee on Grammatical Terminology.

[2] J. C. Nesfield, *English Grammar Past and Present* (Macmillan, 1898).

know, explains how English lost its case-inflexion and simplifies the matter to *Subjective Case*, *Objective Case* and *Possessive Case.*

(b) *Gender.* Gender is an inflexional characteristic of the nouns in inflected languages. We find it, for example, in Latin and Old English, and in those modern languages in which the qualification of a noun by an adjective is shown by the accidence, i.e. the adjective is inflected according to the gender of the noun-form. English lost its grammatical gender with the loss of its inflexions, but it was re-imposed in grammar (though not in the more important *usage*) not as a noun-distinction, which was now impossible, but by an association with the sex-distinction of the persons and animals named by the nouns, 'neuter' being used as a gender-distinction for the inanimate objects named by nouns. To describe the noun *cock* as masculine gender and *hen* as feminine because the animals named are male and female respectively is bad grammar. It is significant that most exercises on gender in text-books are on sexual counterparts, e.g. *landlord, landlady: buck, doe: cob, pen.* Such exercises would be irrelevant in Latin and French as exercises in Gender, and the teaching of 'Gender' in English can only hinder and not help the teachers of other languages. Gratton and Gurrey are sensible in their treatment of Gender; they explain the absence of grammatical gender in Modern English, discuss 'Natural Gender' and speak of 'words denoting men and words denoting women' (to which they might have added 'male' and 'female' in the rest of the animal world).

(c) *Preposition.* The Preposition is a difficult concept to teach, as young pupils find it difficult to distinguish from the Adverb (e.g. *Put on your cap* and *He stuck a badge on his cap*), and when the text-book states that 'it connects the noun or pronoun with the rest of the sentence', from the Conjunction. The almost universal definition of the Preposition is 'a word which precedes a noun or pronoun and governs it in the Accusative Case'. The Preposition does not always, of course, precede the noun (e.g. 'That's a question I shall look *into*') and to speak of one word governing another word, whether in a non-existent case or not, savours of a mumbo-jumbo which can only mystify pupils and can even hinder their training in fluent and accurate English if they are led by the teacher to believe that the learning of such 'grammar' is a pre-condition of the correct use of English. Nor are they helped by the teacher's joke (which I first heard in 1917) that 'A preposition is the wrong word to end a sentence *with.*'

'The differing definitions of the Gerund (and indeed the direct contradictions of definition of Gerund and Verbal Noun which have appeared in text-books), the confusion of the Possessive Adjective and Possessive Pronoun and the 'definition' of the Adjective as 'limiting' or 'describing' the Noun are three further examples of the inconsistencies and the slovenly reasoning which are perpetuated by force of tradition in our grammar text-books. Where we have been successful in training pupils to write correct English it has been, among other methods such as reading, through a more opportune (and even *ad hoc*) instruction in English usage than through a planned syllabus of a grammar which is obsolete, unrealistic and so fallacious in its abstractions. Grammar can be a fascinating study for middle and upper school pupils of a high verbal intelligence, but to others it is puzzling and largely irrelevant: if they cannot perceive the inconsistencies and inaccuracies, it is only because they are not mature enough to grapple with the abstractions. Many books are used which combine grammar, usage, vocabulary, style, proverbs, etc., but the text-book entirely devoted to grammar is still extensively used. It is started at too young a level, before the child can grapple with abstract concepts, the niceties and fine distinctions, and before he has acquired sufficient practice and fluency in written language, a sufficient skill in phrase and sentence and an adequate knowledge of words. Intelligent pupils can repeat definitions of parts of speech, recognize them in sentences and fill up gaps with the correct words, but the fact that so many pupils can do this and yet write ungrammatically shows that there is no real connection at this stage between correct writing and that superficial knowledge of grammar which they have acquired. The study of grammar based on the eight parts of speech is analytical, but one must have the material and extensive familiarity with the material before one can subject it to an analytical process.

In any case, we might well examine more critically than we have done this basic conception of the division of words into eight categories. With a highly inflected language such as Latin it would seem to be a fair enough rationalization. The word *mensam* is a noun in the accusative case, the word *amo* is a verb (First Person, Singular, Present, Indicative, Active) and both are capable of definition and particularization outside their use in sentences. It would not be possible to use a verb as a noun or a noun as a verb in Latin or in any language with the same freedom as in English. Since the sixteenth century, however, English has increasingly broken away from a formal grammar which would assign one particular grammatical function to each word. Shakespeare was particularly bold in extending these functions. The well-known *to out-Herod Herod* and *But me no buts and uncle me no uncles* are not exceptional, only conspicuous examples. Today there are no restrictions: for example, the word *table* has three functions (*a table*, *to table a motion*, *table cloth*) and the word *round* five (*a round of golf*, *a round table*, *to round the corner*, *he came round*, *round the corner*). We have also extended the functions of words beyond the eight parts of speech, and have no pigeon-hole into which they can be squeezed without considerable strain. For example, in the sentence *There was a boy* . . . , it is extremely difficult to assign the word *there*, for it does not fit in with the conventional definition of adverb. Is it an impersonal pronoun? We can trace the development of the construction *That wants looking into*, but the word *into* is neither adverb nor preposition.[1] The assigning of words to the eight parts of speech has driven us to use such subterfuges as 'a noun used as a verb', 'a verb used as a noun', 'a noun used as an adjective'; it has given us the misconception of 'the compound noun' in describing such constructions as *clothes horse*, *boat house* and *hair brush*.[2] It has given us such extraordinary definitions as 'Adverbial Accusative' for the word *ankle* in the sentence *The mud was ankle-deep*.[3]

There is no easy solution to this problem, for, after all, most words will fit according to their functions into these eight parts of speech, and the recognition of additional functions (e.g. possibly, the particle) leaves the main problem unsolved. But

[1] See Grattan and Gurrey, *Our Living Language*, cap. xiii, for an illuminating discussion on the Verbal Particle.

[2] For a discussion on this point see Professor Allen Mawer, *The Problem of Grammar in the Light of Modern Linguistic Thought: The Problem of Grammar*. English Association Pamphlet No. 56.

[3] S. C. Glassey, *The Groundwork of Grammar*, part II (Oxford 1937).

we could as a beginning reject the assumptions that every word, in isolation, conforms to a particular grammatical term and that if it is used in any other way than that by which it normally conforms to such a term, then it retains its original function as well as the function defined by a different grammatical term. For, at present, if we say that the word *table* in *to table a motion* is a noun used as a verb, or that *morning* in *morning dew* is a noun used as an adjective, we are confusing definition with function. The well-known Churchillian marginalium *This is something up with which I will not put* shows how modern English usage has developed beyond the formal rules of grammar. Such a construction conforms with the strictest grammatical rules but it is not correct English. Here *up* is not an adverb and *with* is not a preposition: the verb is *put up with*. We must start on the true basis of function, that the part of speech to which a word can be assigned depends entirely on the work which it is doing in a particular sentence, whether in meaning or in syntax.

# *The Teaching of Formal English Grammar*

R. J. HARRIS

THIS article was prompted by boys' questioning the value to them of the study of formal English grammar, by the writer's subsequent review of the place of grammar in his own studies and experience, and by attendance at a conference where it was assumed by the majority as axiomatic that a knowledge of formal grammar was essential in teaching English.

## HISTORY

It is sometimes said, fallaciously, that there is no such thing as English grammar, and indeed at one time in the teaching of English there was none. Its place was supplied by a Latinized English grammar, and this and the English language proving as disjunct as the sheets in Leacock's *Boarding-House Geometry*, grammar as a part of the English syllabus fell into a disrepute from which compromise, the establishment of a native grammar, and the passing of time have to some extent redeemed it. The teaching of formal grammar in English now normally occupies one-fifth to one-quarter of the time allocated to English studies in grammar schools. After the G.C.E. (that is, when it might be really of value) it is dropped. Teachers abandon what presumably they have felt to be a vain attempt, and boys do not touch the subject again until their children's homework, or their own entry into the teaching profession, compels revision.

## ADVANTAGES CLAIMED FOR THE TEACHING OF FORMAL GRAMMAR

What are the pupil, the language and the teacher said to gain from formal grammar? The pupil, it is claimed, is trained in logical and abstract thought; the study of sentence-structure aids him in expression and comprehension; he learns to conform to a social discipline, submission to which is not without value, both in conferring prestige on him and in other ways; and he is trained to answer one or two specific grammar questions in the G.C.E., and to read and write foreign languages more quickly than he otherwise would. The language is codified, its forms are crystallized, its definition sharpened, its purity defended. The teacher is helped by the feeling that he is guarding the golden apple, the incorruptible language which is in the book and cannot rot, he has something definite to teach and to mark, and thus is enabled to share with his colleagues who teach logarithms or atomic weights the comfortable status of 'specialist'; he has a breathing-spell in a busy day, for the formal grammar period involves no new reactions to new and unexpected situations; he is praised by his Modern Language and Classics colleagues, in so far as his terminology can be squared with theirs; he is taking 'something the boys like'; he is on the safe side (authoritative about forms of language, condemning the slip-shod), and yet progressive in that he teaches a 'functional' grammar and allows for usage in so far as he can stomach it; he has an instrument, useful in disentangling eighteenth-century inversions or in filling-in with paraphrase the irreverent gaps in some modern poems, by which the meanings of complicated sentences can be made to seem comprehensible; and he can relate the errors so continually repeated in boys' compositions to general principles, and so achieve an economy of correction.

At a later stage, it is true, close study of a text will usually show that the form is an essential part of the meaning – that sentence-structure is an image, a reinforcement, or even the only indication of an important aspect of meaning: even this, however (as will be later suggested), is first perceived and then by formal analysis confirmed – the meanings of the rhythms of thought and of sound are intuitively apprehended, after which, according to the completeness of the apprehension, their forms may be traced. It is a craftsman's delight to trace out these forms – a difficult Sixth Form study.

### SCOPE OF THE TERM 'FORMAL GRAMMAR', AND A NOTE ON THE FORM/MEANING RELATIONSHIP

Before attempting to assess the worth of the more respectable of the claims made on behalf of formal grammar, I would clarify two points. First, the word 'grammar' covers many related ideas, from 'a logical use of an accepted terminology to analyse the form of groups of words' (e.g. clause-analysis), to 'the rote acceptance of an orthographical convention for representing the phrasing of thought' (e.g. punctuation); in the opinion of some it includes even 'etymology'. I am using 'grammar' to represent only the first of these. The second point, which is the focus of the whole article, is that understanding of meaning can always, and in the great majority of instances does, precede analysis of form; or, in another mode of statement, recognition of function follows that of meaning. Take as an example the lines:

> No, this my hand will rather
> The multitudinous seas incarnadine,
> Making the green one red.

Embarrassed by the evidently identical paraphrastic meaning of the last two lines, some scholars suggest the reading

> Making the green one, red.

but the majority would probably agree that there is sufficient formal dissimilarity to prevent any feeling of tautology. No listener can be enlightened by an analysis of form in these lines, unless he has first felt the weight of the formal difference intuitively. That he should be able to do so at once is the theatrical test of the lines; nor in truth is the meaning even then brought nearer to him by the formal explanation of the juxtaposition of the short, heavy native line with the long-rolling foreign one, for it is only in this play, with this character, that the juxtaposition has this particular weight of meaning. Anyone wishing to prove the truth of this has only to try to reproduce the same power by using the same formal devices, to see how fatally easy is the craft of parody, and how unrewarding is technique without a compelling truth. Thus it is impossible to make a dictionary of forms – and yet this is what all school text-books profess to do. In school grammar-books the meaning of a sentence to be analysed is accidental; and the triviality and dissociation almost prevents its having any form at all, in any sense that matters. It is not correct to say: 'This is grammatical, and therefore has meaning'; if any picture of the actual mental process is intended, one can only say: 'This has meaning, and therefore must be grammatical'. At Sixth Form level, it is worth while to confirm apprehension of meaning by study of form, although even at this level the more gifted the reader, the less gain will eventuate, and the less gifted, the easier it will be to substitute the apparent gain of knowledge for the real want of understanding.

### AN EXAMINATION OF THE ADVANTAGES CLAIMED FOR THE TEACHING OF FORMAL GRAMMAR

Does the formal grammar taught to the eleven to fifteen-year-old pupil achieve the purposes to which it is devoted? I do not think it does.

It is sketchily remembered, and even where remembered, seldom applied. Inconsistency of terminology (a matter not beyond remedy since 1911) is partly to blame for this; but more to blame are certain inherent characteristics of English, of children, of teachers, and of the learning process. English more than most living languages is governed by usage, and it is therefore especially difficult to keep grammatical classifications up to date, even in the usage of educated and thus more conservative speakers. Psychological difficulties arise between pupil and teacher, despite the claim that an efficient teacher can teach children anything however futile. These difficulties spring from the intellectual pragmatism of children, who insist, in effect, on being shown that the processes of formal grammar are useful and practical for them as an aid in understanding. The teacher too contributes to the difficulties, for he may be often uncertain of his right to exclude one form of language and to admit another which he likes and his social equals employ. Thus, the children perceive illogic sometimes defended in the name of logic, and social pressure exerted and personal taste imposed in the name of clarity, euphony, and so on, by a teacher often timid, distrustful of his language's power to survive, perhaps also of the validity of his social status or of the value of what he has to teach. A third reason for the inefficiency of instruction in formal grammar has been touched on already, and is that children learn to communicate by communicating; always it is the meaning of words that matters. Meaning leads to new meaning, and it is this growing perception of relationships which contains the valuable training in method to which formal grammar has pretensions; for it seems most certain that in the Lower School formal analysis leads merely to a restatement in abstract terms of an already understood meaning. Correct habits of expression can be established only by examining and criticizing in terms of meaning the meaning of specific sentences in specific contexts: the qualities which convey this meaning are qualities of style – word order, sound, word choice, economy, power – and these should be introduced directly, so that emphasis is placed on the really functional apparatus; when the child sees this working, he will correct related faults in his own work without ever knowing the name of the general and abstract term of grammar under which the qualities may have been categorized. The grammatical term, being a stage further removed from the fact of meaning, is a distraction, not an aid to correct usage. 'Function', as normally used in teaching grammar, is an incubus, coming after the important event, comprehension. In this, teachers of English are often misled by an apparent similarity of aim in teaching English grammar and in teaching the grammar of foreign languages, in learning which, at least until some considerable fluency and acquaintance is gained, grammar does necessarily precede comprehension.

Whether formal grammar trains a child in logical and abstract thought is disputable; whether it should be used to do so, is even more doubtful, for it can lead to a pedantic, hair-splitting logic-chopping in clever boys, and a superficial arrogance in dull, and in both to a neglect of organic and poetic growth of language and of the ability to receive language sensuously; in so far as school grammar has not this negative influence, it has next to none, save in the phantasy of scholastic piety. It may even cause boys to despise formal grammar: in a recent research among boys in two London grammar schools, the formal grammar lesson was ranked bottom in every year from the first to the fifth, equally by the clever and by the dull boys, though possibly for different reasons. It is not difficult to show that school grammar is an illogical instrument with which to teach logical method: the arbitrariness of some grammatical categories at the early level is often admitted, and pupils must feel frequently that this 'abstract thought' is no more than a child's game at shops with coins that are cardboard. As a result, the terminology is within a short while disused or misused – it is no uncommon experience that you cannot rely on a Fifth Former to recognize a finite verb. The study of formal grammar has been introduced too early. English grammar begins to stimulate, not merely to fill the mind, only when its categories and terms can be used to question rigid language and thought-structures, and to compare formal effects in style. At Sixth Form level this can happen, and it is there that the opportunity for the future scholar exists: within a few weeks he will learn, and using remember, more categories and terms than the Fifth Former after five years and a vacation.

What is the practical value of the 'frame of reference' to which the teacher is said to be able to refer common errors? Is there any ascertainable transfer from the grammar lesson to the pupils' own understanding and expression? These questions, discussed in part already, deserve more attention. The answer to both seems to be 'Very little'; and this not only because there are some stupid exercises in grammar books, but because skill in grasping the relatedness of the parts of a complex sentence, and of sentence to paragraph, and so on, comes from a habitual attention to meaning in reading and listening, and through association with effective communication in speech and writing. Let us consider, as an example for correction, the sentences:

> The man is walking along the street. Now the man is entering the garden.

A grammatical method of correction might involve saying: 'It would be neater to replace the noun which you have repeated by a pronoun'. For this correction to be effective, at least three things are needed: the child must know what a noun is; he must know what a pronoun is; and he must believe that the new version is neater. Of these, the valuable or motivating item is the third. The 'non-grammatical' corrector might say: 'Wouldn't it be neater to say "The man is walking along the street. Now he is entering the garden"?' In this, only one factor is involved, and that is the most important. It is the experience of neatness or economy or power in the one example which will transfer to other examples, and so act as a correcting agent – an aesthetic experience; the knowledge of the other terms is only an added burden. The assumption in teaching such terms is that their knowledge can bring about the aesthetic experience, which in fact it usually supplants. In the same way, children's correctness is a personal habit – that is, imitation in the sense not of a parrot-like following but of a shared experience. It may be essential for the teacher to know the general rules and the technical terms, but they are to him what the doctor's medical terms are to the doctor – he applies them, but does not set the patient to learn them.

### THE USE AND PLACE OF FORMAL GRAMMAR

What then is the place of formal grammar in the teaching of English at school? Its real value appears at Sixth Form level: first, in examining with specialist curiosity the formal structure and abstract pattern of the language; then, in using this knowledge as one of the many instruments in, for example, the comparison of styles of writing. At present, unquestioning custom, the G.C.E., the foreign-language crutch, give the subject a spurious importance earlier in the school.

A language can degenerate. The teacher of English is concerned to keep English alive and healthy. He is therefore bound to search for a means of maintaining the good old and of testing and accepting the good new word or speech habit. The criteria for distinguishing good from bad usage are notoriously fallible and subjective: they are such things as euphony, educated taste and consent, clarity, ability to communicate. In so far as anyone can see and defend a genuine distinction between forms (for example, between 'shall' and 'will') he has a duty to maintain the forms – yet, as is happening in the case of the example given, the distinction may die out. Other factors than defensible logic enter, and powerfully: the language is learnt by imitation, and by acceptance of custom, but it is revivified by a sort of organic growth – by the power of new writing, of new thinking, and of the re-lived experience of old. It is because there is never enough time to ensure this organic growth that the writer has questioned the wisdom of allocating a period or its equivalent to formal grammar in the lower school.

# *English and Intelligence*

D. W. HARDING

THE devising of the original intelligence tests, the standardizations, the revisions, the tests of reliability, the researches into validity, the construction of new types of test, the persuasion of administrative authorities to make fairly wide practical use of them, this achievement, costly in ingenuity, years of patient labour and subtle statistical analysis might be expected to meet with enthusiasm from teachers of English. They, if anyone, should welcome an assessment of intelligence. In fact, their welcome has been tepid, even tinged with distrust. Now that intelligence testing is on its way to becoming a potent engine amongst the administrative machinery of education it may be useful to inquire whether anything more than inertia and professional exclusiveness contributes to the lack of enthusiasm.

The tests measure some quality with remarkable objectivity – far beyond that of an ordinary examination, of course – and they measure it reliably, giving the same answer, within fairly narrow limits, each time they are applied. The effects of coaching can be made negligible without much difficulty by ensuring that all candidates have a small number of practice attempts at the test (this method of dealing with coaching is not everywhere administratively established but appears to be technically sound). A child's efficiency in the tests – relative to other children of the same age – is a quality that remains in the vast majority of children very stable as they grow up, even if the alleged 'constancy' of the I.Q. has been exaggerated. All this the informed teacher of English readily admits. What he may perhaps question is whether the quality measured is of prime importance to him in the children he teaches.

Dr W. P. Alexander offered some evidence, in his valuable monograph *Intelligence, Concrete and Abstract* (Cambridge 1935), of the influence of the qualities measured by intelligence tests on children's success in various school subjects. By comparing scores in 'performance tests', in which problems are framed in terms of concrete materials, with scores in the more usual 'abstract' (largely verbal) tests, he was able to show that the two kinds of test measure partly the same and partly different abilities. The characteristic of the two sets of scores which was responsible, on statistical analysis, for the correspondence between them he identified with '*g*', the statistical factor which expresses the overlapping parts of the abilities needed for all the various intellectual tasks. Scores in the concrete tests yielded evidence of an additional factor which he called '*F*', and scores in the abstract tests yielded a factor '*v*'. Putting aside statistical caution and psychological precision, we can reasonably say that the concrete tests measure 'practical ability' (i.e. general intelligence plus a special facility for handling problems framed in concrete terms), and the abstract tests measure 'verbal ability' (i.e. general intelligence plus a special facility for handling problems framed in verbal terms).

Alexander then went on to find out how much the three different 'factors' contributed to the marks obtained by children in various school subjects, including English. In the first place, as one would expect, he found that success in school subjects depended not exclusively on these abilities but to a large extent (varying from subject to subject) on other features of personality, among which he suggests that persistence was perhaps predominant. These latter qualities have not been brought within range of simply psychological measurement in any effective degree. Alexander represents the statistical influence of the most important of these qualities by his factor '*X*'. He then shows that success in English is accounted for to the extent of 23 per cent. by *X*, 10 per cent. by *g* (general intelligence) and 67 per cent. by *v* ('verbal facility' as I have called it). Similarly he shows that for mathematics the relative contributions are: *X*, 48 per cent., *g*, 31 per cent. and *v*, 19 per cent.; for science: *X*, 55 per cent., *v*, 31 per cent. and *g*, 12 per cent. This last extraordinary result prompts Alexander to comment that 'science' here means science as taught in the particular American school in which his study was made, and that science as a school subject varies from school to school.

This, of course, is the crucial point; and it applies equally to English as to science or any other subject. Yet, like many psychologists, Alexander seems much happier about the use of tests for predicting success in English. He writes that, 'testing *g* and *v* with intelligence scales we should have covered 73 per cent. of the total variance. We know from experience that scholastic guidance in this sphere is fairly successful when based on verbal intelligence tests alone. That we occasionally meet cases where pupils do not succeed, despite the fact that they scored well in such tests, is to be explained by the fact that we neglected '*X*'. It is just this note of confidence that makes me, for one, a little uneasy.

The question is whether minds possessing the verbal ability measured by the tests are necessarily the minds that are most rewarding for a teacher of English. It seems a reasonable surmise, for instance, that teachers effectively influenced by I. A. Richards might want general intelligence to count for more than 10 per cent. of a child's success in the English they taught. The aptitude indicated by *v* is not yet by any means clearly identified or intimately understood; it is some kind of facility in the understanding of words and the handling of problems framed verbally. But not all kinds of verbal facility are equally welcome to all teachers of English. Some kinds may make for lapping up Macaulay and others for enjoying Cobbett. Nor do the tests necessarily reveal much about the child's ability to express himself in language, as distinct from understanding it. The nature and quality of a particular English course alone determines whether a given test will be a useful instrument in selecting children for the course. The fact that a test had fair success in predicting children's relative success in the English course at two American schools, or at hundreds of English schools for that matter, would be no guarantee of its validity in selecting children for the English course that this or that teacher gives at this or that school.

This point of view may seem to the administrator unworkably anarchic – a fact that points to one of the ultimately fatal weaknesses of large-scale centralized administration. For the possibility of development in the teaching of English depends on advances and experiments, and the taking of risks, by this or that teacher; advances have to be made first in salients, not on the whole broad front. If we take the view that centralized control should be concerned with maintaining equivalent standards at different schools and not imposing uniformity of performance (an easier and administratively more tempting task), it follows that a standard psychological test will not necessarily be the best method of selecting children for any given school. It follows that we must look with some anxiety at the ideals suggested by Alexander in 1935: 'If the loadings in a test are such that it is good for prediction of success in English, it necessarily follows that these loadings are wrong for prediction of success in mathematics. This being so, we must either have a different test for every subject (as is the general tendency in practice today) or measure these factors one at a time and then combine the measures according to the needs of the situation. This would be really scientific guidance. For example, if we had a measure of *g* and also one of *v* we should simply load these in the ratio of 6 of *v* to 1 of *g* for English, and 2 of *v* to 3 of *g* for mathematics. With, in addition to these, a measurement of *X*, we could load appropriately and make a most accurate prediction of future success.'

However far from practical realization these ideals still are, they none the less represent an unwelcome tendency. Dr Alexander, it is true, seemed to see the snag where science teaching was concerned and he would perhaps not deny its existence for English, but most administrators are prone to be seduced by the allurements of simplicity. The danger lies in the extent to which a uniform set of selection tests for English must imply the expectation of a uniform achievement.

That the wish to secure uniformity really exists, and in a form vigorous enough to lead to action, was instanced by the production in 1933 of the *Northamptonshire Composition Scale* (G. Perrie Williams, Harrap). I pick on Dr Williams' work only because it was excellent of its kind and resulted in the creation of an effective tool for a purpose which many would regard as good. In this undertaking fifty compositions written by children of eleven to twelve for what was then the free place examination were arranged in order of merit by 199 teachers. It was found, of course, that although the teachers were working to a carefully prepared standard scheme of marking they differed wildly from each other, not only in the marks they gave but even in assigning compositions to one of four grades. This familiar finding was only the first step, however. The author next took the median judgment of the 199 teachers on each composition and ranked the fifty compositions in order of merit according to this judgment. The aim was to provide in this way a permanent scale against which future examiners could match any composition and so decide on its 'correct' mark. And in fact preliminary experiments with this scale showed that it did bring about much closer agreement among examiners when they marked other compositions. That is to say, examiners whose judgments would otherwise have deviated a good deal now subscribed fairly closely to the standard represented by the average (or median) view of the original 199 teachers.

One can only feel dismay at the implication that uniformity of marking seems worth securing at the cost of establishing as a criterion the median view of 199 teachers in one small area in the 1930's. From the compositions that gained good marks it seems clear that the average teacher of this group of judges rewarded fluency in genteel-romantic journalese rather highly; phoney rhapsodies about the English countryside, concocted to the greater glory of a brewer or a bus company, would have gone down well with him. And it is easy to believe that tests with a high loading of *v* and a slight loading of *g* would have given him promising pupils. But no effort of standardization or statistics would have lent him a scrap of valid support against any of his deviant colleagues who saw what this stuff was worth. Nor would it make the least difference in principle if the median view of 2,000 teachers from all over the country had been taken, not even if that view happened to be one that you and I agreed with. We should still be unwise to impose it by means of psychological and administrative machinery on people who judged differently. To do so would be to invite rigidity. Plasticity in a profession, with the possibility of development, is paid for by allowing some of its members to be in the wrong. Even the aim of making examinations less of a lottery may be questionable if it results in the deeper entrenchment of mediocrity and ensures that the best people never can get a prize. We do well to fear an 'objectivity' that really amounts to a majority judgment. Rather than uniformity of expectation among examiners in English we need the tolerance and flexibility of mind that can recognize equivalent levels of merit among pupils who have been offered widely diverse ideals.

It may be argued that this is perfectly compatible with a greatly increased use of intelligence tests in the selection of pupils for English courses. The tests, it may be said, are meant only to select generally 'intelligent' children, and the teacher is then left to make what he wants or rather can of the 'intelligence'. But this is where we came in. As one sees from Alexander's work, the usefulness of tests is measured in practice by their prediction of achievement in some particular curriculum. If we keep them general enough to be relevant to all kinds of curriculum they will only serve Binet's original purpose, that of identifying children who are too unintelligent to benefit by any ordinary schooling. It still is as tests of 'unintelligence' that they are most indisputably useful; presumably no teacher regrets the establishment of a minimum level of whatever quality the tests measure as a prerequisite for ordinary classroom teaching. But above that minimum it becomes exceedingly difficult to show any close relation between *g* and success at particular school subjects such as English. It is then tempting to supplement the general tests of intelligence with measures of more limited qualities, and the choice of these qualities and the relative importance given them depend upon our particular view of the proper nature of, say, an English course.

It is only the teachers who can ultimately provide means of measuring the validity of tests used in school allocation, just as employers must provide criteria for the validity of vocational selection tests. It must not be assumed that the success of vocational tests within their limited range guarantees equal success for tests used in educational guidance. Only limited guidance can be given for complex vocational work, and we should do well to recognize that the intellectual demands even of complex occupations – medicine, the law, scientific research, public administration – are less extensive and subtle than the requirements for a highly developed understanding of the English language and its literature. The English teacher takes his pupils some little way into this extraordinarily complex activity. It can ultimately be no ones' responsibility but his to judge whether he is receiving the right pupils for his own approach and his own part of the task.

If psychological tests are to be given more weight than at present in the selection of children for English courses they must be subtler tests than we yet possess. The aspect of mental functioning on which they shed very little light, if any at all, is the relation between the highly differentiated cognitive surface of the mind – solving its straightforward problems with precise words and numbers or clearly organized spatial designs and cubes – and the much less manageable aspects of the personality where interest, sentiment, desire, mood and attitude are in a fluid condition, a condition which literature may render less inchoate by means additional to the precisely differentiated, cognitive 'sense' of words and descriptions. The simple (and for a time doubtless useful) device of psychologists was the fiction that intelligence could be clearly distinguished from the emotional and conative aspects of the mind, and dealt with separately. There are plenty of signs that that fiction is being abandoned. There always were psychologists who denied it, notably L. L. Thurstone in *The Nature of Intelligence* (Kegan Paul, 1924). Quite recently David Wechsler, an American authority on intelligence testing, argued explicitly against the older assumptions and maintained that 'general intelligence cannot be equated with intellectual ability, but must be regarded as a manifestation of the personality as a whole' (*American Psychologist*, March 1950). In various other directions psychological attention is nowadays being given to the non-cognitive movements of the mind out of which cognitive meaning is differentiated. But I suspect that some kinds of concern with 'English' offer a closer familiarity with these mental activities than does 'psychology' at present.

The special kind of precision of experience that is needed for, and encouraged by, an understanding of literature and a sensitive use of language seems to be different from the precision needed for intelligence tests. The latter depends on the clear reference-signs employed in cognitive activity from which emotional significance has been as far as possible eliminated. Their precision is gained by exclusion. A great part of our thinking is analogous to the naming of colours, where our 'violet', 'indigo', 'blue', 'green' and so on are labels which, for all their seeming precision, are crudely approximate compared with the real subtleties of colour experience. In getting to know more about the matrix of our formulable thoughts the psychologist can make small progress without taking into account facts which are working materials for the more sensitive use of English. Until he has gone much further in this direction the contribution he can properly offer towards the better teaching of English is strictly limited.

# V

# *ENGAGING WITH A LITERARY HERITAGE*

As soon as the child is reading and writing with confidence, part of the teacher's responsibility is to introduce the literary heritage of the race. In the profoundest sense this is what literacy is *for* – not to read the papers or the 'trespassers will be prosecuted' notices, though these may be necessary and valuable consequences – but to find release from the experience of the here-and-now into 'the best that has been thought and known'. This can be a difficult and paradoxical task. The hardest thing to do with a child who has learned to read is to teach him how to *read*. In a civilization where literacy is general, where so many commercial interests combine to exploit it in flimsy and ephemeral ways, where to concentrate and to attend to language is to live quite against the buoyant mood of the age – then everything works to blur the child's sense of language. The unique charge of this word and of that becomes obscured, and inoculated against the Shakespearean use of language the young boy or girl is also inoculated against the Shakespearean realm of experience.

Given literacy, the teacher's next task is to teach *reading*. This means, often enough, the concentration on limited passages – a speech, a page, a verse – picking up tone and rhythm and image, all the metaphorical drive and resonance, until the reader begins to open himself fully to language under the pressure of genius. The succeeding essays on the novel, the play, the poem, tackle problems of reading in this sense. After them come two reminders. Firstly, mediaeval drama – a little-tapped source of fine dramatic work, which can perhaps better support the centrality of Shakespeare than the more common excursions into Restoration comedy or the drama of the 'nineties. Secondly the Authorized Version, where again we have a line of strength formerly handed down by the home and the community, but which now (like folk-song or John Bunyan) has to be largely preserved and communicated by the school.

# *Twelfth Night*

CHRISTOPHER GILLIE

'Twelfth Night' is a frequent set book; this means that it is one of the plays commonly regarded as a safe introduction to Shakespeare. Unfortunately, the underlying assumption about this quality of 'safeness' is apt to be that it is synonymous with lack of difficulty, absence of challenge, even sheer innocuousness. Of course, if these qualities are really true about the play, then, as an introduction to Shakespeare it is of small use; such a work could only be an evasion of the problem. My aim in this article is to indicate an approach to the play which shows it to be more complex and interesting than is usually recognized, and consequently that it may be a satisfying challenge to teacher and student.

The usual assumption about it seems to be that it is a kind of circus embroidered with a sentimental fairy tale; in fact, an Elizabethan Christmas pantomime. But this view endows the play with an apparent inconsequence that is irritating to many students, especially perhaps to the more intelligent ones. Such readers allow to Viola her 'charm' and to Sir Toby and company their 'funniness', but they are apt to be impatient with the Duke 'in love with love' and with the extraordinary vagaries of Olivia. The conclusion of the play, in particular, is apt to be shrugged off, with the result that as a dramatic organisation it makes no total effect; the experience is fragmentary, unsatisfactory and mystifying.

I was myself led to what I think is a more coherent and rewarding view of *Twelfth Night* by a question in a test paper: 'How many different attitudes to love can you distinguish in the play?' I believe that a full answer to this question disposes of the apparent incoherence that I have indicated.

It is obvious and easy to begin with Viola and Orsino; in fact it is by contrasting the two that the attitude of each can best be understood. In scene 4 of act 2, having been employed by Orsino to woo Olivia, Viola tries to persuade the Duke to give up hope:

VIOLA: But if she cannot love you, sir?
DUKE: I cannot be so answer'd.
VIOLA: Sooth, but you must.
  Say that some lady – as, perhaps, there is –
  Hath for your love as great a pang of heart
  As you have for Olivia: you cannot love her;
  You tell her so; must she not, then, be answer'd?
DUKE: There is no woman's sides
  Can bear the beating of so strong a passion
  As love doth give my heart; no woman's heart
  So big, to hold so much: they lack retention.
  Alas, their love may be called appetite –
  No motion of the liver, but the palate, –
  That suffer surfeit, cloyment and revolt;
  But mine is all as hungry as the sea,
  And can digest as much: make no compare
  Between that love a woman can bear me
  And that I owe Olivia.

What are the implications of this speech of the Duke? One may notice that his passion is expressed entirely in physical terms. It is apparently 'A motion of the liver', and 'as hungry as the sea, and can digest as much'. Moreover, if no woman can love as Orsino loves, then presumably Olivia lacks this capacity too, and what then of the high price he professes to place on her? She must be at best the most prized of his physical possessions, and he a bitterly jealous husband believing that her feeling for him may at any time suffer 'surfeit, cloyment, and revolt', and be distracted to someone else. In what, then, does Orsino's love itself differ from mere appetite, and what is his reason for supposing that it is different, except that he has not yet been surfeited?

And now, in reply, comes Viola:

VIOLA: Ay, but I know –
DUKE: What dost thou know?
VIOLA: Too well what love women to men may owe:
  In faith they are as true of heart as we.
  My father had a daughter lov'd a man,
  As it might be, perhaps, were I a woman,
  I should your lordship.

DUKE: And what's her history?
VIOLA: A blank, my lord. She never told her love,
But let concealment like a worm i'th'bud
Feed on her damask cheek: she pin'd in thought
And, with a green and yellow melancholy,
She sat like Patience on a monument
Smiling at grief. Was not this love indeed?

It is noteworthy that Viola's craving is *to be* loved, whereas Orsino has only a craving to devour, and expects, apparently, no love in return – only right of possession. The fact that Viola is as reckless in her love as Orsino in his, is unimportant beside the fact that her capacity for real feeling is authentic, whereas he is self-deluded. If Viola is deluded about Orsino then she is exposing herself to tragedy; but this is more than Orsino himself is capable of.

It is now time to consider Olivia. She is a great Lady, and her personal dignity is in proportion to her status. She is the daughter of a count, is desired in marriage by the sovereign of the country (and probably many others – Sir Andrew is a suitor), keeps a great household, and even her riotous hanger-on of an uncle, Sir Toby, is in awe of her. It is important that these facts about Olivia should be given full weight, because they are a clue to her behaviour in the play. Like Portia in *The Merchant of Venice* she is bored by the candidates for her hand, whom she may well suspect of desiring to marry her rank rather than herself. Her state of secluded mourning for her dead brother need not be taken too seriously; it is a useful defence against her wooers.

The second important characteristic of Olivia is her witty good sense. This appears in her humorous indulgence of the clown, and in her strictures on Malvolio, who will not indulge him:

O, you are sick of self-love, Malvolio, and taste with a distemper'd appetite. To be generous, guiltless, and of a free disposition, is to take those things for bird-bolts that you deem cannon-bullets: there is no slander in an allow'd fool, though he do nothing but rail; nor no railing in a known discreet man, though he do nothing but reprove.

The salty good sense of this does not suggest a woman without penetration, or one likely to be easily infatuated. How, then, are we to account for her behaviour later in the play? For the solution to this puzzle, we must consider the scene in which Viola appears, disguised as the page Cesario, to woo Olivia on behalf of the Duke. Olivia is bored by the Duke, as what woman of sense would not be by a man who wooed only by proxy, but she consents to see Viola because Viola is importunate, and because she expects to make a fool of the page in such a way as to deter a second visit.

There follows a fencing match, in which all Olivia's passes are foiled, and at the end of which she is pierced through the heart. This defeat comes about because Viola is different from Olivia's expectation of her in two ways. First, instead of being a boring, mannered courtier, she is as poised and nimble-witted as Olivia herself; second, and far more important, she is sincere. Sincerity is a weapon Olivia is not equipped to meet; she has probably, at least in her wooers, never met it before. We must remember that Viola is in love, and debarred from expressing her passion except in the desperately frustrated way that we have seen. Orsino's relationship to Olivia resembles Viola's to Orsino in one respect; the object of the passion is, though for very different reasons, out of reach. Viola is, therefore, in complete imaginative sympathy with her master, and can address herself to Olivia in the very terms in which her heart would address him:

> VIOLA: If I did love you in my master's flame,
> With such a suffering, such a deadly life,
> In your denial I would find no sense,
> I would not understand it.
> OLIVIA: Why, what would you?
> VIOLA: Make me a willow cabin at your gate,
> And call upon my soul within the house;
> Write loyal cantons of contemned love,
> And sing them loud even in the dead of night;
> Holla your name to the reverberate hills;
> And make the babbling gossip of the air
> Cry out, 'Olivia!' O, you should not rest
> Between the elements of air and earth,
> But you should pity me!
> OLIVIA: You might do much.

Olivia is, in fact, already lost; she is lost less because she is in love with Viola, than because she has been given a vision. This bored, lonely woman of high estate, who has nothing to fill her days except the flattery of courtiers, the witticisms of clowns, and the staling memories of a fading sorrow, now sees that she might fill her life with love, if only she can find a mate as worthy of being loved, and as capable of love, as Viola is. This explains the otherwise unaccountable marriage to Sebastian, or rather the fact that Olivia is evidently content to abide by this marriage even when she discovers the confusion between the brother and sister. Like Orsino, Olivia becomes in love with love, but whereas to him it is the most interesting of all forms of recreation, to her it is a matter of life itself. Sebastian, after all, is willing to love her: he can be taught, just as Olivia herself has been taught by his sister.

The loves of Orsino, Olivia and Viola are, as is so often the way with human love, by turns comic and moving, sometimes both simultaneously. But there is another kind of love in the play which, here as in life, arouses only the more brutal sort of mockery; this, of course, is the self-love of Malvolio. Space does not allow me to expatiate on his part in the play, and it is probably needless to do so, but it is worth noticing that he is, in his own way, as much 'in love' as the others; Olivia's pointed rebuke early in the play is not there for nothing. His role completes the pattern of attitudes to love; he is, so to speak, at the comic end of the spectrum of which Viola is at the tragic end, and the grotesqueness of his self-delusion balances the phantasmagoria in which the romantic theme is played out.

It is dramatic irony that in this phantasmagoria the only character to have a true measure of affairs is herself consciously unreal and a deceiver. Viola has the inner truth in her grasp but at the cost of being a conscious liar, rather in the same way as Feste alone is entitled to free comment before all just because he is an 'allow'd fool'. The fool and the liar alone are the wise and the true – unless we make another exception, the sot.

Sir Toby owes his privileged position in the play to the fact that he does not care to have one. Everybody else wants something or someone – even Fabian, perhaps, Feste's position in Olivia's household. Sir Toby wants nothing and nobody but his licence, and that, in the nature of the thing, he takes. It is on this rock of unconsciousness – his continuous, uninhibitedly coarse enjoyment depends on his being unconscious – that the brittle structure of error and delusion smashes, leaving the characters face to face with the truth; for it is his device of setting Viola and Sir Andrew against each other in a duel that eventually, though unintentionally, exposes the shams and reveals the realities. He represents, if one wishes, the coarse actuality with which all 'fancy' must sooner or later and for good or ill come to terms; in this play, being a comedy, it is for good.

*Twelfth Night* can thus be regarded as a marvellously complete pattern of attitudes to love, in which the psychology, instead of being merely whimsical and clownish, is in fact subtle, varied and balanced; it is a play of profound sanity. As a pattern of humour it is no less comprehensive in its range, but the humour is intrinsic to the main theme; the chief protest to be made against the common acceptance of the play is that the coarser element should not be allowed to dominate, leaving the rest as a mere golden, sentimental backcloth.

# *An Approach to 'Nostromo'*

J. D. HAINSWORTH

THE notes that follow are the fruit of an attempt to bring to bear upon the teaching of a novel the experience of the practical criticism class. The work we were dealing with was Conrad's *Nostromo*. The class read the novel through in their own time, and in class periods we looked together at particular passages. Occasionally, these passages were suggested by members of the class, but usually, at this stage, I selected them myself.

To make the points I wish to make, it will be sufficient to refer to only three of the passages. The page references are to the volume in Dent's Collected Edition of Conrad's works.

The first passage (pp. 51-52) is a description of the drawing-room at the Goulds' house:

Then giving up the empty cup into his young friend's hand, extended with a smile, he [Señor Avellanos] continued to expatiate upon the patriotic nature of the San Tomé mine for the simple pleasure of talking fluently, it seemed, while his reclining body jerked backwards and forwards in a rocking-chair of the sort exported from the United States. The ceiling of the largest drawing-room of the Casa Gould extended its white level far above his head. The loftiness dwarfed the mixture of heavy, straight-backed Spanish chairs of brown wood with leathern seats, and European furniture, low, and cushioned all over, like squat little monsters gorged to bursting with steel springs and horsehair. There were knick-knacks on little tables, mirrors let into the wall above marble consoles, square spaces of carpet under the two groups of armchairs, each presided over by a deep sofa; smaller rugs scattered all over the floor of red tiles; three windows from ceiling down to the ground, opening on a balcony, and flanked by the perpendicular folds of the dark hangings. The stateliness of ancient days lingered between the four high, smooth walls, tinted a delicate primrose-colour; and Mrs Gould, with her little head and shining coils of hair, sitting in a cloud of muslin and lace before a slender mahogany table, resembled a fairy posed lightly before dainty philtres dispensed out of vessels of silver and porcelain.

At first sight, this is merely a preliminary sketching-in of a scene which, throughout the entire length of the novel, is never far from the reader's consciousness, and which is itself the centre of a good deal of important action. Yet what the passage conveys is much more than just a description of scene, as a query about what the room can tell us of past and present Costaguanian history will soon elicit from the class. The very furnishings illustrate the social and economic pressures to which the province is subject. From them, we learn not only of the existence of a Spanish tradition, and of imports from Europe and America, but also of the aesthetic and cultural values associated with these facts. While the 'heavy, straight-backed Spanish chairs' help towards an impression of 'the stateliness of ancient days', the European furniture is 'low and cushioned all over, like squat little monsters gorged to bursting', and Don José Avellanos, himself a relic of ancient days, enjoys 'the simple pleasure of talking fluently' as he *jerks* to and fro in a rocking-chair 'of the sort exported from the United States'.

The paragraph ends in an expression of Mrs Gould's personality, and what it means in the life of Sulaco. This transition from furnishings to a person involves no felt breach in the unity of the paragraph, for Mrs Gould, seated before a slender mahogany table, is a tableau-vivant rather than a character, a part of the scene rather than an intrusion on it, and this is as it should be. This is the scene and situation to which, above all the others in the book, she really belongs. Here it is that she dispenses her hospitality, and it is as a high-priestess of hospitality or fairy-godmother to those in need of it, that she sits, 'resembling a fairy posed lightly before dainty philtres dispensed out of vessels of silver and porcelain'. Discussion should bring out, too, how the qualities of littleness and beauty, present, either singly or in conjunction, in the words with which Mrs Gould is associated ('delicate', 'little', 'muslin and lace', 'slender', 'fairy', 'lightly', 'dainty'), are appropriate in a moral as well as a physical sense. For she pits her puny idealism against the might of social and economic pressures, and fully deserves the suggestion of a halo in the 'shining coils of hair'.

In its ironical, unillusioned quality, the second passage (pp. 80-81) illustrates what Dr Leavis says in *The Great Tradition* about Conrad's own attitude being much akin to that of his character, Decoud:

> Of course, he [Mr Holroyd] was too great a man to be questioned as to his motives, even by his intimates. The outside world was at liberty to wonder respectfully at the hidden meaning of his actions. He was so great a man that his lavish patronage of the 'purer forms of Christianity' (which in its naïve form of church-building amused Mrs Gould) was looked upon by his fellow-citizens as the manifestation of a pious and humble spirit. But in his own circles of the financial world the taking up of such a thing as the San Tomé mine was regarded with respect, indeed, but rather as a subject for discreet jocularity. It was a great man's caprice. In the great Holroyd building (an enormous pile of iron, glass, and blocks of stone at the corner of two streets, cobwebbed aloft by the radiation of telegraph wires) the heads of principal departments exchanged humorous glances, which meant that they were not let into the secrets of the San Tomé business. The Costaguana mail (it was never large – one fairly heavy envelope) was taken unopened straight into the great man's room, and no instructions dealing with it had ever been issued thence. The office whispered that he answered personally – and not by dictation either, but actually writing in his own hand, with pen and ink, and, it was to be supposed, taking a copy in his own private press copy-book, inaccessible to profane eyes. Some scornful young men, insignificant pieces of minor machinery in that eleven-storey-high workshop of great affairs, expressed frankly their private opinion that the great chief had done at last something silly, and was ashamed of his folly; others, elderly and insignificant, but full of romantic reverence for the business that had devoured their best years, used to mutter darkly and knowingly that this was a portentous sign; that the Holroyd connection meant by-and-by to get hold of the whole Republic of Costaguana, lock, stock and barrel.

The passage epitomises the novel as a whole in the pervasiveness of the sardonic contemplation, and also in the objects towards which that contemplation is directed. There is, for instance, the clear recognition of a cleavage between apparent or declared intention and real motive – 'He was so great a man that his lavish patronage of the "purer forms of Christianity" . . . was looked upon by his fellow-citizens as a manifestation of a pious and humble spirit.' The class should not be slow to recognize that Mr Holroyd is not unique in this respect. Charles Gould's declared motive of bringing security and justice to an oppressed people by his pursuit of material interest (p. 84) does not long remain credible to either Mrs Gould or the reader. It is the occasion of Decoud's comment to Mrs Gould (pp. 214-15) that an Englishman 'cannot act or exist without idealizing every simple feeling, desire, or achievement' – Decoud being, appropriately, very concerned in his own case that he shall not mistake for patriotism that love for Antonia Avellanos which inspires him to political activity.

Comment should be invited on the manner in which Mr Holroyd's building is described. No less than the Casa Gould, the 'eleven-storey-high workshop' characterizes the civilization of which it is part. What is not said about the building is as important as what is said. There is nothing here of artistic disposition or aesthetic effect, which occupy such space in the description of the Casa. What is offered is mainly a catalogue of the materials used – 'an enormous pile of iron, glass, and blocks of stone at the corner of two streets, cobwebbed aloft by the radiation of telegraph wires'.

The class should also be asked about the effect of Mr Holroyd's activities on those who work for him, and what evidence there is of this in the passage. The 'scornful young men' are 'insignificant pieces of minor machinery', and the business is said to have 'devoured' the best years of their more elderly but still 'insignificant' colleagues. Here, at an early stage in the novel, is a foreshadowing of the devouring and dehumanizing effect that material interest is to have on more prominent actors in the story, on Charles Gould and Nostromo, and the contrastingly simple Sotillo; and a hint of the vision which Dr Monygham finally communicates to Mrs Gould: 'She saw the San Tomé mountain hanging over the Campo, over the whole land, feared, hated, wealthy; more soulless than any tyrant, more pitiless and autocratic than the worst government; ready to crush innumerable lives in the expansion of its greatness' (p. 521).

But what, most of all, deserves discussion in the passage is the contemplation, rather than the objects contemplated, and the predominant note of that contemplation is the note of unillusion. All the way through, a contrast is evident between the view the reader is invited to take up, and the views of other people (Mr Holroyd's 'intimates', his 'fellow-citizens', 'the heads of principal departments', 'the office', etc.), who are themselves part of what the reader is looking at. The contrast produces an amusement not incompatible with compassion. It is the kind of amusement exhibited by Decoud in his memorable tête-à-tête with Antonia Avellanos, behind the long damask curtains of the Casa Gould. Conrad's reversions to this spirit are just as vital to the unity of the whole as is his preoccupation with 'theme'.

The third passage (pp. 384-5) describes the victorious entry of the combined forces of Señor Gamacho and Pedrito Montero into Sulaco:

During the night the expectant populace had taken possession of all the belfries in the town in order to welcome Pedrito Montero, who was making his entry after having slept the night in Rincon. And first came straggling in through the land gate the armed mob of all colours, complexions, types, and states of raggedness, calling themselves the Sulaco National Guard, and commanded by Señor Gamacho. Through the middle of the street streamed, like a torrent of rubbish, a mass of straw hats, ponchos, gun-barrels, with an enormous green and yellow flag flapping in their midst, in a cloud of dust, to the furious beating of drums. The spectators recoiled against the walls of the houses, shouting their *Vivas*! Behind the rabble could be seen the lances of the cavalry, the 'army' of Pedro Montero. . . . They rode four abreast, mounted on confiscated Campo horses, clad in the heterogeneous stock of roadside stores they had looted hurriedly in their rapid ride through the northern part of the province; for Pedro Montero had been in a great hurry to occupy Sulaco. The handkerchiefs knotted loosely around their bare throats were glaringly new, and all the right sleeves of their cotton shirts had been cut off close to the shoulder for greater freedom in throwing the lazo. Emaciated greybeards rode by the side of lean dark youths, marked by all the hardships of campaigning, with strips of raw beef twined round the crowns of their hats, and huge iron spurs fastened to their naked heels. Those that in the passes of the mountains had lost their lances had provided themselves with the goads used by the Campo cattlemen: slender shafts of palm fully ten feet long, with a lot of loose rings jingling under the ironshod point. They were armed with knives and revolvers. A haggard fearlessness characterized the expression of all these sun-blacked countenances; they glared down haughtily with their scorched eyes at the crowd, or, blinking upwards insolently, pointed out to each other some particular head amongst the women at the windows. When they had ridden into the Plaza and caught sight of the equestrian statue of the King dazzlingly white in the sunshine, towering enormous and motionless above the surges of the crowd, with its eternal gesture of saluting, a murmur of surprise ran through their ranks. 'What is that saint in the big hat?' they asked each other.

The two sections of the 'army' are kept distinct, but, in either case, the question may be asked whether the description is meant simply to repel us, or whether there are any grounds given for sympathy. The degradation of the 'Sulaco National Guard', who stream through the street 'like a torrent of rubbish', is not without its pathos, and the 'expectancy' of the populace, who, however, recoil against the walls of the houses to shout their *Vivas*! is another reminder of the deprivations and aspirations which lie behind the popular response to Montero. The evidence of loot and pillage which Pedrito's 'cavalry' bear about them on their bodies, and their uninhibited insolence, cannot but repel us, but, at the end, their surprise and ignorance suddenly make even them human, and we grant them a share in that sympathy for the common people which the novel so consistently evokes.

The statue which causes their surprise is, like others in the novel – the broken-nosed bishop at the Amarilla Club and the Madonna and Child on the staircase of the Casa Gould, used significantly, and the thoughts and feelings it provokes will probably be worth inquiring into. Like the heavy, straight-backed chairs of the Casa, it recalls the Spanish past of the continent, whose traditions linger on in such families as the Avellanos and the Corbelàns. But the title of 'King', through the nickname 'King of Sulaco', has become closely associated with that other equestrian, Charles Gould, who, the novel has demonstrated, is as tragically aloof from the common people and their aspirations, as ever was his Spanish counterpart, 'towering enormous . . . above the surges of the crowd'. Both the contrast between the old- and new-style wielders of power, and the characteristics they have in common, are surely meant to be part of the reader's awareness. Perhaps some will catch, too, in the description of the statue, a hint of that tragic irony crystallized elsewhere in the novel in the characteristic pose of Giorgio Viola, as he meditates on his dead leader, Garibaldi:

> . . . the Garibaldino could be seen . . . with his big bush of white hair, his arms folded, his legs crossed, leaning back his leonine head against the lintel, and looking up the wooded slopes of the foothills at the snowy dome of Higuerota (p. 26).

In both descriptions is a conjunction of white (suggesting saintly idealism), motionlessness (of the statue and of Viola), deadness (of the King and of Garibaldi), and towering height (of the statue and of Higuerota), which serves to underline the idea implicit in the action of the novel, that idealism can exist unsullied only in dissociation from life. Viola, alone of all the principal figures in the novel, plays no part whatever in the political events of the day. Charles Gould's idealism has to compromise with things as they are, and finally becomes no more than a blind for his ambition, while Mrs Gould's is thwarted and pathetic, and that of Dr Monygham complicated by an awareness of human fallibility amounting almost to cynicism.

I have tried to set down the kind of comments that can arise when particular passages from a novel are discussed, not in isolation from their source, as so often in practical criticism, but in relation to the novel of which they form part. Setting the passages against their context has drawn attention to Conrad's characteristic mode of giving symbolic life to physical objects and qualities; to such recurrent themes as the cleavage between apparent intention and real motive, and the corrosion of idealism in a materialistic world; and to the unillusioned and often compassionate contemplation of the human situations in which the themes are bodied forth. The particular passages have helped to illuminate the novel as a whole, and the novel as a whole to illuminate the particular passages.

My contention is that adequate reading requires a sense of context which is not developed by the practical criticism of isolated passages. The study of such passages has its place in the teaching of reading, but only as a preliminary to the study of passages in their contexts.

The transition from one kind of criticism to the other will probably raise problems. 'How', I have heard it asked, 'can we read a whole novel at the rate at which we have been reading these short passages? It would take months.' To draw a distinction between 'intensive' and 'extensive' reading can be an unhelpful and, indeed, harmful comment, if it suggests to the class that there are two different methods of reading. There are not. 'Extensive' reading involves no less of a full response to the words on the page than does 'intensive' reading: it is only that the words are less demanding. To discriminate, to give to each word and to each passage the degree of attention that it merits, neither less nor more, is one of the abilities that can be developed, and should be aimed at in the preliminary stage of dealing with passages in isolation.

# *Conrad: The Shadow Line – Form in the Novel*

G. D. KLINGOPULOS

'The actual story of a novel eludes the epitomist as completely as character; few great works are not ridiculous in synopsis. And for this reason – that the form of a novel only exists as a balance of response on the part of the reader.' (C. H. Rickword in *The Calendar of Modern Letters*.)

A DISTINCT stage in the process of 'trying to learn to use words' is reached when the schoolboy or adult begins to extend his command of critical terms to cover all kinds of reading-matter, not only the classics, but the poems, plays and novels of the day. It is by no means easy to persuade even quick-witted readers to go beyond summaries of plot and character when describing the effect of a Shakespeare play. A large proportion of them never succeed in putting into words an adequate impression of the living centre of interest in a great work of literature. Such readers will offer any amount of historical and biographical annotation to a poem, say a satire of Pope's or an ode of Keats's, with observations on the versification, but the final, sharp recognition of the 'life' which has been given 'form', is beyond them. No experienced teacher would pretend that he does not share, in relation to many works of literature, the same feelings of difficulty and intractableness. Great works may appeal at several levels, but there is always, as understanding deepens, a sense of difficulty, in the resolution of which much of the 'value' of literature resides. A poet and critic, William Empson, has written in this way of the process of writing poetry:

When you are holding a variety of things in your mind, or using for a single matter a variety of intellectual machinery, the only way of applying all your criteria is to apply them simultaneously; the only way of forcing the reader to grasp your total meaning is to arrange that he can only feel satisfied if he is bearing all the elements in mind at the moment of conviction; the only way of not giving something heterogeneous is to give something which is at every point a compound.

The 'moment of conviction', when the 'total meaning' of a poem flowers in the mind, is hardly to be reached without difficulty. Nor is the case essentially different when novels are studied. There may be a clear plot and distinctive characters, as in *Pride and Prejudice* or *Washington Square*, but to arrive at the 'total meaning' of these works one has to keep at a distance a number of inadequate, over-simple alternatives. It is true, of course, that the average novel is more likely to be 'something heterogeneous' than 'at every point a compound', and that even some great novelists, like Scott or Dickens, were frequently content with heterogeneity. The novel has often been made a synonym for formlessness. 'A novel was a novel, as a pudding is a pudding.' The sheer bulk of some novels creates problems in the classroom. But there are various ways by which readers may be brought to understand the formal organization of prose fiction as something more than symmetry of plot and neatness of arrangement.

Because it can be read comfortably in four or five two-hour sessions, I have used Conrad's *The Shadow Line* for this purpose. True it is a simple tale when compared with *Nostromo*, and several critics have seen in this late work signs of something resembling sentimentality. Here there is none of Conrad's characteristic probing of the ambiguity of idealism and goodness. But there is no falsification in this entirely successful story, in which an attentive reader would not fail to notice numerous astringent touches, such as the use made of the lunacy and death of the previous skipper ('in all essentials but his age just such another man as myself') and the closing references to Death – 'our common enemy it was Ransome's hard fate to carry consciously within his faithful breast'. In his prefatory note Conrad himself suggests that this novel is, despite its brevity, 'a fairly complex piece of work'. The art it reveals is that of the realizing novelist, welcoming the challenge of his chosen subject-matter, controlling, directing response from sentence to sentence, with a masterly completeness. And the tale offers little to the collector of characters and plots. As with poetic drama, one can only answer the question 'What is it about?' by entering more and more thoroughly into the significance of a phrase here, a choice of words there, by connecting the implications of one image with those of another, and so recreating a whole structure of experience and judgment.

The sub-title is 'A Confession', and Conrad writes in his preface, 'as a matter of fact it *is* personal experience seen in perspective with the eye of the mind and coloured by that affection one can't help feeling for such events of one's life as one has no reason to be ashamed of'. The story is told, like so many of Conrad's, in the first person, but we run no risk of merely equating this with the author. From the first words the experience is distanced. 'Only the young have such moments'. The narrator is a young man, the first mate of a steamship in the Far East. Abruptly he throws up his job when his ship touches at a Malayan port. He takes lodgings at the Sailors' Home there, and meets an older seaman, a Captain Giles, who gives him advice which, though amusingly paternal, is felt to be profound. The narrator is surprised to find such a steady character in such a place. The steadiness of Captain Giles in that hard climate is contrasted with the behaviour of another officer at the Home, who allows himself to become hopelessly useless. By chance a message comes through from the Harbourmaster asking for a skipper to be sent out immediately to a port in the Malay Archipelago. The narrator thus wins his first command – the command of a sailing vessel. Like Captain Giles, the Harbourmaster, also an ex-skipper, is made to seem a pillar of strength, representing on land the moral order of the Merchant Navy. The narrator goes off. In some way the whole story is to be an initiation as well as a test. When the narrator reaches his ship, he finds that the former skipper had died mad and had been buried at sea. The ship had since been commanded by the mate, a gaunt Scot named Burns, who resents being superseded, and is suffering from the shock of the dead skipper's derangement. The crew also is in poor shape, with the exception of the cook, Ransome, a finely built man who is ironically a semi-invalid with a weak heart.

They put to sea and are becalmed. Fever strikes the crew and Burns becomes unmanageably obsessed. The narrator hopes for a change in the weather and meanwhile puts his faith in the ship's store of quinine, which he feels he must carefully administer. But he discovers, when he examines the medical stores, that the quinine phials had been emptied to buy drink for the dead skipper.

The ship continues becalmed. The young second officer proves to be worse than useless. A storm breaks. Only the narrator, the cook and an old deckhand named Frenchy keep the ship afloat, forming an oddly assorted comradeship. The change in the weather restores Burns and some others of the crew. They reach port.

That is all there is of plot. Yet out of these far from unfamiliar materials Conrad creates a tale of such authenticity and power that it makes *The Ancient Mariner*, with which it is sometimes compared, appear slight and fanciful. The prose works, like poetry, through the pressure and interaction of words, and only by responding to them and to their rhythm, as one responds to poetry, can one discover what the story is 'about'.

At the beginning of the story, the wilfulness of the narrator's abrupt decision to throw up his job is brought out by showing him, for a few pages, on the defensive against the entreaties of several of his colleagues. They only make him 'more discontented, disgusted, and dogged than ever. The past eighteen months, so full of new and varied experience, appeared a dreary, prosaic waste of days. I felt – how shall I express it? – that there was no truth to be got out of them. What truth? I should have been hard put to it to explain.' The explanation is, of course, the novel itself.

He meets Captain Giles at the Sailors' Home. 'To me (I know how absurd it is) he looked like a churchwarden. He had the appearance of a man from whom you would expect sound advice, moral sentiments, with perhaps a platitude or two thrown in on occasion, not from a desire to dazzle, but from honest conviction.' The experience of life of Captain Giles is not merely asserted but demonstrated. His moralising is interesting. 'Things out East were made easy for white men. That was all right. The difficulty was to go on keeping white, and some of these nice boys did not know how.' The narrator is sufficiently uncertain of his own aims and motives to be made uncomfortable by these remarks. 'I said to myself that I ought to shut up that moralist.' But the 'twilight and stuffiness' of the Home, and the wretchedness of a drunken fellow-lodger, add point to the moralizing. 'I wondered what sort of complicated debauch had reduced him to that unspeakable condition.'

The unexpected offer of a captaincy from the Harbourmaster is given a special significance. It is not inappropriate to find a resemblance between the Harbourmaster and the status of the Duke in *Measure for Measure*. ' "This is your appointment to the command," he said with a certain gravity. "An official appointment binding the owners to conditions which you have accepted" . . . He shook hands with me: "Well, there you are, on your own, appointed officially under my responsibility." He was actually walking with me to the door . . . I opened it with the sensation of dealing with mere dream-stuff, and then at the last moment the fellowship of seamen asserted itself, stronger than the difference of age and station.' The tone and rhythm of that last sentence are moving. The tone is that of youthful idealism, confirmed in retrospect by further experience, and, as always in Conrad, it carries an implication of precariousness, of something all the more intensely valued because dependent on the resoluteness of fallible men.

The Harbourmaster says: '*You* are the right man for that job – if there had been twenty others after it. But no fear of that. They are all afraid to catch hold. . . . Afraid of the sails. Afraid of a white crew.'

A captaincy is felt to be an elevation to a new state of being in which the responsibilities of life are greater and more complex. The narrator was 'still too much on this side of the shadow-line'. But his earlier 'obscure feeling of life being but a waste of days', his restlessness under 'the menace of emptiness', are suddenly obliterated by the full realization of his good fortune. 'A sudden passion of anxious impatience rushed through my veins and gave me such a sense of the intensity of existence as I have never felt before or since. I discovered how much of a seaman I was, in heart, in mind, and, as it were, physically – a man exclusively of sea and ships; the sea the only world that counted, and the ships the test of manliness, of temperament, of courage and fidelity – and of love.'

These passionate affirmations express a normal sense of dedication and, at the same time, a youthful ignorance of the manysidedness of failure. In the course of the story, in the darkness before the storm, before 'the darkness turned into water', the narrator is to experience his own 'moral dissolution', and to acknowledge with new, astringent, humility 'the weight of my sins' and 'my sense of unworthiness'. The book is, indeed, very far from being a simple celebration of nautical virtues. It was written in the middle of the First World War, and the author's preface suggests Conrad's state of mind at the time.

Captain Giles tentatively warns the young skipper of the hazardous navigation ahead. 'He remarked casually that from Bankok to the Indian Ocean was a pretty long step. And this murmur, like a dim flash from a dark lantern, showed me for a moment the broad belt of islands and reefs between that unknown ship, which was mine, and the freedom of the great waters of the globe. But I felt no apprehension.' There is room only for eager confidence in the narrator's mind. 'Extreme patience and extreme care would see me through the region of broken land, of faint airs and of dead water to where I should feel at last my command swing on the great swell, and list over to the great breath of regular winds.' This lyrical anticipation, which by its tone, its movement, and the poetic force of words, gives essential form to the novel, comes to mind later when the winds have shown themselves anything but 'regular'.

The new Captain boards his ship, and, as he sits in the captain's chair for the first time, he experiences to the full a sense of 'succession'.

A succession of men had sat in that chair. I became aware of that thought suddenly, vividly, as though each had left a little of himself between the four walls of these ornate bulkheads; as if a sort of composite soul, the soul of command, had whispered suddenly to mine of long days at sea and of anxious moments. . . . Deep within the tarnished ormolu frame, in the hot half-light sifted through the awning, I saw my own face propped between my hands. And I stared back at myself with the perfect detachment of distance, rather with curiosity than with any other feeling, except of some sympathy for this latest representative of what for all intents and purposes was a dynasty; continuous not in blood, indeed, but in its experience, in its training, in its conception of duty, and in the blessed simplicity of its traditional point of view on life.

The 'simplicity' does not imply any degree of obliviousness to complexity. The effect of crossing the shadow-line is to make one more grateful for rules, training, tradition and 'distinct ideals', and to teach the use of them. Nor does the word 'blessed' imply any condition of comfortable serenity. The dead skipper had been 'just such another man as myself'. The decent but neurotic mate stands midway between the living captain and the dead. Part of the function of Burns is to reinforce, by his delusions, the latency of 'the late captain – ambushed down there under the sea with some evil intention'. As the author's note points out, Conrad makes no Coleridgean play with 'the supernatural'. Conrad writes: 'The world of the living contains enough marvels and mysteries as it is. . . . No, I am too firm in my consciousness of the marvellous to be ever fascinated by the mere supernatural, which (take it any way you like) is but a manufactured article, the fabrication of minds insensitive to the intimate delicacies of our relation to the dead and to the living, in their countless multitudes.'

As in the word 'ambushed', image after image creates the sharp grotesqueness of Burns's fears, and conveys the large and vague misgivings of the dispirited crew. 'It was impossible to distinguish land from water in the enigmatical tranquillity of the immense forces of the world.' Still more of the crew fall sick. 'And as I looked at them from the poop I could not keep from my mind the dreadful impression that they were moving in poisoned air.' But in the dark, the helmsman's strong brown hands grasping the spokes of the wheel appear 'like a symbol of mankind's claim to the direction of its own fate'.

The store of quinine is described in terms with associations as definite as those of the opening speech of *Volpone*. 'I went into the spare cabin where the medicine chest was kept to prepare two doses. I opened it full of faith as a man opens a miraculous shrine.' The discovery that there was no quinine, like the derangement of Burns, is not an extraneous complication, a twist in the plot. The loss shakes the complacency with which the narrator had reproved Burns's 'nonsense', and narrows the gap between the two men. 'I said to myself disdainfully that it should take much more than that to affect in the smallest degree my fortitude.' After the discovery, the Captain rushes into Burns's cabin. 'The wildness of his aspect checked my mental disorder.'

The ordeal has to be lived through, the mind can only suffer and try to find courage to fulfil its 'training become instinct'. And the trial is not only the narrator's. There is the quiet usefulness of the cook Ransome, who bears up better because death is ever present to him. There is the deckhand Frenchy. 'To see him coming aft to the wheel comforted one. The blue dungaree trousers turned up the calf, one leg a little higher than the other, the clean check shirt, the white canvas cap, evidently made by himself, made up a whole of peculiar smartness, and the persistent jauntiness of his gait, even, poor fellow, when he couldn't help tottering, told of his invincible spirit.' Like Wordsworth from the Leechgatherer, the narrator draws comfort from other people.

The storm hits the ship at last, when it is almost crewless. Unobtrusively Ransome joins in the struggle with the main sail, and suffers afterwards. 'Every man was alone where he stood.' If the story can be said to have a hero, it is not the narrator but Ransome. He has no glamour of command to sustain him. But it is he who unconsciously gives encouragement. 'I dared not look at Ransome as we worked side by side. . . . I could hear him panting close to me and I avoided turning my eyes his way for fear of seeing him fall down and expire in the act of putting out his strength – for what? Indeed for some distinct ideal.'

Yet the man who helps most to keep the community of seamen in being, is also the one who has to endure during his life's voyage the starkest form of 'moral isolation'. At the end of the story, when the ship has reached harbour, there is no triumph. Ransome 'was like a man listening for a warning call'.

> 'Won't you shake hands, Ransome?' I said gently.
>
> He exclaimed, flushed up dusky red, gave my hand a hard wrench – and next moment, left alone in the cabin, I listened to him going up the companion stairs cautiously, step by step, in mortal fear of starting into sudden anger our common enemy it was his hard fate to carry consciously within his faithful breast.

An adequate appreciation of the significance of *The Shadow Line* would fill a book at least as long as the novel itself. This story, like others of Conrad's, is such a thoroughly created structure of words, rhythms and contrasting judgments, that it may seem to exemplify what is exceptional in prose fiction rather than the rule. But it is the exception of all major art. When a reader has learnt to grasp its form, and to feel satisfied only 'if he is bearing all the elements in mind at the moment of conviction', he is much better prepared to do justice to some of the larger canvases of fiction, such as *Martin Chuzzlewit*, *Mansfield Park*, or *Nostromo* itself, than if he were merely equipped to summarize plot and give impressions of 'character' – which are so often only personal impressions. True, much fiction requires only a superficial attention. But the great novels in the language require quite as much effort of mind and feeling if their form (or 'subject' or 'meaning') is to be understood, as *Lear* or *Antony and Cleopatra* or *The Winter's Tale*.

# *Looking at a Poem*

## DAVID HOLBROOK

*The poem:*

What is our life? A play of passion
Our mirth the music of division.
Our mothers' wombs the tiring houses be
Where we are dressed for this short comedy.
Heaven the judicious sharp spectator is
That sits and marks who still doth act amiss.
Our graves that hide us from the searching sun
Are like drawn curtains when the play is done.
Thus march we playing to our latest rest,
Only we die in earnest, that's no jest.

*Sir Walter Raleigh*

In one of my W.E.A. classes we compared three 'religious' songs – the popular song *I Believe*, the folk-song *Matthew, Mark and Luke and John*, and the above poem, which was set to music by Orlando Gibbons. One student said that *I Believe* was 'written by a very sincere religious man', and another said of the Raleigh 'I don't care for this modern stuff'. I hesitated until the end of the period to reveal that *I Believe* was in fact written by four people, and that *What is our life?* was Elizabethan. But the two remarks drew attention at once to the relation between 'technique' and sincerity: their point was that *What is our life?* could not be sincere, because it was such an 'artificial' comparison between life and the theatre, and because it was sophisticated (containing 'unpoetical' words like 'judicious'), and required thought. 'Searching sun' seemed awkward and calculated to be 'obscure'. *I Believe* on the other hand, made an immediate impact, and one's feelings were aroused at once – though this 'depended on who sang it'. A few said it was 'trite', but found it difficult to justify that comment; while, preferring *What is our life?*, they couldn't but agree that the comparison of life with the stage-play was a common one in literature, a cliché itself ('Each man in his time plays many parts' in *As You Like It*;

'Life's but a poor player' in *Macbeth*). The folk-song was generally overlooked – perhaps because its simplicity was embarrassing.

Interestingly enough, whenever I've done this exercise discussion settles down at first around the Raleigh, which is the poem least liked at first sight. This fact itself is enough to show that, if one is encouraged to pause on it, its complexity and ambiguity do their work – they appeal because they are the outcome of an intense personal pressure controlled by the formal urbanity of the poem. This poem has something of the quality attributed to Marvell by Mr T. S. Eliot: 'a tough reasonableness under the slight lyric grace'. The thought can be tested: the analogy between life and the theatre is complete at all points, and, what makes it more than a conventional hackneyed comparison, it is from this completeness that a rich ambiguity develops. There is a play on 'division' (the division between acts of a play, and also strife and dissension), on 'act' (to act a part, and to do acts in life), and on 'dressed' (for aren't we in the womb 'undressed' – in our birthday suits, in popular cant?). But this last has more activity than the two former – which could be taken simply as puns – for the word suggests the body being dressed on to the soul, or, more disturbingly, the flesh being dressed on to the bones – and it is in the grave that we are 'undressed' – behind the 'drawn curtains' (like the stone draperies) of the tomb. The butcher's use of the word isn't far away: Raleigh sees 'the skull beneath the skin' – and the humility achieved in the poem is seen to be achieved by a great maturity, by the poise and balance of a mature civilization – in the face of a terrible perception of the glory of life, the burden of time and death, and the brevity of human existence. The point can be underlined by stopping on the word 'searching' – to ask, why 'searching', and not 'shining', for instance?[1] Words with such 'rightness' aren't chosen in any random way, and this departure from the ordinary is for no purpose of simply being 'obscure'. 'Searching' powerfully suggests *movement* – the continual revolution of the sun, the harassing nature of daily life in time, the sun

[1] Isn't it that habit, which expects the word 'scorching', is being defeated? (A hasty student who too-quickly skims over the poem may actually think he *sees* 'scorching'.) For the finest 'practical criticism' of this poem the reader is referred to Gibbon's madrigal. It is recorded by the Deller Consort on APM 14056. – B. J.

as the Eye of Heaven watching man 'act' (the world 'hide' suggests his awareness of his imperfection) – and at one and the same time the desire to be part of the activity of sunlit life, and to accept the end of that life in the oblivion of the grave. The poem isn't bitter, isn't seventeenth-century melancholy indulgent and unrelieved – the last couplet reveals with its 'that's no jest' that there is an underlying bitterness – but the 'artificial' sustained conceit itself which is the means of achieving balance. That this control by wit of an underlying agony was an essential means whereby Raleigh ordered his own experience (and in reading it and experiencing it we are helped to order ours) is shown by reading his poem *His Pilgrimage*, written the night before his death, and comparing it with these words as we find them in Orlando Gibbon's madrigal.

## *A Further Comment*

### MacDONALD EMSLIE

Raleigh's fine *What is our life?* which Mr Holbrook discusses has its uses in speech lessons for adults. Its problems include that of the way in which to read the final couplet (a much more worthwhile speech-class activity than, say, pointing out sound effects in line 5). Problems of this kind (the poem has several), involving decisions on tone and attitude, lead back to the necessity of a thorough reading of the text to begin with. (Poems used for speech training should at least be *worth* this attention; but how much interest has been lost in such lessons because of the embarrassing triviality of the practice material?) I pass on some results.

Raleigh's quibbles operate on three levels: the explicit moral meaning, the series of theatrical terms, and the musical terms. 'Thus march we *playing*' is either 'not taking life seriously', 'performing, like actors – not being our real selves', or 'playing music, trying to cheer ourselves along life's journey' (the whole phrase suggests an Elizabethan stage army's entrance with drums: 'They march about'). 'Our latest *rest*' has the same three levels: 'to the grave, our last resting-place', 'to the leisure following a hard day's acting' (I don't suggest the modern actor's 'resting' – though some students have), and – the musical term – 'our last long silence'. The musical quibbles have been set going by the first two lines: 'our life is essentially tragic; even its mirth depends on conflict', and 'even our music, which should bring us mirth, is "passionate" and full of florid *variations*' (the last word is some sort of equivalent modern quibble). Perhaps *judicious sharp* serves to keep the suggestion of deliberate musical quibbling alive, and 'sits and marks still' may have the notion of the continuous beating away of the time, the musician's *tactus*. The threefold quibbling meets, we have seen, at the end of the poem in *playing* and *rest*, *playing* harking back to '*A play* of passion' ('filled with nothing but conflict and unhappiness', and also 'these are not even genuine emotions at that'). The last line's subtleties thus include: 'All our life is a play, an elaborate "seeming", except for the fact of death'; 'actors only simulate death, but our death is in earnest; don't let us be deceived by our own imagery here'; and 'after all of this poem's wit – there is enough of it to appear at first self-regarding – we cannot but speak sad brow and true maid and see death as simple, serious fact'. The poem turns round in its last line and talks about itself.

# *A Plea for Mediaeval Drama*

JOAN CHARLTON

ONE of the problems of planning the English work of children in the first year of a secondary school is that of finding suitable material for drama lessons. Few people would deny that classroom acting at this stage has great value, far outweighing the difficulties with which an acting lesson is beset: but few, I imagine, would not agree that finding a good play is one of the greatest of the difficulties. Such a play must have many, and almost contradictory, virtues. It must be simple in content, within the intellectual and emotional grasp of eleven-year-olds, yet it must provide ideas which will interest them and which they will treat seriously – for they will regard anything which appears to talk down to them as 'kids' stuff'. It must be simple in language, too, for many still find difficulty in reading, and consequently distrust or dislike unfamiliar ways of writing, feeling (often quite rightly) that when they read verse it does not make sense. It must be short, capable of being acted in a lesson; yet a series of unrelated short plays will be felt to lack purpose and so again the acting lesson will not be taken seriously. It must, moreover, be capable of being acted in the normal classroom, with little costuming or scenery and little space to move between the blackboard and the pushed-back desks – yet the children will want to do it 'properly', and will be conscious, all too often, of a vague disappointment that the performance is so cramped, so lacking in the glamour of a proper play. Yet one more problem faces the teacher – how to bridge the gap between the plays of the first year and the work which he plans to do later. How are form-room plays to be made to lead on to Shakespeare? – or anything else, for that matter?

The answer to these problems lies, I would suggest, in the use of mediaeval drama. For some years I have followed this course, finding in it not only a solution to the difficulties I have mentioned, but the beginning of other, more constructive ideas as well. We possess a magnificent inheritance of such plays, in the Chester, York and Towneley cycles of mystery plays as well as in the more familiar isolated plays such as 'Everyman' and the Coventry Nativity Play. What better prelude to the study of Shakespeare could be found than a study of this earlier tradition? If this source of plays can be exploited, moreover, not only the English syllabus will benefit, for the mystery plays provide a rich source of information about the lives of people of all classes in mediaeval England which the historians may also rejoice to have available.

A selection of mystery plays, I would suggest, provides the eleven-year-old with ideal material for acting; the stories are familiar, but presented with such individuality that they never threaten to become dull – for who could fail to delight in King Herod's thunderings or in the wrath of Mrs Noah? The plays are simple, but without any sense of being 'written down' – indeed the high seriousness and sincerity of the Coventry Seeker and the Towneley Kings are most moving, even in the class-room, and the pathos of Abraham and Isaac has a realism which frees it from any taint of sentimentality.

ISAAC: Wood and fire are in my hand:
Tell me now, if ye have space,
Where is the beast for our offrand?
ABRAHAM: Now, son, I may no longer feign.
Such will is unto my heart went;
Thou didst ever love me plain,
Ever ready to fulfil mine intent,
But certainly thou must be slain,
And it must be as I have meant.
ISAAC: I am heavy and nothing fain,
Thus hastily that shall be shent.
ABRAHAM: Isaac!
ISAAC: Sir?
ABRAHAM: Come hither, bid I.
Thou shalt be dead, whatsoever betide,
ISAAC: Ah, father, mercy, mercy!
ABRAHAM: That I say may not be denied;
Take thy death, therefore, meekly.
ISAAC: Ah, good sir, abide!
Father!
ABRAHAM: What, son?

ISAAC: To do your will I am ready,
Wheresoever ye go or ride,
If I may ought overtake your will –
Let me be beaten for my trespass!

. . . . .

ABRAHAM: Now, my dear child, thou may not shun.
ISAAC: The shining of your bright blade,
It makes me quake for fear to die.
ABRAHAM: Therefore grufling shall thou be laid,
That when I strike thou may not see.
ISAAC: What have I done, father? What have I said?
ABRAHAM: Truly, no shade of ill to me.
ISAAC: And thus guiltless shall be dead?
ABRAHAM: Now, good son, let such words be!
ISAAC: Father!
ABRAHAM: What, son?
ISAAC: Let me arise
For my mother's love!
ABRAHAM: Let be, let be!
It will not help that thou thus cries.
But lie still till I come to thee,
I need somewhat for the sacrifice.

In contrast, from the same cycle, we have the comedy of the shepherds:

GIB: I go to buy sheep.
TOM: Nay, not so!
What, dream ye or sleep? Where should they go?
Here shall thou none keep.
GIB: Ah, good sir, ho!
Who am I?
I will pasture them free
Wheresoever please me!
Here shall thou them see!
TOM: Not so hardy!
Not one sheep tail shall thou bring hither.
GIB: I shall bring, without fail, a hundred together.
TOM: What, art thou in ale? Now thy wits gather!
GIB: They shall go, sans fail. Go now, bell wether!

TOM: I say, tyr!
GIB: I say, tyr now again!
I say, skip over the plain!
[*They drive imaginary sheep in opposite directions.*]
GIB: What, wilt thou not yet, I say, let the sheep go?
Whop!
TOM: Abide yet!
Wilt thou but so?
Knave, hence I bid thee get, 'tis good that thou do,
Or I shall thee hit on thy pate, lo –
Shalt thou reel.
I say, give the sheep space!
[*They begin to fight about the sheep which Gib has not yet bought.*]

Both the sensitive child who responds to the beauty of words and the little ruffian who enjoys farce and rough-and-tumble can be satisfied – and neither is going to be disappointed by the limitations of classroom production, for these plays were expressly designed to be performed by amateur actors on small and inconvenient stages. Unlike most plays written for the young, they have no elaborately pictorial stage directions, so that ingenuity and invention are given free play. (I still cherish the memory of a performance of the Towneley 'Pharaoh' triumphantly produced by a certain Form Ic, broad of accent and ignorant of orthography, which exploited electric light for the burning bush but rolled out a red carpet for the Red Sea in true mediaeval style.)

Not only does mediaeval drama offer good plays which can be acted satisfactorily by children in classrooms, but it provides a solution for the teacher's less immediate problems. It is possible to select, from a cycle such as the Towneley, a series of plays which are self-contained, each short enough to be acted in one lesson, and contrasted in style and material, without losing a sense of continuity, since the series was planned as a whole. The needs of a term's drama work can be amply satisfied, for instance, by using the 'Creation', 'Cain and Abel', 'Abraham', 'Shepherds' and 'Herod' of this cycle, which provide comedy and tragedy, stateliness and clowning, in effective contrast.

This particular group also made one of the most satisfactory school plays in my experience. 'Everyman' offers a different type of material and needs rather more time spent in discussion, but I have found that children in the second or third term of secondary school respond to its greater intellectual challenge. Discussions of costume and movement here lead directly to discussion of the symbolism of the various characters. There is ample scope for miming, and the play lends itself to a great variety of experiments in production. It is, I feel, a summer term play, best acted out of doors, for while it demands little or nothing in the way of scenery it gains greatly by having ample space for deployment. A flight of steps is an asset, but the main interest is in working out patterns of grouping and movement. Unlike the mystery plays, where a small number of children present the play to the rest of the class, 'Everyman' offers opportunities to involve the whole group. Even with the cutting necessary for school use, the play has a large number of small parts, and those who do not have speaking parts can provide the background of the activities of the world against which the first part of the action takes place. This filling out in action of a rather spare text is valuable both as a challenge to imagination and as preparation for the later reading of Shakespeare. It is all too common for older children to regard a Shakespeare play just as a text to be studied; those who have worked through such a course as is here outlined find it less difficult to think of the text as something from which a living play can be created. Even in classroom conditions the speeches of Brutus and Antony in 'Julius Caesar' become a very different matter when the rest of the class is prepared to become the citizens of Rome, muttering unscripted lines, interrupting and having to be dominated, changing in mood in response to the appeals made to them (sometimes with the added realism of the child who has created a deaf old gaffer at the back of the crowd).

Indeed, a further very considerable virtue of the mediaeval plays is that they offer opportunities for really creative acting. The outlines of the characters are clearly and simply laid down – Mrs Noah is a rollicking scold, Pharaoh and Herod bullying cowards, Cain's Boy a pert little guttersnipe – but within these outlines there is room for imagination and understanding to develop a fuller personality. At first there will be need here for judicious direction from the teacher – for instance a discussion of how the shepherds in the Prima Pastorum are to be distinguished can lead to consideration of the hints given in the text:

> Here comes Slow-pace
> From the mill-wheel
>
> Ye are of the old store,
> Go you first therefore

and so to further ideas of how such a person would behave in such a situation (e.g. 'Slow-pace' is obviously very poor; he probably would have nothing to give the child. He is miserable and ashamed, and then suddenly remembers his own water-bottle – evidently a treasure – which he presents with an anxious explanation and defence – 'It holds a full pottle!')

Later, children more readily build into the play's outline their own observation of people – often disconcertingly shrewd. The school production of the Towneley plays to which I have already referred produced a memorable performance of an Abel of such sickening smugness that one could not but share the mounting exasperation of Cain – unorthodox but provocative!

So far I have not attempted to carry this creative process further. It would be interesting to see what effect the experience of acting mediaeval plays might have on the composition work of a class – to see, for instance, what a group of eleven-year-olds might do with the story of David and Saul. I have myself used mediaeval drama mainly as a preparation for the critical reading of plays at a later stage of the grammar school curriculum, but there are, I think, exciting possibilities of a different kind of development. In any case, however, the choice of these plays for first-year dramatic work seems to me to be amply justified by the enjoyment they give and by the kind of discussion they provoke.

There remain, of course, two practical problems – books and language. The teacher who feels that even his older pupils find Shakespeare's English difficult to understand will probably view with astonishment the suggestion that children in the first year, who often cannot manage the English of their own time, should be offered that of the fifteenth century. But experience has shown that modernized spelling and a surprisingly little modification of the language, together with judicious cutting, is enough to make the plays easily accessible to children, without dislocation of metre or loss of vitality. I might add that where there is a local accent which can be drawn on for the appropriate persons – especially if it is a country one – the plays are enriched by it, and the local speech given a status which is all too often denied. Accessibility is a more difficult problem. Various collections of classroom plays contain the occasional mediaeval play and a school version of some of the Chester plays has recently been published, but otherwise one has to depend on typescripts, which are clumsy to handle and disintegrate easily. Further school editions of mystery plays, suitably cut and modernized, would provide a much needed source of material and a means of making 'drama lessons' a more valuable part of first-year English than one often feels them to be.

# *The Authorized Version of the Bible*

## *A Literary Approach*

SUSIE I. TUCKER

I

THE roots of English Literature reach deep into the classics of the ancient world, whether Greek, Latin or Hebrew. But all three Literatures are in danger of being less studied in these days of modern science and technology, so that the English teacher cannot now assume the common stock of knowledge that nourished our literature in the past. The loss of general understanding, of sheer pleasure in the quickly caught allusion, grows greater in proportion to our neglect. What follows is an attempt to suggest some lines of approach to the ancient Literature that in its English dress has become the greatest prose classic of our language as well as the most pervasive influence on the national character.

Scholars in the last century have analysed many masterpieces, giving us all kinds of knowledge about authorship, date, historical setting, and transmission: but the sixteenth- and seventeenth-century translators who gave us the Authorized Version of the Bible had little idea of the complicated historical and textual problems that worry the moderns. They used such texts as they had, and we should take the Book as it stands if we are to appreciate their work, asking ourselves two questions – What was there for them to translate, and how did they do their work?

The Old Testament and the Old Testament Apocrypha are a complete national literature, of wide range, in antiquity, treatment and subject-matter. Judaism and Christianity both claim that the Old Testament recounts the special dealings of God with Man – at first with the Jews only, or on their behalf, later, with a deepening spiritual perception, with all mankind. But this concept is conveyed through history and legend, folk-tale and battle-song, elegy and lyric, legal document and priestly code, by allegory and apocalypse, by proverb and meditation, in verse or in prose. They represent men at differing stages of growth and understanding, with a very varying capacity for spiritual insight. On the one hand, there are the all too human war-songs, exultant and ruthless. Some are mere scraps, like Miriam's verse after the Israelites' escape from slavery in Egypt:

Sing ye to the Lord, for he hath triumphed gloriously; the horse and his rider hath he thrown into the sea. (Exodus xv, 21.)

Some are poems at full length, like the song of Deborah and Barak in Judges v. The prose narrative of the defeat and slaying of Sisera, captain of the host of Canaan is given in chapter iv: the poem is a dramatic sequence:

Blessed above women shall Jael the wife of Heber the Kenite be, blessed shall she be above women in the tent. He asked water, and she gave him milk, she brought forth butter in a lordly dish. She put her hand to the nail, and her right hand to the workman's hammer: and with the hammer she smote Sisera, she smote off his head, when she had pierced and stricken through his temples. At her feet he bowed, he fell, he lay down; at her feet he bowed, he fell; where he bowed, there he fell down dead.

The mother of Sisera looked out at a window, and cried through the lattess, Why is his chariot so long in coming? Why tarry the wheels of his chariots?

Her wise ladies answered her, yea, she returned answer to her self, Have they not sped? have they not divided the prey, to every man a damsel or two? to Sisera a prey of divers colours, a prey of divers colours of needle-work, of divers colours of needle-work on both sides, meet for the necks of them that take the spoil?

So let all thine enemies perish, O Lord: but let them that love him be as the sun when he goeth forth in his might. (Judges v, 24-31.)[1]

On the other hand, we can look at Psalm 104 with its awed approach to God, its humanity, its tenderness and resignation, its feeling of fellowship with the brute creation: or the ninetieth, with its regretful contemplation of frail and transient human life, and time that will not stay:

[1] Passages quoted are in the spelling and punctuation of the edition published by John Baskett for the University of Oxford, 1732.

. . . for a thousand years in thy sight are but as yesterday, when it is past, and as a watch in the night. Thou carriest them away as with a flood; they are as a sleep: in the morning they are like grass which groweth up. In the morning it flourisheth, and groweth up; in the evening it is cut down and withereth. (Psalm xc, 4-6.)

Sometimes the two styles – the fiercely vindictive triumphing and the melancholy elegiac strains – are found together. One of the most often quoted of the Psalms is the hundred and thirty-seventh:

By the rivers of Babylon, there we sat down, yea, we wept when we remembered Zion. We hanged our harps upon the willows, in the midst thereof. For there they that carried us away captive, required of us a song; and they that wasted us, required of us mirth, saying, sing us one of the songs of Zion.

How shall we sing the Lord's song in a strange land?

If I forget thee, O Jerusalem, let my right hand forget her cunning.

If I do not remember thee, let my tongue cleave to the roof of my mouth; if I prefer not Jerusalem above my chief joy.

That is the song of the exile and patriot, the cry of the anguished heart calling across the centuries. But the poem is not finished:

Remember, O Lord, the children of Edom in the day of Jerusalem; who said, Rase, rase it, even to the foundation thereof.

O daughter of Babylon, who art to be destroyed: happy shall he be that rewardeth thee, as thou hast served us. Happy shall he be that taketh and dasheth thy little ones against the stones.

It is hardly for us, with our powers of mass destruction, to take a superior moral attitude to this sort of sentiment: but the contrast of moods in the psalm is appalling, and one sympathises with the charitable fourteenth-century translator who thought that the enemies to be destroyed were allegorical and stood for evil deeds. (Early English Text Society, 97.)

There are other contrasts. At one point, righteousness consists in absolute fulfilment of ritual observances – hence so many documents dealing with ceremonial – and at another it depends on the purity of the inward heart and just dealings with one's fellows. The second point of view is put with force in the words of Micah, chapter vi:

> Wherewith shall I come before the Lord, and bow my self before the high God? shall I come before him with burnt-offerings, with calves of a year old? Will the Lord be pleased with thousands of rams, or with ten thousands of rivers of oyl? Shall I give my first-born for my transgression, the fruit of my body for the sin of my soul? He hath shewed thee, O man, what is good; and what doth the Lord require of thee, but to do justly, and to love mercy, and to walk humbly with thy God? (Micah vi, 6-8.)

The rhetorical amplitude of the question is most effectively offset by the simple finality of the answer.

Beside the writings which deal directly with conduct and belief, the Old Testament contains some political propaganda such as the Book of Daniel and that exciting and (quite literally) Godless, historical novel, the Book of Esther. And Solomon's Song was admitted to the Canon, after considerable opposition, by the grace of allegory.

The narrative portions of the Old Testament contain a magnificent series of tales and dramatic episodes. We have only to think on those that have most impressed artists, poets and preachers alike: the history of Joseph; the heroic saga of David, now so chivalrous, now so barbaric; Elijah's challenge to the priests of Baal; the fall of Queen Jezebel; Elisha and the enemy soldiers whom he leads blindfold into their opponents' capital; the exploits of those mighty men of valour, Samson and Gideon; the story of Naaman, the Syrian, the captain of the host who was also a leper; the highlights of the story of Daniel, including the burning-fiery furnace, Belshazzar's feast, and the lions' den: the Apocryphal addition to this – the tale of Bel and the Dragon which is one of the earliest ancestors of the detective-story; the idyll of Ruth which captivated Keats: or, again in the Apocrypha, the patriotic history of Judith and that other detective story about Susannah and the wicked Elders, which begins, as the Elizabethan ballad-mongers knew – 'There dwelt a man in Babylon' – and the wholly delightful Book of Tobit with its kindly humour, its mixture of grotesquerie and romance, its human tenderness, its demon-ridden heroine, and the Archangel Raphael disguised as a hired man.

Apart from narrative power, one of the most valuable qualities of style demonstrated in the Authorized Version and, of course, one that it owes to its originals, is its direct dealing with concrete things. All the senses come into play, so that nothing is left vague, ill-defined or abstract.

We may consider the sensuous delight in perfume in Psalm xlv, 8:

All thy garments smell of myrrh, and aloes, and cassia; out of the ivory palaces, whereby they have made thee glad.

Archaeology has proved the reality of the ivory palaces,[1] but the power of words alone takes us into eastern splendours here and again in the colourful opening of the Book of Esther, where King Ahasuerus holds festival in the court of the garden of the King's palace 'where were white, green, and blue hangings, fastened with cords of fine linen and purple, to silver rings, and pillars of marble: the beds were of gold, and silver, upon a pavement of red, and blue, and white, and black marble. And they gave them drink in vessels of gold (the vessels being divers one from another) and royal wine in abundance, according to the state of the King.' (Esther i, 6, 7.)

There are glimpses of nobles in scarlet and wearing chains of gold: of a queen with a vesture of gold wrought about with divers colours, of the time when the singers went before, the players on instruments followed after; amongst them were the damsels playing with timbrels. (Psalm lxviii, 25.)

The detailed descriptions of Solomon's Temple are overwhelmingly magnificent, with their unlimited gold, silver and cedar-wood: but the Old Testament can deal with equal precision and emotive power with ruin, desolation, misery, famine and death. Sometimes it is direct and merciless description: sometimes the effect is obtained by the use of strong metaphor.

This is one picture of a great kingdom fallen:

Come down and sit in the dust, O virgin daughter of Babylon, sit on the ground: there is no throne, O daughter of the Chaldeans: for

[1] See the Guide to *From the Land of the Bible: An Archaeological Exhibition at the British Museum* 1954.

thou shalt no more be called tender and delicate. Take the milstones and grind meal, uncover thy locks, make bare the leg, uncover the thigh, pass over the rivers. . . . Sit thou silent, and get thee into darkness, O daughter of the Chaldeans: for thou shalt no more be called the lady of kingdoms. (Isaiah xlvii, 1, 2, 5.)

Babylon was indeed fallen, that great city: and the poet is seeing her here with cold and devastating clarity as a woman who had once been a queen – but is now a slave.

It is interesting to compare two other treatments of the same theme. One is an eerie picture of Babylon given over to desolation:

And Babylon the glory of kingdoms, the beauty of the Chaldees excellency, shall be as when God overthrew Sodom and Gomorrah. It shall never be inhabited, neither shall it be dwelt in from generation to generation: neither shall the Arabian pitch tent there, neither shall the shepherds make their folds there. But wild beasts of the desert shall lie there, and their houses shall be full of doleful creatures and owls shall dwell there, and satyrs shall dance there. And the wild beasts of the islands shall cry in their desolate houses, and dragons in their pleasant palaces. . . . (Isaiah xiii, 19-22.)

A parallel occurs in chapter xxxiv, on another enemy of Israel:

But the cormorant and the bittern shall possess it, the owl also and the raven shall dwell in it, and he shall stretch out upon it the line of confusion, and the stones of emptiness. They shall call the nobles thereof to the kingdom, but none shall be there, and all her princes shall be nothing. And thorns shall come up in her palaces, nettles and brambles in the palaces thereof, and it shall be an habitation of dragons, and a court for owls. The wild beasts of the desert shall also meet with the wild beasts of the island, and the satyr shall cry to his fellow, the scrichowl also shall rest there, find for her self a place of rest. There shall the great owl make her nest, and lay and hatch, and gather under her shadow: there shall the vultures also be gathered, every one with her mate.

We know chapter xxxv much better ('The wilderness and the solitary place shall be glad for them: and the desert shall rejoyce and blossom as the rose'): it is much more effective when not torn from its contrasting context.

From vivid observation of real scenes and persons, we pass to the concrete imagery that clothes abstract ideas and brings them down to earth. If an Old Testament writer wants to impress us with the idea of the protecting power of a great man, he gives us a series of similes which draw their force from the Palestinian climate but which our imagination can seize:

And a man shall be as an hiding-place from the wind, and a covert from the tempest: as rivers of water in a dry place, as the shadow of a great rock in a weary land. (Isaiah xxxii, 2.)

Of the hypocritical, we read:

The words of his mouth were smoother than butter, but war was in his heart: his words were softer than oyl, yet were they drawn swords. (Psalm lv, 21.)

A man in distress beset by foes cries out 'My soul is among lions, and I lie even among them that are set on fire, even the sons of men, whose teeth are spears and arrows, and their tongue a sharp sword' (Psalm lvii, 4). So the tongue of a tyrant 'deviseth mischiefs: like a sharp razour, working deceitfully' (Psalm lii, 2) and the unjust turn 'judgment into gall, and the fruit of righteousness into hemlock' (Amos vi, 12). Wasted years are the years 'that the locust hath eaten' (Joel ii, 25) – and this last reminds us how much Biblical imagery is drawn from nature and the life of the soil:

Israel is a scattered sheep, the lions have driven him away: first the king of Assyria hath devoured him, and, last this Nebuchadrezzar king of Babylon hath broken his bones. (Jeremiah l, 17.)

Sow to your selves in righteousness, reap in mercy: break up your fallow ground: for it is time to seek the Lord, till he come and rain righteousness upon you. Ye have plowed wickedness, ye have reaped iniquity, ye have eaten the fruit of lies. . . . (Hosea x, 12, 13.)

Because of Ephraim's idolatry,

. . . they shall be as the morning cloud, and as the early dew it passeth away, as the chaff that is driven with a whirlwind out of the floor, and as the smoak out of the chimney. (Ibid. xiii, 3.)

The allegory of the Good Shepherd begins with Psalm xxiii; keeping company with it, but less well-known is the allegory of the bad shepherd in Ezekiel xxxiv:

> Woe be to the shepherds of Israel that do feed themselves: should not the shepherd feed the flocks? Ye eat the fat and ye cloath you with the wool, ye kill them that are fed: but ye feed not the flock.

These are the ancestors of Milton's 'blind mouths' in *Lycidas*. And finally we can try to visualize that astounding shepherd metaphor in which Jeremiah says that Nebuchadrezzar 'shall array himself, with the land of Egypt, as a shepherd putteth on his garment'. (Jeremiah xliii, 12.)

'Mr Spectator' spoke with some truth when he said 'There is a certain Coldness and Indifference in the Phrases of our European Languages, when they are compared with the oriental form of Speech; and it happens very luckily, that the Hebrew Idioms run into the English Tongue with a peculiar Grace and Beauty. . . . They give a Force and Energy to our Expression, warm and animate our Language, and convey our Thoughts in more ardent and intense Phrases, than any that are to be met with in our own Tongue.' (*The Spectator*, No. 405, 1712.)

## 2

NEW Testament writers were saturated with Old Testament literature: this is obvious when they use quotations with little respect for the original context, as it seems to us. But the link may be as much literary as theological. In Ezekiel xlvii, 12, we come on the imagery of the trees:

> And by the river upon the bank thereof on this side and on that side, shall grow all trees for meat, whose leaf shall not fade, neither shall the fruit thereof be consumed: it shall bring forth new fruit according to his months, because their waters they issued out of the sanctuary, and the fruit thereof shall be for meat and the leaf thereof for medicine.

This passage reappears in chapter xxii of the Revelation, concentrated and heightened:

And he shewed me a pure river of water of life, clear as crystal, proceeding out of the throne of God and of the Lamb. In the midst of the street of it, and of either side of the river, was there the tree of life, which bare twelve manner of fruits, and yielded her fruit every month: and the leaves of the tree were for the healing of the nations.

Similarly, the four horses of the Apocalypse (Revelation vi, Zechariah vi) – white, red, black and pale, are a new manifestation of Zechariah's beasts, red, black, white and bay. The picture of Death on his pale horse has seized hold of European imagination: so has another haunting figure – Death the Reaper – which comes from Jeremiah ix, where 'death is come up into our windows, and is entered into our palaces, to cut off the children from without and the young men from the streets. . . . Even the carcases of men shall fall as dung upon the open field, and as the handful after the harvest-man, and none shall gather them.'

Personification and allegory are useful devices, but they need watching to make sure we do not see fact in what is patently allegory or allegory in what is really fact. For example, the little story of Jonah, the miraculous fish (not said to be a whale, though the mediaeval author of that entertaining poem *Patience* was sure it was, like many lesser men since), and the fate of Nineveh which has been a sad strain on the literally minded. This allegorical plea for tolerance of other nations will make its point if for 'Nineveh' we substitute Moscow, Pekin, Washington, London – whatever 'great city' stands for the policies we most dislike.

On the other hand, what about Solomon's Song? Like *Hamlet*, it is full of quotations – 'the rose of Sharon and the lily of the valleys'; 'stay me with flagons, comfort me with apples'; 'the winter is past, the rain is over and gone'; 'my beloved is mine and I am his'; 'fair as the moon, clear as the sun, and terrible as an army with banners'; and that most misapplied of phrases 'until the day break and the shadows flee away'.

The expressions have been applied in mystical writings as symbols of the love of Christ for the church, of the response of the devoted heart, of the relation between God and the individual soul. The Jews had interpreted the book as an allegory of Solomon's love of wisdom. Not many in the heyday of mediaeval mystical literature would have agreed that wisdom's name was woman, but there seems no doubt that what we have here is really a collection of sheer secular love lyrics, some perhaps almost too sensuous for western taste, but often exquisite. To let them make their own impact, we should read them in forgetfulness of the allegorical chapter-summaries provided so carefully by the Vulgate, the Geneva Bible and the Authorized Version alike.

Not all the imagery of the Old Testament is beautiful: there is a strong strain of realism in the more sordid sense of that word, as this selection of similes will make plain:

As a bowing wall shall ye be, and as a tottering fence. (Psalm lxii, 3.)

The earth shall reel to and fro like a drunkard, and shall be removed like a cottage. (Isaiah xxiv, 20.)

Moab shall be troden down under him, even as straw is troden down for the dunghill. (Ibid. xxv, 10.)

. . . they have caused Egypt to err in every work thereof, as a drunken man staggereth in his vomit. (Ibid. xix, 14.)

And the people shall be as the burnings of lime: as thorns cut up shall they be burnt in the fire. (Ibid. xxxiii, 12.)

At greater length, the beginning of Micah iii will show what can be done in English with curt, stark monosyllables: it is an appeal to the princes of Israel:

Who hate the good and love the evil, who pluck off their skin from off them, and their flesh from off their bones: Who also eat the flesh of my people, and flay their skin from off them, and they break their bones and chop them in pieces as for the pot and as flesh within the caldron. Then shall they cry unto the Lord, but he will not hear them: he will even hide his face from them at that time, as they have behaved themselves ill in their doings.

For satire, we can look at the little vignette in Isaiah iii, which has caught for ever 'the daughters of Zion' who are haughty and 'walk with stretched forth necks and wanton eyes, walking and mincing as they go, and making a tinkling with their feet'. Some of the best pieces of satire are on the makers and worshippers of idols, for example in Isaiah xliv, 9-20, and Jeremiah x, 1-16.

Judas Maccabeus, the Jewish leader in the second century B.C. against the oppression of Antiochus Epiphanes, was regarded in the Middle Ages as one of the Nine Worthies. Much of the two books on his times is occupied with pretty dull history and with ritual problems hard for us to share: but they have their moments. Before the last battle, one of his followers tries to persuade him to a prudent retreat from overwhelming odds. Then Judas said, 'God forbid that I should do this thing, and flee away from them: if our time be come, let us die manfully for our brethren and let us not staine our honour' (I Macc. ix, 10). That has the authentic ring of heroic saga.

The Wisdom Literature is well represented in Proverbs, Job and Ecclesiastes in the Old Testament Canon, and in Wisdom, Ecclesiasticus and parts of the first two books of Esdras in the Apocrypha. The Book of Job should be included in any reading of Old Testament Literature, and indeed some of the noblest meditative writing is to be found in these books, as well as some of the shrewdest social comment. And at times there is a sudden flash of magnificence, like the two verses of II Esdras vii, 12, 13 which contrast the ignoble present with that lost golden age which the human heart finds it so difficult to give up:

> Then were the entrances of this world made narrow, full of sorrow and travail: they are but few and evil, full of perils and very painful. For the entrances of the elder world were wide and sure, and brought immortal fruit.

It is not so long ago that those who looked to the Bible as a body of doctrine rather than as literature thought all parts of it to be of equal value: probably now most Christians would agree that the much shorter New Testament, as a spiritual document, is worth all the Old Testament put together. But the same cannot be said of it as literature in its original form. Very little of it could claim any literary qualities beyond clarity and cogency. The Greek texts were written in the ordinary everyday language of the time, neither archaic nor high-flown, and there is no denying that the Authorized Version produces effects that are quite at variance with those of the original. St Luke's Gospel and the Book of the Acts are the work of a cultured Hellene, though the hymns he inserts owe their force to Hebrew tradition. In the Acts, it is the eye-witness account of perils and adventures by land and sea that is compelling. St John's Gospel deals with events and ideas that deserve a lofty style, and get it in our version. Vigour and speed characterize St Mark. And the Parables, wherever recorded are perfect cameos, clear-cut, vivid and compact. The Pauline Letters are the closely reasoned arguments of a man of deep learning and the impassioned appeals of a man of burning moral and spiritual experience, but the Authorized Version is not the best approach to them. The poet speaks in the hymn of love in I Corinthians xiii, or in the hammer-blows of the rhetorical questions at the end of the Epistle to the Romans viii, 31-39. And in the courteous little note to Philemon about his runaway slave, it is the Roman gentleman who writes as well as the Christian pastor.

The finest piece of writing in the New Testament in English is probably The Book of the Revelation, and that, so Greek scholars tell us, is due entirely to the fact that the Authorized Version translators rendered it into the highest style they knew, regardless of the quality of the writing they had before them. The Revelation has been described as hardly Greek in the original, but full of foreign idioms abrupt and barely grammatical.[1]

But if we look at the Authorized Version as a work of art in its own right we can be glad of the perversity which gave us this sort of thing:

> And I saw another mighty angel come down from heaven, cloathed with a cloud and a rainbow was upon his head, and his face was as it were the sun, and his feet as pillars of fire. . . . (Revelation x, 1.)

or the profound simplicity of this:

> And when I saw him, I fell at his feet as dead: and he laid his right hand upon me, saying unto me, Fear not; I am the first and the last; I am he that liveth and was dead; and behold I am alive for evermore, Amen; and have the keys of hell and of death. (Ibid. i, 17, 18.)

[1] E. E. Kellett, *Reconsiderations*, C.U.P. 1928

Or consider the vivid picture at the beginning of chapter xii:

And there appeared a great wonder in heaven, a woman cloathed with the sun and the moon under her feet, and upon her head a crown of twelve stars:

'Sublimity', said Coleridge,[1] 'is Hebrew by birth' – and the Revelation is Hebrew by inspiration. 'Longinus' had seen the same quality centuries earlier, for he quoted by way of illustration in his treatise *On the Sublime* the passage in Genesis which runs in the Authorized Version: 'And God said, Let there be light: and there was light'. (Genesis i, 3.) From the first book of the Bible to the last, it is a quality which is never lost and is often enhanced in the translation produced by the learned divines to whom the Hampton Court Conference entrusted the making of the Authorized Version of the Bible.

[1] *Table Talk*, 25th July 1832.

VI

# *A CRITIQUE OF TEXTS*

SCHOOLS are centres of education, but they are also markets for furniture, sports equipment, texts. It is important that anything the school buys, aids education and doesn't cripple or control it in any deadening way. No one would buy a cricket bat that lowered the standard of play in the school, but don't we sometimes buy and use texts that lower our standards in teaching? Certainly *The Use of English* has seen part of its function as being a defence against this, as preserving standards of serious and stringent reviewing in the face of the huge numbers of texts loosed on a thinly protected and very attractive market.

It is important that teachers remain critical of texts provided for either the teaching of literature or the teaching of drills. It is all too easy for the poor text to combine with the natural difficulties of the classroom situation, to turn attention away from the arduous and elusive to the markable but trivial. Publishing houses are not extensions of the education system, but intelligent commercial ventures with special responsibilities. A constant critical tension between teacher and publishers is good for both, and a symptom of soundness and vigour. In all kinds of subtle and recurring ways the quality of work in the classroom is governed by the quality of work coming off the printing presses. This next section opens with three representative articles making criticisms which need, for the health of English teaching, to be repeated year after year. It concludes with a sample of more welcoming and hospitable reviewing – 'Taking Bearings' – in which three teachers establish markers by which to consider and direct their craft. The first marker points back to George Sturt. His prose, like that of Hardy, Jefferies, and in another direction, Joseph Conrad, transmits the cultural vigour of work well and cleanly done in a meaningful environment. Its economic moment may have passed for ever, but the prose to which it gave life commands a permanence in the training of the youthful sensibility. The second marker indicates Caldwell Cook's presence behind contemporary English teaching, and tries to make distinctions between what was bold and lonely advance, and what was boyish and protective regression. A third marker establishes the boundaries of teaching in schools and colleges today, and shows where and how an advance beyond the conventional and the cognitive is being made.

## *The Making of Text-books*

### A TEXT-BOOK MAKER

*The writer of this article is the Senior English Master in a Grammar School. He has written and edited a number of text-books.*

IT has been pointed out how unsatisfactory the content of many text-books is, especially those published for use in grammar schools. If we would know more about the circumstances in which such books are written we ought, I suppose, to apply to the publishers; but we should probably apply in vain, for it is unlikely that any publisher will ever reveal the secrets of his mystery. However, there are other sources of information; and from conversations with the travellers who visit our schools, from scrutiny of the publicity matter they bring with them and from an examination of the books themselves, we can form at least a general idea of why most text-books are not what we would have them be.

It is worth noting, to begin with, that the majority of class-books are written or edited by school teachers. Of course, there are others engaged in this sort of work: university professors, school inspectors, lecturers in various colleges, novelists and free-lance journalists. The author of one successful series of composition books is said to be also a traveller for the firm which publishes it. But these others are in a minority; and it is probable that the educational publisher, all things being equal, prefers that the author of his text-books shall be also a teacher. And there is good reason for this preference; though not, indeed, the reason which the teacher himself might like to give – that he, more than anyone else, knows the real needs of the child. In point of fact, the special value of the teacher-author is that he does not forget that it is the teacher who inspects the specimen copies, his hand which writes the requisition list – that it is the teacher, not the child, who is the publisher's real 'public'.

The publisher, then, feels safest with a teacher-author, and he chooses him with care. But he does not necessarily choose a very extraordinary person. The writer of text-books is not always a 'literary man'; usually he has never written anything else besides text-books; his exceptionally close acquaintance with figures of speech has not imparted to his style any special vitality or grace; and when he ventures on the writing of a piece of connected English – which is often only in the preface of his book – he frequently gives the impression of awkwardness and of some constraint. Yet he is undoubtedly the right man for the job: ordinary he may be, but who better than the ordinary teacher is likely to know what the ordinary teacher wants?

And what *does* the ordinary teacher want? His wants may be stated briefly. In a grammar and composition book he expects to find a large number of questions requiring 'black or white' answers – exercises of a type easily marked, and not too unfamiliar to himself or too exacting for his pupils. Unlike the best specialist teacher – who always regards the practice of small skills as subordinate to the work of free composition, and indeed of little importance except in so far as it can be related to that work – he looks upon the various exercises in grammar, punctuation and vocabulary as ends in themselves. He prefers clause-analysis to sentence-building: the latter exercise may be worked in several ways, the former in but one. He requires little help with the composition lesson, for he seldom gives one; what he does expect is a long list of subjects from which the composition 'prep' can be chosen. Even that list is sometimes superfluous. A boy of eleven (taught, it is true, by a non-specialist teacher) admitted towards the end of his first term in a grammar school that, while he had worked a great many mechanical exercises, he had done but one piece of free composition – the writing of a business letter. 'And I lost most of my marks because I hadn't put the firm's name at the top.'

In an anthology of poems or prose-extracts the ordinary teacher looks for material that has been familiar to him since his own schooldays, for he cannot help feeling that what he himself was taught to consider good must also be the right thing for his pupils. There must be some respectable names – Dickens, Scott, George Eliot, Milton, Wordsworth, Tennyson – as guarantees of excellence. He does not mind if the material is difficult or dull: he will listen complacently when an inspector of schools tells him that he is aiming too high. For is he not an upholder of scholarly standards, a champion of our literary heritage? Inspectors may challenge his wisdom as a teacher – but who shall dare impugn his literary discernment?

For requirements such as these the teacher-author must cater; and his closeness to classroom conditions ensures that he will do so. The whole matter was put very clearly by a publisher's traveller when he remarked to me recently: 'You see, they don't really want a man who's years in advance of his time. They just want someone who'll freshen things up a bit – approach the job from a new angle.' Even so, he was speaking, I imagine, for his own employers, and I am not sure that a 'fresh approach' is so real a necessity. A reviewer of an English course, writing in *The Use of English* said: 'The book merely reproduces many existing courses, and has nothing fresh to recommend it.' Such a book is probably, from the selling viewpoint, the ideal, and should go successfully through a number of editions.

So far I have suggested that the publisher caters for the needs of the ordinary teacher; but it does not follow that the ordinary teacher in any one school can always get the book he wants. This is because so many books are planned to sell on a very wide market. It is told that the author of one English course, when interviewed for appointment to the staff of a training college, was asked why he had put so much grammar into his book. 'For you do the London exams, don't you? And there's not much grammar in their syllabus, and none of it compulsory. Couldn't you have left out the grammar altogether?' An ingenuous suggestion! No publisher's reader would dare approve such a book. For not only must an author consider the full requirements of the London syllabus – he must keep in mind those of the other examination boards as well; he must write for girls as well as boys, for country schools as well as town, for the colonies as well as Great Britain. More than that – he may have to cater for several grades of school simultaneously: grammar, technical and modern all at once. Nor must he aim to meet the average requirements of children of only one specified age; to state in plain terms that a book is intended for the average twelve-year-old is wantonly to restrict sales. In short, we are up against the concept of 'wide general usefulness', and books produced according to this concept may well be of so generalized a character that they cannot possibly be considered of real educational value. Meanwhile the puzzled teacher goes on complaining: 'I just can't get the book I want.'

Even a brief survey of the conditions under which text-books are produced would be incomplete without reference to the question of copyright; for considerations of copyright have always markedly affected the choice of reading matter for schools. Where copyright matter is used we are usually made well aware of it: neither author nor publisher is slow to point out how much material has been drawn from copyright sources – as though that in itself were a guarantee of high quality. Yet it *is* a guarantee, if not of high quality, at least of variety, and it ensures that the child shall sometimes be permitted to read the English of his own day. The difficulty is that – whatever contrary impression may be given by the profuseness of an editor's thanks to various authors and publishers – copyright material is not usually to be had for nothing; and if we imagine that, for example, the fee for the use of a short poem or a prose extract is as little as two guineas, we may see how easy it is to add a hundred pounds to the cost of producing a book. Moreover, these fees, though deductable from an editor's royalties, must be paid initially by the publisher, and their payment naturally sends up the price of the book. Consequently, in order to capture a cheap market, some publishers prefer to issue lower-priced books and to avoid the use of copyright matter altogether. There are still being published books of prose reading, purporting to be suitable for 'the middle school', which include hardly anything written during the last fifty years. Several school certificate courses do not include among their passages for précis any copyright matter whatever – and that in spite of the fact that examiners nowadays show a strong leaning towards contemporary sources. This practice of battening on the un-copyrighted past is not at all defensible. No publisher should allow considerations of price entirely to outweigh those of suitability.

In writing of the production of text-books I have purposely dealt with only its worst aspects. It would be unfair not to admit that, in spite of everything, a number of good books do come on to the market. These books are put out by scrupulous publishers – publishers who choose real educationists for their advisers, who plan for limited and specified markets, who make generous use of copyright matter, and whose pride will never allow them to sponsor anything shoddy. The sad thing is that even these publishers cannot afford entirely to ignore commercial considerations. To do so would be to fall behind in the race against less scrupulous rivals. After all, no publisher produces books for the joy of seeing them piled high on his warehouse shelves.

# *The Present-day Debasement of the Language*

## R. J. HARRIS

THE rival courses of English multiply. Does none of these tracts please the teachers, and is this the reason for there being so many? Most have some merit, but that is not surprising – they all contain a large part of a traditional store of material. Too many are clogged filters of abstractions, opaque with the names of names. I do not expect their language to answer life with a life of its own; but in any museum, to delineate, clearly and perspicuously though without song, is the least to ask. To make money, to please everybody, to instruct everybody, and in one Course, this cannot be done, and yet is every day attempted. Janet and John read at different paces; nor is my teaching voice like yours. Our lesson-notes themselves diverge in order and content. Nevertheless, we should not need to look on school textbooks as on certain Sunday newspapers, which fiercely inveigh against the very vices they represent. 'Sense, but not complete sense' and 'the present-day debasement of the language' are phrases appearing in the same book. Generally speaking, linguistic vices are avoidable – nor would their avoidance commit compilers and publishers to any general aims of education which might seem to them too radical or coherent.

I list below, some of the avoidable vices exemplified in one or more of a dozen recently published books.

(*a*) Clumsy or inappropriate diction. Forms inelegant by any standard, or unsuited to the people supposed to use them. Examples: the phrase '*he or she*' eight times in eighteen lines; '*My dear aunt*' – the beginning of a letter by a child of eleven; a spelling rule – '*If the suffix begins with a consonant symbol the final -e usually remains but if it begins with a vowel the -e is normally dropped; but in certain words ending in -ice and -ge the -e must be retained before a, o, or u to keep the consonants "soft".*' Or: '*You have a good chance to clean up the business world when your turn (to write business letters) comes, for many business people are still churning out these atrocities*'; '*The Sonnet. . . . There are two different types. All have fourteen lines*'; a recommended start to an essay: ' "*There is no such thing as an ideal holiday, since one man's meat is another man's poison.*" *Such a beginning conveys its meaning in a sharp, concise manner. Moreover, it conveys a feeling of surprise. . . .'*

(*b*) A blinkering tone, with which no disagreement is allowed – magisterially pompous, discouraging, or patronisingly facetious. Examples: the title of this piece; '*There are two uses of language, the scientific and the emotive. In the emotive we do not usually refer directly to what we are talking about*'; '*We have in the twentieth century many more ideas in our heads than the Greeks and Romans, and therefore we have a much wider range of linguistic devices to deal with all that.*'

(*c*) Jumping-Jackism: breath-taking leaps from the elementary to the advanced; disconnectedness and lack of graded development of an idea. Examples: on page 1, the alphabetical arrangement of simple words in a dictionary; on page 3, homonyms, synonyms, antonyms and homophones. From another book: insistence that knowledge of subject and predicate as terms is necessary as a tool, followed by exercises in which such knowledge is presupposed before it has been taught.

(*d*) Irrelevant material – most common in the early books of a course; it is difficult to say what is irrelevant to the GCE once that stage is reached. Examples: telegrams at age 11, and business letters too. Exercises such as, '*Substitute a simple English word for: prognosticate, effulgent, malediction, impecunious, domicile.*'

(*e*) False analogy, and other deceptions. A popular analogy is that between a carpenter's tools and the parts of speech. I have heard a master craftsman in one trade say, ' 'andmeanevvyammer, Bert', but never one in the writer's trade who exclaimed, 'Give me a noun, collective or abstract, to replace the blank in the following sentence'. Another: '*Here is a riddle. What is the difference between a house without a roof, and a sentence. . . . The answer is, the house without a roof is not complete, but a sentence is.*' Compare this with '*Nearly all sentences contain verbs*' – from a still more recent book. Another: '*Adjectives are to the writer what colours are to the artist. A plain black and white drawing is neither as interesting nor as realistic as a picture in rich natural colours.*' O Dürer, O Kodachrome!

(*f*) Visitors from abroad – especially those weak comprehension questions demanding extraneous information and leading away from the close study of the actual words supposed to be under consideration. Examples: '*Why are several snowstorms unusual in the New Forest?*' – no clue is given in the passage, which happens to mention the New Forest. Another, from an effusion on England, written by Earl Baldwin: '*What important offices of State has Earl Baldwin held?*'

(*g*) Doubtful assumptions, obscure aims. Examples: that a thorough grounding in grammatical terminology is needed to help children to write clearly, or even that this knowledge may be presumed to exist. Thus, in Book 1 of a course for secondary modern schools, an inaccurate classification of masculine, feminine, common and neuter gender. Again, that an exercise or idea which has worked in class is thereby shown to be educationally valuable. An obscure aim: '*The feeling for rightness of sentence and grammatical form rather than technical achievement is aimed at.*' What are 'rightness' etc, if not 'technical achievement'?

(*h*) Exercises in the habituation of error and cliché. The practice of blunders, and other forms of negativism and of deliberate confusion. Examples: the typical 'correct the punctuation' exercise; the juxta-position without context of easily confused pairs of words; *as – as a cucumber, as – as a lion.* '*Some lazy folk pay no attention to the choice of adjectives*' is the sentence immediately following this last exercise.

(*i*) Dragons and chimeras – exercises in correcting mistakes that are never made, and in overcoming difficulties that would be such folly if in fact they existed. Examples: '*Correct the following sentences: "I had not scarcely sat down for my meal than the telephone rang". "He was almost a year junior than me."*' *Another, from Book* 3 *of a Course:* '*Correct the following: talbe, pulbish, odrre.*' *Another:* '*Dear sir,s*

*i have seȝn yor advert. inthe JUNIO4 woRLD" an I wo uld lick to by "THE detecto dISGUISESET" whi ch costs*15/*qqd.* 8 *have enclosed a postl* 9*rdeR.*

*yors tuwly&*"

Another: '*Gretty swam bacefully bo the toat. Ge are woing for our tolidays homorrow. Flave your wags*'. Another: '*With who did you go to the match?*' None of these examples is taken from a commercial Course.

(*j*) Parasitism on the literary body – as in the use of poetry and prose in ways which suggest a total dissociation of language and literature. This happens not so much when a poem is used to reveal parts of speech, as when comprehension questions direct attention away from the meaning of the original or to trivial details of it. Examples: replacement of the real thing by the names for the real thing, as in technical chapters on versification and figurative language – 'Tricks of the Trade'; mechanical rigidity of treatment of rhythm – e.g. *Thus the pattern of line 1 is*

x / x / x / x /

His horse who never in that sort

Is it?

(*k*) Uncertainty of audience – is the book written for the pupil or for the teacher? A great volume of ink would be saved if those little talks and exhortations were omitted which usurp the teacher's place. The space so saved could be used for further exercises and for illustrations of points made.

(*l*) False promises – lip-service, in the introduction, to some typical educational theory, which is not however exemplified in the body of the work. A characteristic example is the promise to establish a clear relationship between grammar and meaning, '*the constant practical application* (*of grammar and its terms*) *to composition, both written and oral*'. All that this usually means is the interpolation of formal grammar exercises into chapters on narrative and other writing.

(*m*) Burst suitcases – sometimes superficially repaired by hand-sewn examples made to fit the rule, but sometimes unashamedly paraded. Examples: '*The, a, an, are really adjectives though they have no adjectival force*'; '*Sun, moon, are common nouns, whereas Englishman and German are proper nouns*' – despite the usual definition. (I owe these examples to Mr Ian Michael.) One is always meeting 'sense' that is not 'complete', or, just as surprisingly, sense that *is* complete, e.g. '*He went galumphing home.*' Sometimes one is commanded to '*understand*' a word which is not expressed (as in '*Halt!*' – '*you*' understood). At other times it is forbidden to do this (as in '*He studied at Oxford*' – studied what? – a question one may not ask here, for the verb is intransitive). Or the sceptical reader is assured that '*alas*' is '*not an essential part of the sentence* – "*Alas! we shall never see him again*" – *it is merely an exclamation of grief*'. In short, enormous confusion between objective description of structure and pedantic conscription into categories.

(*n*) Contextless commands – many books contain such instructions as, '*Add suitable adverbs to the following: The wind blew . . . through the trees. The student did his work. . . .*' Or, '*Fill in the most suitable noun: The children travel to . . . by . . .*' The most suitable! Mere recognition grammar, shamming literature.

I look forward to seeing the perfect text-book. I secretly feel that it may be a child's new exercise book, an immaculate blank.

# *Young Readers' Digests: A Note on Shorter Versions*

DOUGLAS BROWN

I HAVE been studying some texts of Shakespeare and of nineteenth-century novels that abbreviate and dilute their originals for young readers.[1] These books seem to be aimed at the classrooms and probably the library shelves of junior and middle forms in secondary schools – in grammar schools chiefly. I pass on, here, some of my reflections. I have expressed them in a downright way, but without meaning to be dogmatic. I have tried to get over a strong reaction of mere vexation, and to immerse myself, with the texts, in a variety of imagined teaching contexts. I shall pass in review, first, what a cross-section of these abridgements actually make of their originals; second, what effective uses they may have for teachers in particular situations; third, what merits and demerits the abridgements have, given their context; and fourth, what deeper consequences their use may have and what line one ought to take regarding them. The methodical procedure is there to check the whirl of contradictory thoughts, and irreconcileable pros and cons, in my head. For we cannot have certainties about what a work of art means or could mean at this point or that in the growth of an adolescent. There are no limits. And we have a responsibility to be flexible and adventurous in trying to bring the work near enough for impact and encounter. Equally there is a responsibility towards the integrity of the work of art also, to its uniqueness and its exaction of effort. From abbreviation to dilution to active damage runs a continuous process. Neither kind of responsibility – to young people at this or that point of growth and in need of varied kinds of help; to works of art having their own finality – should allow us to endorse the publication, as a

[1] *The Merchant of Venice*, *Julius Caesar*, *As You Like It*, and *King Henry V* ('A Shorter Shakespeare', arranged by H. S. Taylor, M.A., Ginn.) Dickens, *David Copperfield* and *Bleak House*. Emily Brontë, *Wuthering Heights* ('The Sheldon Library', Oxford, Clarendon Press.) H. Melville, *Moby Dick*. M. Irwin, *The Stranger Prince* ('The Queen's Classics', Chatto and Windus).

text representing a work of art, of something by way of being a defeat for the work of art itself.

I

First, abbreviated plays of Shakespeare, with editorial matter to compensate, and to drive home the approach intended. Mr H. S. Taylor bases his text upon classroom experience. He wants to preserve immediate liveliness, a narrative line, some of the more obvious dramatic values, and easy comprehensibility, for the middle school experience of Shakespeare. His text is well printed, in a light, handy format with stiffish paper binding. His introduction is brief, his textual notes (short, rather arbitrary in choice of material) are collected into a few paragraphs at the beginning and addressed to the teacher; *dramatis personae* are set out prominently, with simple 'leads' on how to envisage them. Then we get about two-thirds of the play. Scene divisions are obtrusive, and the verse has been sieved through for what is plain, narrative and easy of contemporary access. These siftings have been threaded together (with occasional verbal alterations) and manipulated into new wholes. The editor prefaces each scene with a passage visualizing setting and action, and many speeches have a parenthetical note on interpretation. Mr Taylor has done it cleverly. But it will lend force to the problems raised if I allow myself two quotations from the text of *The Merchant of Venice* (a play I am used to acting through complete but for one scene with twelve- and thirteen-year-olds). These do not fairly represent Mr Taylor's skill, be it said. The touch is a good deal less than nice. Here Gratiano has left Antonio and Bassanio in the first scene, the whole of his 'Let me play the fool' having been deleted:

ANTONIO: Farewell.
[*Exeunt Gratiano and Lorenzo. There is a short pause while Antonio looks at Bassanio searchingly before broaching his question.*]
Well, tell me now, what lady is the same
To whom you swore a secret pilgrimage,
That you to-day promised to tell me of?

BASSANIO [*with youthful enthusiasm*]:
In Belmont is a lady richly left,
And she is fair, and, fairer than that word,
Of wondrous virtues: sometimes from her eyes
I did receive fair speechless messages.
Her name is – Portia . . .
Nor is the wide world ignorant of her worth,
For the four winds blow in from every coast (etc.)

I say nothing of what is missed, at any age, when Gratiano's robust and trenchant language no longer rests within call of Antonio's and Bassanio's formalities. What happens here to Bassanio's speech is itself an offence both to Shakespeare and to any pupil who is developing an ear and a feeling for Shakespearean verse movement and ceremony of statement. It strikes a note of extraordinary crudity. That note in turn matches some of the italicized guidance continually before the eye. As here –

ANTONIO [*suspiciously*]:
This were kindness!

SHYLOCK: [*eagerly, and pretending to treat the whole business as a joke*]:
This kindness will I show!
Go with me to a notary, seal me there
Your single bond; and, in a merry sport,
If you repay me not on such a day,
In such a place, such sum or sums as are
Expressed in the condition, let the forfeit
Be nominated for –
[*Here Shylock hesitates and looks at Antonio, as if searching in his mind for some ridiculous object as a security, then, with a laugh.*]
– an equal pound
Of your fair flesh, to be cut off and taken
In what part of your body pleaseth me!

ANTONIO [*enthusiastic, because he considers this a most sporting gesture*]:
Content i'faith: I'll seal to such a bond,
And say there is much kindness in the Jew!

BASSANIO [*anxiously*]:
You shall not seal to such a bond for me:
I'd rather dwell in my necessity.

The tendency nowadays is to have editorial comment either tangled into the texts, or page by page facing. At least when it was at the back it could be ignored. Confronted by such a passage I sigh for the safety of Verity. In fairness I should say that I have gone through four of these texts, and found few intrusions so mischievous and so footling as these; most are merely stereotyped to the level of a television serial, and an embarrassment to a teacher. But the editorial guidance is not a side-issue, and at its most absurd it declares its intentions most candidly. It is very much a part of the approach through abbreviation, it goes out to meet the pupils where they are supposed to be (with comic strip, with *Eagle* and *Girl*, and Blyton a little receded in memory, and mass entertainment) and makes sure that even Shakespeare keeps them there. It is complacent, it deals in the platitudes of serial psychology, and always it keeps things very simple.

I pass to the *Sheldon Library* abridgements. Reserving judgment (with an effort) at this point, I say only that the novels chosen are nineteenth-century 'classics' in the slack sense of that term – *Ravenshoe* goes alongside *Wuthering Heights* in the first six; that apart from the illustrations the presentation is good and unencumbered – the books look like novels, not text-books. The abbreviating method is that of the blue pencil tracing a course in and out of every paragraph, with a view to keeping up an appearance of the original's structure (the same number of chapters) and otherwise making the story plain in about a third or half the words it took the novelist to make it a work of art. The tampering is persistent – almost the same amount chapter by chapter – and the author's syntax and paragraphing, movement and detail, suffer every sort of interference. We have précis without paraphrase; it reads baldly. Just in what degree the diluted story and disembodied characters stand up it is hard to tell, for I cannot read the degraded text without bringing to it memories and associations from the real one.

Third, one or two texts from the *Queen's Classics* (again, looking down the titles, one wonders with what intention the term 'classics' is tacked on). The editors here have applied a different principle. The omissions are of chapters, or of sections, or (occasionally) of odd paragraphs. They are bulky. But at any given place the texture of the author's writing is undamaged. As a result the superficial 'architecture' of the novel is quite transformed, but the thing itself where you do get it is real. And the editors make clear what they are about (the *Sheldon* editor is not candid). These books, too, are well produced and a pleasure to read.

It will readily be seen how different are the principles at work. To balance the whole account I ought to refer to those texts of Shakespeare for the classroom that offer a variety of isolated but unshortened scenes from the plays, with no pretence of doing more or other than this. (I believe someone has also presented 'scenes from the plays' as a linked succession of the most exciting and accessible scenes from one play at a time. Either way, we have only a part of the whole, but in what we have the texture is true.)

## 2

Before we come to the performance, what are the relevant considerations about the situation to which these abridgements address themselves? Shakespeare first: I think many teachers will concede that the plays aren't sufficiently *enjoyed* in the middle school; that verbal difficulties obtrude more than they are worth; that heavy annotation is irrelevant and obstructive; that (having in mind the classroom time available) there must be guidance in advance of reading or acting, so that response can come immediately and not – tempting word – posthumously; that simple dramatic values, real caring about character, a strong narrative line, do form an intrinsic part of the enjoyment most middle school children can discover. And it could be urged that even if this is the limit of their enjoyment, at least Shakespeare is being kept alive for them as something worth going on with, and the future may yield more. With whatever measure of success, the texts before us address themselves to this situation. I think we can say the editor is right to try. Besides, we should balance reluctance to take his tactics against perceptions of another side to the situation. Comic strip Shakespeare, televised Shakespeare (and passages from Shakespeare) and filmed Shakespeare also direct themselves to our pupils, and may blur and limit their experience of his work in their own fashions. The distortions and inadequacies involved there (not invariably) far outmeasure the editorial treatment here: it is where the editor most lapses that these other media come to mind. Where these texts are in use, at least Shakespeare's words still occupy attention, and the interpolated commentary is there to animate the children's dealings with the words. It may not be too much to say quite simply that with drama now, the mass media of visual experience are at work upon our pupils, stereotyping expectation and dulling response: and even abbreviated and unduly simplified Shakespeare, made sufficiently telling in the classroom, may a little penetrate to those deeper levels otherwise untroubled.

Similar reflections hold for Dickens, Emily Brontë, Melville: at least the situation justifies experiment, one feels. Television, broadcast serials, the cinema, (at worst) the picture strip, all offer aggressive versions of the great novels, compared with which abbreviations of the text seem to be the thing itself. They are versions which filter into and out of relaxed imaginations, and lend themselves to the psychological needs and impulses of the moment; at best they offer only hints of something that requires quite other energies than it is getting. The material in hand dwindles to the level of whatever entertainment and diversion surround it. At the same time the public and probably the family background is such as to suggest that it makes no *real* difference whether you read these novelists or whether you don't; and that for purposes of growth and culture the tabloid equivalent will certainly do as well. Where the reading habit itself survives the easier media and the subtle and growing discredit, plenty of momentary and inferior fiction offers itself, shorter and more appealingly episodic than the great novels, and very much less demanding. So perhaps every real encounter with a novel of classical stature (although as an experience of the novel it may leave a lot to be desired) has value for the adolescent. Some notion of what a novel *can* be infiltrates, some notion of deeper possibilities – not necessarily an explicit notion. And when the encounter takes place, much more than that may happen – we can set no limits. Evidently, then, the abridgers are right to make some move to meet our pupils where they may be more willing to come; and bulk, completeness, the whole organization of the novel are perhaps not indispensable. A caveat occurs, though. Is the bulk, the length, itself an obstacle? Sometimes, obviously; especially to the slower reader. But I think much depends on what makes up the bulk. The introductory note to the *Sheldon* series refers to the last century as 'a more leisurely age': the reference should attach to a social class, for it has no general truth for the past. We, and our pupils, use our leisure differently, but the leisure is there, abundantly. The note goes on to indicate 'long discussions of topical events' and 'the repetition necessary in books written in serial form': only 'this kind of material', we are assured (falsely) has gone. What has really gone, in the Emily Brontë and Dickens novels, is detail, profusion of detail, depth and solidity of impression. And that holds good, too, of the Melville abridgement, only the editor is more candid and explicit. I want to leave wide open the question, whether this solidity of impression in the great novelist really is a major obstacle. If it is, so much the stronger appears the case for abridgement by preserving only passages in full texture and abandoning the shape of the whole. If it is not, then the case for abridgement itself begins to lose force.

## 3

Now to see how these particular attempts to create a neutral ground where contemporary youth can meet the classics, succeed. The Shakespeare texts first. I am ready to admit, at least in more doubting and depressed moods, that what this editor presents as a text of Shakespearean drama is perhaps much like what many middle school pupils *recognize* in the complete text they're more used to. This wan verse, scooped away, simplified and interpreted in terms of inferior adolescent fiction, constitutes perhaps what many do encounter. And I can see that to offer them just this, in the first place, means a faster pace, an easier enjoyment, a sense in them of dominance, and probably more coherent classroom performances. Yet I feel most dissatisfied. The sheer pretence involved is a worry. Can it be right to offer as Shakespeare's, in printed form, this thinned out verse and stock psychology? Besides, doesn't such a text imply a very limited confidence about what adolescents can find for themselves in undiluted Shakespeare, and be helped by a teacher to discover? (A less defeatist mood now insists upon being heard.) We've a duty, too, to those in the class who can be sensitive to detail, to poetic movement and energy, to the unfolding process; and we've certainly a duty to those who *like* to know that they are confronting the real thing. And between the very sensitive whom we know of and the less sensitive whom we know of, how can we be sure enough of what does go on in the borderworld of response, when we take Shakespeare uncut into the classroom?

I am worried about the element of pretence; I am worried about the underlying assumptions to be made. Even if what we meet in these texts is all that our pupils see and find attractive when confronted with their originals, ought we to confirm and solidify the impression that Shakespeare's art is this and no more? No; it's a stage *towards* the experience of Shakespeare, it oughtn't to have the permanence of print and the sanction of teaching. And it is hard to resist an equivalent note on the parentheses and the Dover Wilson stuff printed before each scene: oughtn't the teacher to have more room to move in, to illuminate and to help? I feel that it isn't the pupil only, whose potentialities are slighted. The implication is (on the one hand) that there really is no more for the pupil to find out from the words, nothing to work imagination upon, and (on the other) that the essential teaching is there, in parenthesis, given editorially.

So I am not persuaded. I feel that a plain, full text of Shakespeare's own play is still the best – not just the best in principle, but the best for the human situation we have thought about. I feel that cutting should be part of the teaching process, public and accountable: by the scene, the episode, or the page, as Elizabethan playhouse practice warrants. What else may be needed is a teacher's responsibility and privilege. He can gauge need, gauge potentiality, judge the moment, through direct experience of the class. I prefer the Penguin text for every purpose from acting in class with twelve-year-olds to studying with undergraduates. For there we can find Shakespeare's verse, with an approach towards his punctuation, the proper absence of later stage directions and of obtrusive scene divisions, so that the imagination has to work. And even if we have to grant that lots of our pupils may in fact take no more from that text than Mr Taylor's gives them, still, oughtn't they to know (even at this stage) that there is more to take? I look back at those elements in the contemporary situation discussed earlier, and I conclude that one by one they can be met on the basis of a plain complete Shakespeare text and a teacher who cares to meet them. Failing that, let us have (with no pretences) 'scenes from Shakespeare'; not diluted 'wholes' in make-believe.

The editorial performances in the *Sheldon* abbreviations can be given shorter shrift, and ought to be. I respect the aim, for the situation requires experiment. But to do *this* to the art of a great writer is scandalous, and deserves no support whatever. The blue pencil has traced its way in and out of the paragraphs, taking a phrase here, a sentence there; has taken here a paragraph and there a page: and the result is a travesty of the pace, idiom, tone of voice, mood, narrative procedure – of all the constituents of art. It is a pretence, and it is made the more a pretence by the editorial preface: 'We have cut out this kind of material . . . but we have not altered the author's words. There is no break in the continuity, no paraphrasing; but by careful selection we have tried to leave intact the character of the original.' Technically there may be no untruth in that, but in spirit it is a plain lie. The blue pencil has not 'altered' the author's words, but it has taken away one context or supplied another, dashed out a qualification, re-worked syntax and paragraphing. It has altered, often from line to line, his way of doing things with words. I can't feel that the editors have any perception what kind of art they are destroying so casually; and I can't feel that the Oxford Press are justified in supporting that editorial disclaimer – nor, indeed, the whole appalling venture. Emily Brontë's nervously articulated syntax, the pungent qualifications, the life and motion of her impressions, all subside; and for this

. . . Heathcliff gradually fell back into the shelter of the bed, as I spoke; finally sitting down almost concealed behind it. I guessed, however, by his irregular and intercepted breathing, that he struggled to vanquish an excess of violent emotion. Not liking to show him that I heard the conflict, I continued my toilette rather noisily, looked at my watch, and soliloquized on the length of the night: 'Not three o'clock yet! I could have taken oath it had been six. Time stagnates here: we must surely have retired to rest at eight!'

'Always at nine in winter, and always rise at four,' said my host, suppressing a groan: and, as I fancied, by the motion of his shadow's arm, dashing away a tear from his eyes. . . .

we have this –

. . . Heathcliff gradually fell back into the shelter of the bed, finally sitting down almost concealed behind it, as if struggling to vanquish an excess of violent emotion. I continued my toilette rather noisily, and soliloquized on the length of the night. 'Not three o'clock yet! Time stagnates here: we must surely have retired to rest at eight!'

'Always at nine in winter, and always rise at four,' said my host, suppressing a groan: and, as I fancied, dashing away a tear from his eyes. . . .

Not even the great climaxes are respected. I underline, here, the editorial excisions:

. . . 'It would degrade me to marry Heathcliff now; so he shall never know how I love him: and that, <u>not</u> because he's handsome, Nelly, <u>but</u> because he's more myself than I am. Whatever our souls are made of, his and mine are the same; <u>and Linton's is as different as a moonbeam from lightning, or frost from fire.</u>' . . .

That first excision ought to be pondered: how it degrades the entire statement to reduce it so, how it drugs the valid passion. What besides mere grossness and some insistent wish to stabilize young complacency, leaving fantasy undisturbed, could have sanctioned the excision (from Cathy's final passionate claim) of

. . . 'I cannot express it; but surely you and everybody have a notion that there is, or should be an existence of yours beyond you. What were the use of my creation if I were entirely contained here?' . . . ?

And then, by way of gratuitous insult alike to Emily Brontë's art and to contemporary youth, this –

. . . 'If all else perished, and *he* remained, I should still continue to be; and if all else remained, and *he* were annihilated, the universe would turn to a mighty stranger: I should not seem a part of it.' . . .

becomes this –

. . . 'If all else perished, and *he* remained, I should still continue to be; and if all else remained, and *he* were annihilated, I should not seem a part of the universe.' . . .

'We have not altered the author's words.' In justice to their public, and to the novelist whose name is still attached to this *Wuthering Heights*, the publishers should have the introduction to the series reworded. But it shows scant respect for any public to offer such a series at all. This is not Emily Brontë's prose and therefore it is not her novel. And indeed, many of the deletions are calculated to reduce even the 'story' to the *Woman and Home* level. What is the real case for abridging this novel, anyway? It's so economical a performance; and any middle school pupil who is capable of interest in the *Sheldon* dilution is surely capable of wanting the vitality, the firm and thorough emotion, the pressures of original experience that buoy up and thrust into every paragraph of the novel itself? Are readers who once take it up bored with the length of *Wuthering Heights*?

Well, but *Bleak House*? It seems a fairer case for abridgement. No, Dickens's syntax and prose movement are every bit as vital as Emily Brontë's; and, in fact, the editorial insensitiveness is as marked, the interference as damaging. For what disappears ('repetitive', presumably, and 'topical') is the wealth of incisive detail, the sardonic flourishes, the humorous or passionate proliferation: all that *abundance* which is the life of Dickens's prose and therefore of his art itself. He is one master whose language must never be thinned out. And the price paid for making him 'readable' after this fashion, is to make him (if that were possible) hardly worth reading. If *Bleak House* is to be abridged it must be by omitting large chunks; or by deliberate re-disposing of a few fine elements (after the style of Mr Emlyn Williams's published *Readings*). In the *Sheldon* version, even the obviously exciting things – the suspense of Tulkinghorn's death in chapter 48, or the more subtle suspense of chapter 41, things that even an editor anxious only to get the Wilkie Collins element out of Dickens would have kept uncut – are so peeled and shorn as to lose their force.

I can imagine an argument for eliminating the sardonic from the text, though I would hope to refute it. I can't imagine, even, any argument for eliminating or raking over the Dickensian tenderness. I know from experience what response that elicits from the young, even from the apparently callous (indeed, especially from the apparently callous: Dickens's art deliberately addresses them). I think that in the modern setting nothing is more apt to make for sanity and a cultured heart than the tenderness of Dickens. But here, in the scenes of tenderness, of protest, of pain, the excisions are as coarse as ever. In places the art and passion do gleam through – how could they not? But the abridgement impoverishes continually; always it is about its business of stereotyping emotion into accustomed and complacent forms. Anyone who wishes to check upon this, and at the same time to refine his feeling for what, in the prose, gives Dickens his saving strength, should compare in detail the chapter called *A Multitude of Sins* with its shortened version; or such a scene as the death of the crossing-sweeper.

In sum, these abridgements reveal no interest in what has made these novels profound works of art and they reproduce no such thing. By excising evenly and continually the editors have tried to preserve a resemblance of the surface, and that they have done; and in doing it they have approximated these surfaces to any and every other, made them altogether insignificant.

I take the *Queen's Classics* edition of *Moby Dick* as the best instance of the opposite approach. The surface has suffered extremely; the proportions and appearances are changed: but in those places of Melville's art which the editor has chosen to suggest what kind of experience the book offers, the texture remains untouched. Here is a good test-case, because *Moby Dick*, like *Bleak House*, really is very long. There are substantial sections likely to bore any but the most persistent young reader; and it could fairly be argued that an encouraging, a satisfying experience of the original novel as imaginative art is especially out of reach of the young. It is often a difficult book, it hasn't the intermediary richnesses of (say) Shakespearean drama. But it has a story of strange magnificence, it has – from the first – the *inexhaustible* quality, its methods and procedures are so original and fascinating that they may awaken the young mind to new possibilities in the novel as a form, as an experience. However far out of reach at twelve or fourteen or sixteen may be a firm possession of the art, the sense of adjacent depths does come through; the notion that the tale means more than a sailor's yarn and means it with unyielding energy. A good test-case: and this abridgement comes out well. It respects the integrity of the prose, it gives prominence alike to the disquieting lure of the opening and to the marvellously exciting end – one of the very great narratives of literature. More important, the abridged version contains enough material from the obscurer levels of the real novel, not to be self-sufficing. Such a version hints at meanings beyond, leaves suggestion tantalizingly in the air. And that is as it should be. Personally I would have welcomed rather more of this material. I can't understand why the abridgement is so very brief. It isn't a publisher's ruling as to length, for the abridgement of Margaret Irwin's *The Stranger Prince* in the same series runs to some 15,000 more words. Merely to have equalled that would have given the editor the chance to add a couple more of those haunting preludial chapters like *The Lee Shore* and *The Symphony*, which do more to prepare a reader (any reader) to receive duly the departure and the tragic climax than anything here included. And I am puzzled why *all* the encounters with the ships returning are not there. These would have enhanced the subtler reaches of the narrative, and preserved a juster balance in the proportions of the small book. As it is, the beginning of Melville's novel receives undue preponderance. There may have been good reasons. Anyhow, I think a valid purpose is served by abridging a novel such as *Moby Dick*, and doing it this way. The abridgement as it stands could be a valuable experience for a young reader; and there would remain the likelihood of its stimulating a wish later to tackle the whole novel.

## 4

In what direction do these particular findings take us? Evidently we must test out abridgements against a variety of criteria and apply them generously. Does the version offer anything like as much as the young reader in the library, or the pupil in the classroom, can receive? Does it answer those needs we ought to be providing for? Does it point, ultimately, away from itself and towards the real thing? Does it bear candid witness to its own shortness, and does the editorial material give due weight to what has been left out for the time being? Does the version offer a worthwhile experience as it stands, or has something that was worth while become impoverished, undistinguished? We have our responsibility to the pupil and we have our responsibility to the work of art too. That work is part of our heritage, something given, something that ought to be present as itself, sooner or later, to the educated imagination; it makes its own claim. So we have no right to present it subtly travestied, or concealed, or spoiled, or (while shortened) apparently self-sufficient. Criteria appear again: does any part of the author's imaginative act come through in strength? Does the version deceive the reader about the kind of experience its original offers? Is there a profitless guiding of interest towards 'story' understood in nebulous or daydream terms? How far does the abridgement amount to an abstraction from the life of the original?

To bring such tests into play, in turn, requires more from us who teach. On the one hand we have to exercise juster perceptions of what our pupils can profit from; of their growing points, of where they *are*. On the other hand, before we accept or guide towards an abridged version, we need renewed perception of where the life of the original resides, so that we can properly see what has been done. We shall have to cultivate, it may be, a surer sense of the interplay inside the great novels. Prose syntax and vocabulary and movement work with economy or abundance of detail, work with the placing and weighting of incident, with analysis and assessment of character, with the clarification of tone and stress through growth from page to chapter; work, again, with the emergence of plot in movement and stillness, with inward and outward structures. It is all interplay, interpenetration: these are the charged particles. Of course an abridgement that duly recognized all this would be no abridgement at all. At his most repetitive and proliferating, the Dickens of *Bleak House* still bodies forth, uniquely, his imagined world, cast in a certain inimitable mould. There's probably not a paragraph out of place in *Moby Dick* (despite the rather deprecatory remarks of the *Queen's Classics* editor about 'the history and methods of whaling'). The vast interior theme has taken its weight from a tireless construction of actuality given in minute particulars and insistent technical detail. And the narrative which, in the abridgement, seems nearly all, Melville has constantly set aside or gone beyond, as if towards the condition of poetic drama. For a set artistic purpose he has put immovable obstacles in the way of reading *Moby Dick* simply as a sea yarn. Very well: an abridgement that tried to stand by all this could not abridge. But only as we quicken our own power to receive that life within, can we properly gauge the value for teaching, or for the junior library shelf, of a shorter version. We can't enquire if 'enough' comes through, unless we have a working notion of what there should be 'enough' of.

# *TAKING BEARINGS – THREE REVIEWS*

## *George Sturt*

*Change in the Village*, by George Bourne. (Duckworth.)

*Change in the Village*, published in 1912 when its author was nearly fifty, is the first of George Sturt's two important books, but it is the second, *The Wheelwright's Shop*, which makes clear his qualifications for writing this first. For in *The Wheelwright's Shop* Sturt tells how the early death of his father and the disdain which, through reading Ruskin's *Fors Clavigera*, he had conceived for the teaching occupation, led him in 1884 to abandon his post as schoolmaster and assume the headship of the family's wheelwright business, largely ignorant though he was of the duties of both man and employer. To the 'men', master craftsmen some of them, he was for many years merely 'George'; even when he became 'the Guv'ner' he remained in intimate association with them, receiving their advice and help in the business, and becoming in his turn their adviser and helper in matters of their personal lives. So that when, in 1891, Sturt removed from the wheelwright's shop in Farnham, Surrey, to the village of Bourne three miles off, and assuming the pen name of 'George Bourne' turned himself to authorship, he approached the labourer's life with a directness of knowledge which distinguished him from some others who had preceded him. Jefferies and Hudson, for example, had both come to the labourer by way of their love for the countryside. Sturt interested himself in the labourer first, in his immediate needs and purposes, and it was from the starting-point of the labourer's life that he investigated his surroundings and conditions, and ultimately recorded the changes which are the subject of this book.

The principal village changes recorded by Sturt are three. The first had occurred before his time, in the middle of the nineteenth century, when the enclosure of much of the common land spelt virtual doom to the peasant way of living. Sturt recorded this change because he saw – in the vestiges of peasant life which survived, in the villagers' rapidly dying dependence on local resources, in their declining gaiety, in the petering-out of the 'robust tradition' – that many of the older folk were still impelled by the momentum derived from a forgotten cult, and he was thus able to take the full measure of all that had been lost. The second change was a more obviously disintegrating one, more clearly disruptive of a self-contained village life: it was the impact, only obscurely felt at first, of the growth of the great producing industries, which led ultimately to the decay of local crafts and a rise in the importance of the mechanical and distributive occupations. The 'men' were becoming 'machine-hands'; those who should have been apprentices were becoming errand-boys; the steadying influence of working for a perceived end was giving place to the unsettling effects of working for a mere wage. The third change was the arrival in the village of 'villa residents' living according to a new economy, ignorant of a thrift which depended on local resources, and sustained only by their own money-values and by a competitive attitude towards their neighbours. This arrival was completing the work of unsettling the village outlook and was weakening such sense of corporate and self-dependent life as still remained.

The depressing effects of these changes were seen by Sturt not only in a deterioration of the villagers' material circumstances but also in their apathy, bewilderment, anxiety and feelings of humiliation. And it is important for us to see that what Sturt is pointing to is not merely poverty and its attendant misery but a real desiccation of spirit; otherwise we shall fall into the same error as Geoffrey Grigson, who claims in the Introduction to this new edition of Sturt's book that Sturt's hopes for a brighter future have been fulfilled: a new prosperity has come to the labourer – he has 'access . . . to towns and cinemas', 'more papers, more reading, more books from the County Library', and 'the enjoyment of broadcasting, and of television as the H aerials sprout on cottage and council house'. For Mr Grigson, the village problems of Sturt are problems no longer. And, of course, it is true that George Sturt were he alive today, would rejoice at the great improvement in the labourer's material circumstances. But he would see nothing nowadays in the villages of south-eastern England to suggest a return to a genuine corporate life, to a life stabilized by seasonal routines, solaced by skilled handwork, and made reasonable and satisfying by a perceived relationship between work and the benefits it confers; nor would he find a revival of the spirit of self-dependence, serenity and 'laughter in labour' which was once at the heart of rural existence. What he would find is a great many villages, even formerly secluded ones, from which the labourers have been virtually displaced; their cottages, joined and converted, and improved by the addition of telephone, garage, and TV aerial, are now inhabited by people who have made rapid money in commerce and industry. Often vulgar, complacent or rivalrous, these people owe no allegiance to the village; the very mentality which has spurred them on to prosperity is a guarantee of their unfitness for community life, and their ignorance of the countryside is equalled by their indifference to it. The fast car takes them easily to the town, their real 'centre'; in the home their enjoyments and distractions differ in no way from those of their city cousins. As for the labourer, often no longer needed for tilling a land upon which local prosperity does not depend, he has found himself employment in one of the light industries which have been strategically spaced over the surface of the counties, and his home is a council house on the fringe of a town. His thoughts, too, turn townward: they drift in and out of the local cinema, in and out of Woolworth's, and home at last to the bare-shouldered evening gowns of the towny types on television.

Living clear-sightedly in the middle of profound changes, Sturt not only recorded them but also penetrated to their origins and perceived to what they might lead. If he could not prescribe a cure he could point to a cause; and the causes of our present plight are the first things we must investigate if we are to emerge into a new wholesomeness and escape disaster. I say 'we' advisedly; for behind the changes in Sturt's village lay nation-wide changes which affected and continue to affect everyone, and the spiritual plight described by Sturt is very much the plight of us all.

J. H. WALSH

# *Caldwell Cook*

*Play Way English for Today*, by D. A. Beacock. (Nelson.)

The limitations of Mr Beacock's book are implicit in the statement of purpose at the outset: 'Cold and inadequate as mere words must always be, they can at least try to convey something of Caldwell Cook's greatness to a wider public.' A cool and perhaps adequate attempt to weigh Cook's claim to greatness would have been of greater value, both to the reader and to Cook's memory.

To some extent the book is biographical, as is natural with a teacher whose teaching, in spite of his indirect influence, can hardly be imagined separately from his personality. The impact of that personality on those whom he met was obviously considerable; it is unfortunate that Mr Beacock makes no serious attempt to examine the nature of the impact or of the personality. Emotionally charged words (*enthusiasm*, *genius*, *youngsters*, *joy*) set the tone, whilst the timbre is indicated by dreary clichés (*a gallant band of pioneers*, *the secret of his greatness*, *the secret of his success*, *none the worse for a little wholesome guidance*). Chapter VI from another pen is in the same manner: *remarkable*, *inspiring*, *amazement*, remain as key words. Fearing, with reason, that his ardour may have engendered scepticism, the writer gives four tributes from old boys. New voices but the same song: *what fun . . . what fun . . . genius . . . golden age . . . acute enjoyment.* Part of the over-emphasis may be disregarded in what is to some extent obituary writing, but there is no excuse for allowing reporters and school magazines to *make bold to prophesy* and hint at *rather dazzling vistas.* In 'The Critics Speak' (Chapter X) the critics are in fact refuted before they have well cleared their throats. The cumulative effect of this strenuous pleading is not enthusiasm but exhaustion.

Yet Caldwell Cook's work was not so negligible as to need headlong acceptance. 'He dared to be unconventional in a period of conventionality in the teaching of English,' Mr Beacock justly claims. His 'experiments have laid the foundation for much of the progressive work in the teaching of English in our schools today. There are already many teachers who have incorporated features of his technique in their own syllabus', including many, I believe, who never heard his name. Moreover, his influence bore directly on the spirit and the content of education. Parliamentary and administrative reforms can at most create opportunities for teachers: Cook showed how some of the opportunities could be taken. Under his teaching many boys by the age of thirteen had acquired a wide knowledge of Shakespeare's plays, an unaffected liking for literature, the ability to express themselves with simplicity and freshness in prose and in verse, ease and fluency of speech, and a good working knowledge of grammar and prosody. If English teaching in general has shifted from the salutary towards the humane between the two wars, part of our gratitude must go to Caldwell Cook.

This is an achievement that would bear calm exposition, but there seems to have been something in Cook's personality that inhibited discrimination. It is not that he aroused enthusiasm, but that there is in the enthusiasm an element of strain and artificiality. Those clichés, coming not from one but from half a dozen admirers, are by no means the mark of spontaneous, unforced experience. Doubts, once aroused, seize upon many small points. 'Many of us – not just a few prigs – spent our time lavishly on the attractive and congenial homework which we were given to do.' Nonetheless, the remission of homework was, we learn, not a punishment but a reward.

A state of mind that is admirable in a boy of twelve may be less so in a grown-up, even if recaptured; and in straining to recapture boyish enthusiasms grown-ups will often induce a largely spurious emotion. One is uncomfortable, not so much on account of the original intensity as the nature of the recollection, in reading: 'He showed us expression as more than words meaning things. He revealed it as something alive, pulsing, breaking, surging. I can still remember how we wagged our little batons to "Come Unto These Yellow Sands".' Here, perhaps, is a clue to the central defect in Cook's work: his ex-pupils feel called upon to look back at him through the eyes of childhood not those of manhood. He laid excellent foundations, but cared nothing for the completion of his work. In the application of his experiments to other types of school, in the continuation of his work through the critical years of adolescence to maturity, Cook had frankly no interest. His exceptional energy was focused into an exceptionally narrow field. If that is the explanation of his success, it also obliges us to demur at the attribution of greatness and genius. Having applied such words to Cook, we should be left speechless before Matthew Arnold. Arnold brought to his work on education a widely cultivated mind and an attempt to see life steadily and see it whole. It is not possible to be a great teacher (or educationist) and nothing else.

Cook's breakdown and death must have caused pain enough to his friends, and it may seem a breach of taste to point to his shortcomings Mr. Beacock's over-statement and over-enthusiasm, however, oblige me to state the grounds for a more qualified admiration; to mention, in particular, Cook's lack of intellectual distinction, his immaturity, and a certain insensitiveness even in his imaginative understanding of children.

'Modern poetry', he wrote, 'is not of such a popular quality as it might be, nay ought to be, and (may we hope) will be. But if we all resolutely set our shoulders to the wheel and work towards this goal, surely we shall ultimately bring this aim to its destined fruition.' Though literature was one of his chief preoccupations I cannot recall any remark that might lead a grown-up to a deeper appreciation of a particular work. His scheme for a garden town that would gather round the school, where the traditional English festival days would see the national folk-customs revived, is pure day-dreaming. For all I know the London Stock Exchange may clear the floor for country dancing on Budget Day, but Kaffirs are still Kaffirs. The very fact that the folk arts have been (necessarily) recorded puts an end to that process of mutation and selection that is the essence of their growth. The flowers have withered because of something that has happened down at the roots, and it is to the roots that our attention must first be directed. (It does not follow that folk-song and folk-dances are useless in the school community; there, their value is enormous, but for the community at large the significance has gone.) 'Thither would come, he hoped, children of all classes and creeds, to learn and play together. The barriers between rich and poor, manual worker and scholar, would be broken down as each came to realise the contribution to the community that the other could make.' The banality of the aspiration is brought out by a glance at the realities. 'Marsh's studies in Montreal tell us that at the age of seven the average child from a high-income family is two inches taller than the seven-year old from a low-income family, and at the age of fifteen nearly five inches taller. The boy of seven from the well-to-do family is typically four pounds heavier than the boy from the low-income family, and at fifteen, eight pounds heavier.' In literature enthusiasm is the beginning but only the beginning of enjoyment; discipline and integration must follow if the enjoyment is to assert its priority over whisky and winter sports. The distinction between the kind of rhythm that can be set down in musical notation and expressed with a stick, and rhythm of a more complex nature ('That night of now-done darkness I wrestled with (my God) my God'), can have meant little to Cook, who lost interest in his pupils before they were at an age to know the distinction. The problems of growing up, the work of building his foundations, were outside his province.

Time and again the writers refer to his boyishness, his puckishness, his childlike pride in having real swords; 'it is exhilarating', he writes, 'to make one of this company of boy players'. Add to this the car Boanerges, the cream teas, the toy town, the mannered, almost histrionic style and much else, and the suspicion becomes irresistible that Cook found it all too easy to identify himself with his pupils. The boyishness merges into immaturity. 'He was sufficiently a boy himself to be able to share in their pleasures.' That is good, but it is not enough. A teacher certainly needs a penetrating sympathetic power to imagine his pupils' needs and live through their experiences, but equally he needs detachment, perspective, the ability to see those needs and experiences in their context. Such externality Cook lacked. One great fault of conventional, exam-bound teaching was, and is, its excessive devotion to external standards (of a sort). Cook helped to establish a better balance, but not by attaining the balance himself.

Of the vigorous and whole-heartedness of Cook's self-identification with his pupils there can be no doubt; the scope and quality of his sympathy are less certain. Even in *Play Way English for Today* there are many causes for misgiving, but there is space here to mention one only. Though dramatic readings and productions are at the core of his work, he appears to be oblivious of the attendant dangers. In particular, he ignores the all-important distinction between school drama and outside drama. An ordinary production is an end in itself, undertaken purely for its value to an audience. A school production, on the other hand, is – or should be – part of an educational technique, undertaken chiefly for its effect on the cast. The fact the plays have to go 'with a swing' to be of value to any one at all, leads the producer into grievous temptation. The best parts are allotted to the best actors and the other boys fill in the gaps. Such productions give to those they have and take from those that have not – especially self-confidence and social reassurance. Children are acutely and painfully aware of implied aspersions.

> '*No! I am not Prince Hamlet, nor was meant to be;*
> *Am an attendant lord, one that will do*
> *To swell a progress, start a scene or two,*
> *Advise the prince . . .*'

It is not practicable to give the chief parts to the most hesitant, self-effacing pupils, but the best school production, I believe, is the one that comes nearest to doing so without losing its vitality as a production. The meek in spirit are as much the teacher's responsibility as the patently gifted. It is a responsibility that sets up a constant tug-of-war in the teacher producing a play. A dramatic success may be an educational failure, but a dramatic failure also is an educational failure. Some difficult judgments have to be made. By this tug-of-war and by related difficulties Caldwell Cook seems to have been quite untrammelled. Only the bright boys interested him. 'The boy who had acted best as Falstaff the year before claimed the part of Sir Toby Belch.' An understandable claim, but one to be resisted. It is quite possible that Cook's own productions were carried off with such gusto that the humble pupils derived more benefit from humble parts than big parts would have given them in a more calculated production. If that is so, and my inclination is to believe it, his weakness was his strength, but lesser followers must be more circumspect.

Cook's personality, both his qualities and his limitations, were suited to the particular problem he tackled much as a key is suited to its lock. An almost unexampled single-mindedness underlay his achievement. 'He never married, and became more and more engrossed in his work. This supplied him with all the religious belief he felt he needed, for his faith was summed up in the creed that the teacher exists only for the learner, and that the care of the soul of another human being was a sacred trust and responsibility.'

More inclusive creeds exist. Had he mastered the general educational problem of today as completely as he mastered a certain part of it, he would have earned the ascription of greatness. Had he tried and failed, his step would have faltered and his energy have been dissipated. A very large number of teachers would have been the losers.

It should be added that the present book concludes with examples of pupils' work to remind us how lively that could be, and a very useful copy of his detailed working syllabus.

RAYMOND O'MALLEY

# *Free Writing*

*Free Writing*, by Dora Pym and L. V. Southwell. (University of London Press.)

I hope that many of those engaged in teaching writing, never mind in what sort of school or college, will find the opportunity to consult this book. It publishes fieldwork of the most useful kind; it illuminates both the communication of the skills of writing and the possibilities of creative release. For there is here widely drawn evidence from children's work, and a close account of directed experiments; and there is the tang of relevant and unillusioned discussion among teachers themselves, and some cool wisdom and a proper tentativeness from the two authors; and there is a frank offer of doubts, discrepancies, disappointments. I must put it on record that I had doubts enough myself, and half-hostile reservations, as I went through the section called 'Experiments', and every single one got some recognition, some line of answer, by the time I reached the end of 'Reflections'.

I think that most of the teachers who read this note will already have in hand some form or other of 'free writing' – forms they will have developed out of the give and take of their own experiences with classes. They will have in common with the authors of this study a concern with ways to promote the deepest spontaneity in childrens' efforts to order their experiences, their wishes, their identities. Some will have done work much like that unfolded in this series of experiments: providing the opportunity and stimulus for released, plastic writing, by the use of a starting-point – most often an object of sensory perception – that tells, that strikes home, sensitizes some vulnerable place, enables a real flow. It may be a picture; a noise or a series of noises; a shoe passed round the room, or a little cluster of birds' feathers contemplated for a minute or two in quiet. The writing, checked far less than usual by interest in marks, formal correction, and so on, is to move with some abandon along channels suggested from within, at obscure levels of consciousness perhaps, by want and purpose and dream and impulse. It is understood that valuation will not be competitive, conventional, but generous and personal. The reader, too, is exploring; there is appreciation and pleasure to be recorded wherever he finds hints of achieved individual freedom in seeing and saying, wherever he meets the distinct, the forthright, the candid. The most vital parts of the child's attention are to be free, all along, to engage (in territories of his own finding and choosing) words and meanings, and to find a rhythm and an imagery for communication.

Those who have work of this sort in hand will profit from this study because of the variety of fresh suggestion it offers and the evidence it provides to encourage, to vindicate. There is careful thinking about the purpose of such activity. What does it do for the child? and for the teacher? and how does it connect with, or check, progress in more disciplined forms of writing? and so on. Those who haven't yet adventured far in such directions (whatever the gifts, or apparent inertia, in the children they teach) will find sharp stimulus to move. For I don't think any teacher not already practising in some way the techniques here illuminated and exemplified will wish to do without them after judging the evidence and the argument here published. The tone of the discussion is frankly enthusiastic, but sensible and moderate too. I like the plentiful examples from the work of children, and the economy with which commentary, and notions of what is at stake, arise naturally from them. Indeed it seems to me possible that the authors undervalue free writing and assign to it a more marginal importance than it should have. I think of three clear gains in particular: the nourishment of will and tact for finding a language to fit experience; the easy candour that such work disposes the writer to; and the respect, the more adequate sense of individuality, that can emerge between child and child, child and teacher, where such free communication takes place. And then I have to think of the kinds of makeshift, the insidious varieties of the secondhand and the false, and the failures of mutual respect, that so often seem to be inseparable from the teaching and practice of more disciplined forms of writing, however considerately managed. And it begins to seem that while purposive writing we must have, and of course the child needs it too, yet the more free writing there is time for, the better. It's by no means marginal. That falsities and mannerisms and borrowed ways of treating experience can find their way into free writing also, the authors openly acknowledge. The experience of many teachers confirms it. But there is evidence of so many fine possibilities, that we have obviously to apply the parable of the sower and carry on.

It ends, for the teacher, in problems of balance. That's a truism; but this book really does sharpen our sense of diverse claims, of activities to be balanced. The distinctions made here are clear and pointed ones. How well, for example, the authors separate 'language techniques' (which are important, and deal with the use of words, sentence structure and rhythm, organization of material) from 'printing press techniques' (spelling, punctuation, layout, capital letters). By the time you've finished and thought about *Free Writing* you find yourself where you often need to be: trying to adjust more sensitively the recognition of identity and freedom to grow ('For God's sake stand aside and let him be') to the duty of nourishment and training (' – which spontaneity, because it is the hardest thing of all to come by, will need the most careful rearing').

DOUGLAS BROWN

# VII

## *PROBLEMS OF ASSESSMENT*

THE next three essays raise, in different ways, problems of assessing children's creative or critical work. It is well recognized that the same group of teachers may mark the same batch of essays quite differently after a lapse of time, and there has been, and is, much pressure to standardize marking or to omit continuous prose altogether in favour of more quickly examinable 'exercises'. The problem is very real: all the more so since teachers and examiners, over-hurried for time, are driven to elevate the markable in more subtle ways. The situation in which spelling, syntax, or most deep-rooted of all, vocabulary, take an excessive 'weighting' is all too familiar. Because common standards are hard to come by, and because time is altogether too much heeded both in sitting examinations and in getting the marks out, the many short cuts are taken again and again. But for all that, there *are* standards, though the time and patience required to feel a way to them can be considerable.

M

# *Marking Composition*

## W. H. MITTINS

In the Summer of 1960 issue of *The Use of English* readers were invited to rate in order of suitability for grammar school entrance three short compositions by twelve-year-olds on 'A Day at the Seaside'.

### A DAY AT THE SEASIDE

(Age about 12)

A

One day my father took me to the Seaside. It was a boiling hot day, so he let me take off my boots and stockings and wade about in the water. It was great fun. My playmates built castles with sand which was upon the shore. My father sat by a fire making the tea and warming the pies at the same time. At last the tea was poured out, so I had to stop playing and go up to take my tea. After I had taken it I ran down into the water. I was walking about when all of a sudden I let out a squeal. 'Whatever is the matter?' cried an elderly woman, who happened to be passing. 'I-i-its a crab,' I sobbed. 'Nonsense,' she cried, and walked on. I ran up to my father and he soon removed the crab. 'Are you going down to wade again?' Asked my father. 'No,' I said, and to confirm my statement I commenced putting on my boots and stockings. I walked along the shore, but I did not venture near the water. After an hour had passed my father and I walked along the beach in the direction of the village. We arrived home and I told my mother about the crab biting my toe, and she said it served me right for wading.

B

'A day at the Seaside' – what pleasure is in those few words – for with them comes the echo of the waves lapping up on the golden sands, and the memory of those thrilling donkey rides!

To children who live in the smoky towns the experience of a visit to the blue sea is delightful, and one may well notice the eager looks on the faces, pinched and pale, of the slum children, as they are packed into the railway carriages, bound for the seaside.

Poor little mites, is it not sad to think that they have come into this beautiful world only to see the lovely country and seaside once in so long a while. However the train steams into a small station, where the happy youngsters alight, and after their teacher (for doubtless they are some little flock belonging to a Sabbath School) has seen that no one is lost, she points out the shimmering sea in the distance, and laughing with glee, they all march joyfully down the path, perhaps singing some glad refrain.

They at length reach the sands where myriads of gay children are dancing happily in the summer sunshine, and after throwing off their caps and coats they run away along the sands ready to join in their friends' play, or bathe in the cool delicious waters of the deep, blue sea.

C

One fine summer morning I went a visit to the seaside. While trouging along at my ease, I discovered a little querious shell, picking it up I heard a most wonderful noise, putting it to my ear I heard the rusle of waves. With great glee and merriment I put it in my pocket and ran home to the house, and showed it to my mother, she said 'It was only a ordinary sea shore shell.'

When I heard this I was so angry that I layed it on the floor and smashed it. No sooner than I had done this, I was away to the shore again to finish my exploration. The next place I went to was where all the large boulders were strewn all over the place.

Then I went to the water's edge, and there I bathed my feet in the cool water.

These pieces were chosen from twenty-six used by William Boyd in an investigation described in his *Measuring Devices in Composition, Spelling and Arithmetic* (Harrap, 1924). It might be appropriate to consider first the judgments of the 271 teachers consulted by Boyd.

They showed remarkably close agreement for this kind of operation. Using a 7-point scale from *Ex*cellent through *S*atisfactory to *U*nsatisfactory, 213 judged B as Ex., 51 as *V*ery S., and a mere 7 as S plus or S. For A the spread of marks was greater, ranging from Ex. to *M*oderately S., but with a heavy concentration around S plus. The marks for C ranged from a handful at V.S. and S plus to 101 at M.S. and 87 at U. Using the mean scores, the collective order of merit was indisputably

B-A-C, with placings of 1st, 6th and 22nd in the batch of 26.

The most striking point of agreement between then and now is in the middle placing of A. Though the dozen and a half assessments received revealed sharp differences elsewhere, only two rated A first, and none put it third. This simplifies comparison by making it possible to concentrate on B and C. Opinion was almost equally shared between the orders B-A-C and C-A-B. (The numbers are very small, but similar results have been obtained from other judges.) A comparison of the comments of Boyd with those of the present assessors confirms the impression given by the marks that over the years comparative unanimity about criteria has given way to serious differences. Putting it crudely, almost all the original examiners but only half the current ones are assessing primarily verbal technique; the other modern half are mainly concerned with personal communication.

Boyd's position – and presumably that of most of his panel – is clear, consistent, and deliberately adopted. He is well aware of the alternative position. He recognizes that 'The picture called up [by B] is not so effective in appeal as in some weaker but more personal essays' and that in C 'there is a depth of personal feeling rare – perhaps happily – in children's composition'. That qualification 'perhaps happily', coupled with an appreciation of B's 'elevated style and detached point of view – there is no "I" or "we" in all the essay', reflects Boyd's relegation of the personal factor to a subordinate position. In consequence B (a girl, as one or two readers insisted!) with her 'rich and varied vocabulary', 'unusual number of rhetorical devices' and 'adventurous use of punctuation' scores heavily over C, whose essay, 'if all the crude mistakes . . . were removed, would rank high', but whose mark is brought right down by 'very bad spelling, poor punctuation, and one or two weak constructions'.

Boyd was of course concerned, for the purposes of his investiga- to stress the more 'objective' factors. It is not very surprising that the correspondence between the collective order of merit and the order obtained by counting certain objective features was high. With an 'absence-of-mistakes' order, the correlation was ·8; with length, about ·7; with vocabulary (frequency of unique or unusual words), also about ·7; with all three together, above ·9.

What is perhaps surprising is Boyd's insistence in his summing-up that an essay is always more than the sum of its parts and that markers should 'cultivate a temporary blindness to such details [length, frequency of mistakes, kind of words], so that we may be able to feel whether the essay in any measure succeeds in conveying effectively the information or idea or feeling it seeks to convey. Having got that sense of worth, we may have to go on to modify the judgment it suggests.' This seems eminently reasonable, but it is difficult to reconcile the recommendation with the apparent approval of assessments of Ex. for B ('not so effective in appeal . . .') and M.S. for C ('depth of personal feeling rare . . . in children's compositions'). Even if a harsh penalising of 'details' brings C down, could B (presumably without any such deduction) conceivably start at Ex. for total effectiveness?

The same kind of apparent discrepancy occurred in a number of the current assessments received. For instance, one marker found that C had 'most life and reality' but could not, because it was 'least literate in a formal sense', mark it higher than S; while B, 'nauseating in its second-hand unctuousness' but perhaps 'capable of imitating equally well more attractive models' was rated higher (V.S. or S plus). Another assessor acknowledged that C 'feels strongly and writes as he feels' but thought him so inaccurate ('and doubtless untidy') as to merit only M.S.; while B got a V.S. in the 'trust that good teaching and catholic reading will improve his outlook and style'. A third marker, giving the same marks, admitted to 'resisting the temptation some examiners might have to show their own sense of discrimination by marking up C' and gave B preference because of its 'enviable facility' and in spite of its style ('if written by an adult, style loathsome'); the writer of B, it was thought, 'ought to gain more from good teaching than A or C – and needs it more'. From those who favoured B, perhaps the most persuasive comment was: 'The fact that C relates the most important experience is not enough to compensate for the restricted and inaccurate vocabulary and immature grasp of sentence-structure. On the other hand, though B's sentiments are obviously derived from books (or Sunday school teachers), there are signs of capacity to absorb "literary" language and a growing sense of style.'

Those who rated C above B emphasized the contrast between the genuineness of the former and the spuriousness of the latter. One marker, in a thorough and interesting analysis commented (confessedly with possible exaggeration) on the 'logic of poetry' in C, with its 'creative feeling for words that promises a tuned and flexible response to human experience'. He found B, by contrast, unpleasant for its 'implicit snobbery and derivative maturity'.

A rather alarming under-current in many of the comments suggests that while the writer of C is clearly much more likeable, the writer of B is more suited to a grammar school! The English staff at one school agreed on the order C-A-B but felt that if they took the 'injunction about suitability for grammar school places too seriously', they might have to reverse the order. And the warmest advocate of C-A-B from personal preference, reserved as a 'cold and official' assessment a threefold tie. Granting grammar school entry to all three, he would 'place [his] hopes on the writer of essay C, expect to find the writer of A steadily making his way up to the Sixth to study science or modern languages, and pray that the writer of B would go to a girls' school'.

In three schools the exercise was tried out on classes of pupils. Here again, at least in the middle school, a certain ambivalence might be detected. C was commended for its sincerity, its 'modest originality' and its directness ('I like it because of its clear style, and because it reminds me of the moment when I did just about the same thing'), while B was found pompous, condescending and derivative ('A typical "good essay". It looks as if it were copied out of a book'). Yet the consensus of class opinion here was strongly for the order B-A-C. Some consolation can perhaps be found in another school where, though Form III almost unanimously rated B as best, a distinct majority of a Sixth Form group favoured C.

A tentative conclusion from this little exercise might be that, compared with their predecessors of a generation ago, the markers are more acutely and uncomfortably aware of the competing claims of individual authenticity and verbal technique, that there is a tendency to grant the former more nearly equal status with the latter, but that this tendency is restrained both by an awareness that personal quality is less susceptible of reliable assessment and by a feeling that verbal sophistication is the more important factor for grammar school purposes.

# *Measuring the Inner Light*

## RAYMOND O'MALLEY

A REPORT on the meaning and making of imaginative composition has been drawn up by the Composition Group of the London Association of Teachers of English. Imaginative composition is hardly the core, but rather the summit, of English teaching; here, if anywhere, will arise notions of what finally matters in life and what doesn't. Not only will values be discussed: they will be demonstrated, lived through. A piece of imaginative composition, unlike work that is merely technical, is its own justification. Politicians, engineers, economists, teachers and other technicians exist chiefly in order that there shall be artists. Not that the artists are separate people: there is something of the creative artist in everyone; but whereas we have to concern ourselves so much of the time, in schools, with the engineer or the politician in each pupil, there are times when we can turn to the artist, and the lesson in imaginative composition is one of them. Moreover, this present report is a thoroughly painstaking yet modest piece of work. It raises, directly and by implication, some of the most important questions in the teaching of English.[1]

The problem to be investigated was defined thus: 'Here were ten teachers of English who one and all believed that they could recognize an imaginative composition when they saw one, and assess its merit with a mark out of a hundred: we could not, however, reach agreement in discussion as to what we meant by an imaginative composition. What aims do we set before the children when they write one? What criteria do we have in mind when we mark one? What values underlie our belief in the importance of such work?' Many criteria were discussed and three of them selected: (1) Pictorial quality – 'Does the reader see, hear, feel the actuality of the experience presented?' (2) Creativeness – 'To what extent is what the writer has written new, original, individual?' (3) Feeling for words – 'To what

[1] The report is out of print, but further information may be obtained from the Secretary, L.A.T.E., c/o The University of London, Institute of Education, Malet Street, W.C. 1.

degree does the writer use words (*a*) strikingly AND (*b*) effectively?' The question was thus: When teachers are, in the routine of their work, sizing up an imaginative composition, how far are they being guided, consciously or unconsciously, by their estimate of the pictorial quality shown, or the creativeness, or the feeling for words, as just defined? After a pilot experiment that showed some of the snags, a number of examiners were asked to place in order[1] various sets of thirty-one scripts, according to their general impression and according to each of the three specified criteria in turn. Under expert guidance various checks were included in the scheme so as to eliminate (or else to measure) various unwanted influences; and the subsequent elaborate analyses were again carried out with expert statistical help.

As might be expected, there were wide discrepancies between some of the markings, though without the stultifying scatter revealed in some previous investigations. Examiners tended to fall into groups and sometimes to regroup. The self-consistency of markers on a repeated task varied from 40 per cent. to the remarkable figure of 98 per cent. On the main question nothing very definite emerged: different examiners seemed, when marking by general impression, to be guided to different extents by the specific criteria, with 'originality' as the most common. In general the conclusions are given only in their 'crude' or semi-statistical form, because the members of the Group wish merely to start an enquiry of this type, and are very hesitant about the results that may be claimed from their own work. Their only explicit conclusions are that the general approach is profitable; that short compositions (100 words) are worth considering for the purpose of grading; and that certain types of subject are more suitable than others in that they yield more consistent markings from different examiners.

In approaching their statistical material the authors give this disarming footnote: 'We have tried to keep our terms as simple as possible and we hope that those who know more about these matters than we do will not find that we have sacrificed too much

[1] To meet certain objections, such as the fact that there can hardly be much difference between the fifteenth and the sixteenth out of thirty-one, the gradings asked for were: the top one; the next two; the next two again; the next three; four; seven; four; three; two; two; and the bottom one – in accordance with the 'normal' distribution to be expected.

to simplicity.' The reader who knows less about these matters, and who has inevitably given less thought to the present investigation, is in no position to cast doubts on the technical conduct of it. One is obliged to accept the results of the correlations and the factor analyses largely on trust. This raises the incidental question of how much knowledge of statistical method is needed by the ordinary person (and so the ordinary school-leaver) nowadays, and I should like to turn aside from the main argument here to consider it for a paragraph or two. Certainly the older pupils at school cannot afford to be wholly ignorant of statistical method if they are to make sense of public opinion polls (which can be 'cooked' so as to give absurdly divergent results), advertisements ('Five times more lather' – than what?), political slogans ('Soak the rich'), and so on, to which they will be subjected – and are already being subjected. There is a good opening for collaboration between the mathematics teacher and almost every other subject-teacher, for the material arises nearly everywhere. Tentatively I would say that all grammar school pupils need to be introduced to the general idea of correlation (though not necessarily the method by which it is calculated); otherwise they are apt to see black and white in the wrong places – to believe, for instance, that 'the' cause of crime is poverty. Again, they need to know something of random sampling; of how much can safely be inferred from a given number of cases; of 'normal' distributions; of the simpler laws of probability as they bear upon the Pools, gambling, superstitions, heredity and other everyday matters; of the notion of logarithmic scales, perhaps; – but the actual list is matter for a staff-meeting rather than individual guess-work, whether specialist or non-specialist.

The present report on imaginative composition, however, is a reminder of the all-important fact about statistical technique, namely that it *is* a technique, a means, a piece of machinery. Correlation, by measuring something convincingly, can show that it exists, but it cannot in itself show *what* the thing is that exists. Intelligence tests, for instance, give results which are so self-consistent that they must be accepted, beyond reasonable doubt, as measuring something; but whether that something should be called intelligence, or cunning, or is a factor common to intelligence and cunning, is a matter beyond statistics. Again, certain statistical evidence[1] that seemed to point clearly to the working of telepathy, was later found to be open to quite a different interpretation, the working of precognition. The report now under discussion shows convincingly that examiners have certain consistencies, and that some types of subject-matter are more favourable to consistency than others. Something is being measured. But what?

The more one considers the question, the harder a satisfactory answer becomes. The investigation is concerned with the grading of imaginative compositions. We may picture the realities behind it. Thirty-one fourteen-year-old children, let us say, are told to write on a given subject. They have wide differences as well as similarities in their personal histories: some probably went through the blitz; some have parents who squabble; some are masturbating and all are prodigiously puzzled by sex and much else. Each of them has spent fourteen years finding his way through his own particular tangle of problems, not always very successfully. To grade him for anything at all would seem plain cruelty; to choose the power of imaginative composition as the criterion for the grading would seem doubly cruel. He is, for example, told to write a postcard to a ghost, or, after two readings from *Kubla Khan*, he is told to describe a landscape he might have seen in a dream. He may be intrigued, or entranced, or puzzled, or bewildered, or bored by the poem, or indeed practically unconscious of it. He may be much or little interested in dreams, much or little interested in landscapes. He may just be longing for the time to go home and do something sensible, instead of writing words because there will be trouble if he doesn't. Some of his classmates are industriously putting down the stuff which they know from experience pays good dividends. And some, the most vulnerable, are genuinely moved; to them the process of remembering or inventing, and condensing the experience into words, is as 'real' and intimate as their own dreams. Just where their writing will lead them neither they nor the teacher can know, for the essence of creativeness is that its course cannot be predicted. Thus the eventual scripts vary from the unforeseeable to the perfunctory or stupid. They can be graded, and there will be enough agreement amongst different gradings to show that there

[1] Set out by J. B. Rhine in *The Reach of the Mind* (Faber).

is some principle behind the markings. But is it conceivable that the fish consistently caught in the statistical net is anything so elusive and unpredictable as creative imagination? Is imagination susceptible to measurement at all, and if so, can the work of different writers be 'placed' on the same scale? If not, what possible meaning can there be in the marking of imaginative composition? Would compulsory writing on a prescribed subject at a prescribed time have any necessary connection with imagination, whether measurable or not? If pupils X, Y and Z are graded in that order, what useful inferences can we legitimately make? And, more important (for the results are not normally kept secret), what useful inferences can X, Y and Z themselves make?

These are fundamental, not statistical, questions, and the difficulty of answering them suggests that the whole attempt to grade creative work is misapplied. In so far as a piece of work is new and surprising, in so far as it is imaginative, it will incur wide disparity of assessment, and that is both healthy and inevitable. Lawrence's writing was banned and his pictures were seized precisely because what he had to say was so new, shocking and important. In a very general sense one can perhaps argue that Lawrence is less or more important than Mr Eliot, but the attempt to grade them is largely irrelevant. Lawrence's battle and victory were not Mr Eliot's, and what we owe to Mr Eliot is not what we owe to Lawrence – if it were, he would not be significant. In grading the imaginative composition of pupils we are repeating in miniature the same almost meaningless pursuit. Admittedly the pupils are seldom potential Lawrences or Eliots (though these writers too must have submitted their early imaginative compositions to be graded by their teachers);[1] and admittedly the necessities of the class-room impose a somewhat rough-and-ready kind of intercourse. But only the scale or level

[1] In *The Intelligent Heart*, 1955, Prof. Harry T. Moore writes: 'While Lawrence was writing this book [The White Peacock], which was to be accepted by the first publisher who saw it, he was also writing class exercises at college. And, like the geniuses of tradition, he was not always successful with classroom compositions. He was extremely annoyed with one of the women who taught English; she returned his essays heavily cross-marked with corrections in red. And one of the male teachers also angered him by censoring the use of the word *stallion* in one of his essays. "My boy, that's a word we don't use," he told Lawrence, the future author of *St Mawr*. . . .' [Note added 1961.]

is significantly changed. The present report tells how the examiners found themselves at variance on what to look for in the Dream compositions; some upgraded 'anything fantastic, unreal, or otherwise striking', where others seemed to prefer 'undreamlike realism', and in re-marking later some examiners tended to become 'less tolerant of the vagueness and illogicality of the dream'. The inference is made that to get consistent markings one must avoid material in which such problems arise. True enough. But such problems are the very stuff of literary criticism. To evade them is to evade exactly what matters. Moreover, in many cases the consistent markings will arise, not from genuine agreement, but from unconsidered common assumptions; just as in war-time the opinions of Englishmen about Germans were more consistent than in time of peace, but not more reliable. It is the consistency which is here the illusion, or the cause of illusion; and in selecting subject-matter in order to achieve consistency one is diverting the course of creative composition at best arbitrarily, and perhaps even perversely. True, the immediate concern is testing and not teaching, but the distinction is made perilous by the pedagogic craving for ordinals. Those who shape our tests shape, in large measure, the content of teaching and even some of its ideals.

Vocabulary, or at least the *recognition* of words, can be measured by the Inglis and other such tests; proficiency in most of the techniques can be tested, and usefully tested. Even here, however, the main purposes of the testing should be to inform the teacher, and to enable the pupil to measure himself *against his past self*. The fact that X did better than Y can, if one chooses, be made the means of harnessing shame, greed, fear and other extraneous motives to the job in hand, but all that can honestly be said to matter is whether X now has done better than X a term ago. Once we pass to imaginative composition there is (I suggest) even less place for competitive grading. Those classroom compositions that are devoid of imaginative content are outside the discussion; those that have imaginative value are largely incomparable.

The harm done by attempted comparisons is both general and particular. For the imaginative urge is precarious, even at times embarrassing, in a world of curricula, time-tables, bells and compulsory attendance, and grading could readily become a means of tidying it away altogether. It works at many levels – at the level of 'One misty, moisty morning', or of the schoolboy talent for nicknames, as truly as at higher levels; and the intrusion of marking or grading on whatever plane will always favour the substitution of the measurable and technical for the unmeasurable and essential. Further, each imaginative effort, however humble, is a venture of the writer's beyond quantity into the quality of living. Even a Postcard to a Ghost is a dangerous undertaking; it entails delicate commitments, with the cruel possibility of ridicule, and it is an experiment with tools that 'slip and slide' in the most able hands. These private 'raids on the inarticulate' need sympathetic response and criticism, but not assessment. The apparent success of one part, the failure of another, the advance beyond a previous effort, the way in which someone else met a common difficulty, shortcomings of grammar and structure – all these are among the things that can be discussed with profit. Fortunately they *are* still discussed in almost any English classroom, in spite of the size of classes and the search for an easy objectivity.

Not that teachers will or should cultivate what is *merely* personal or idiosyncratic in their judgments: they can only educate their pupils by educating themselves. But the differences that are the mark of living opinion must not be squeezed out in the quest for quick, statistically demonstrable objectivity. The personal reaction is the only possible starting-point – the reaction of the person who reads to the work of the person who created. For children this personal exchange can remain all-important. When a child describes, say, the 'blue misty feeling' of a cat that has just thrown away its ninth life, and allows you to read the description, he is taking you into his confidence. You are entitled to like it or dislike it; but to say that it is better or worse than somebody else's attempt is to be guilty, in the eyes of any healthy child, of an astonishing irrelevance.

Some comparisons and gradings of imaginative work, unfortunately, there will always be. Well-meaning Governors insist on bequeathing money for literary prizes, and there are external examinations to be taken. For purposes such as these, and the preparation for them, the findings of the present report and others like it will be useful; but, as far as it concerns normal imaginative work in English lessons, one must regard the process examined in the report with the same suspicion that a Quaker Meeting would show towards a supposed means of measuring the Inner Light. The supposition would be held to be harmful if false, and shattering if true.

# *An Exercise in Applied Criticism*

## A. P. ROSSITER

I take this labour in teaching others, that they should not be always to be taught; and I would bring my precepts into practice. For rules are ever of less force and value than experiments. Yet with this purpose: rather to shew the right way to those that come after, than to detect any that have slipped before, by error; and I hope it will be more profitable.

Ben Jonson, *Timber or Discoveries*

IN the last ten years, educational publishers have apparently found it worth while to list an increasing number of small books intended to train the examination-public in the art of reading. At the same time it has become a common practice to include in examination-papers a passage of verse, generally without title or author's name, which the candidate is asked to expound or to 'appreciate'.[1] The purpose of this study is to give an account of some results obtained from an exercise of this sort, worked by a considerable number of school children of School Certificate age and accomplishments. It should be noted preliminarily that there was no compulsion to try the exercise, or to attempt a detailed criticism: the question being set in the form given below:

AN IRISH AIRMAN FORESEES HIS DEATH

I know that I shall meet my fate
Somewhere among the clouds above;
Those that I fight I do not hate,
Those that I guard I do not love;
My country is Kiltartan Cross,
My countrymen, Kiltartan's poor,
No likely end could bring them loss
Or leave them happier than before.

[1] The mutations of educational taste which have made the terms 'paraphrase' and 'précis' slightly improper today, so that argument-tracing and thought-outlining replace them, are working against 'appreciation'; and with better reason. None the less, it is hard to avoid, so long as it is felt to be excessive to ask for 'criticism', 'a critical account', etc. The point may seem trivial, but it conceals a real difficulty of examination-technique. The rubric in the present question is only one of the commoner evasions.

Nor law, nor duty bade me fight,
Nor public men, nor cheering crowds,
A lonely impulse of delight
Drove to this tumult in the clouds;
I balanced all, brought all to mind,
The years to come seemed waste of breath,
A waste of breath the years behind
In balance with this life, this death.

*Give a plain prose account of what you understand by this piece of writing, and say, with your reason, why you think it good or bad.*

The line-numbers have been added for the convenience of the present reader, who is invited to lend himself to his own investigation by making up his mind, preferably before reading on, about *what the verse says* as it would appear in a paraphrase, and what sort of feelings it stirs, especially with regard to the airman, if he is 'seen' as a 'dramatic figure'. It may be important to watch the mind's reactions to lines 3-4 and 7-8, and to exercise a sympathetic candour with the work of those who had to commit themselves on paper without the help of this warning. It may add to the detective-interest of this study if the reader can determine forthwith which of the following crude epithets he would apply to the verse after a little consideration: Is the piece *great*, *good*, *passable*, *so-so*, *poor*, *weak*, or *bad*?

(Here it should perhaps be remarked that the comments given below were produced in a time of nominal peace.)

### REACTIONS

In examining the results, a possible first step is to give an impressionistic view of the variety of report, followed by some indication of the overt or latent critical standards applied.[1]

1A good . . . because in ordinary language, simple to understand and conveys what it is meant to.

1B not . . . good. Does not appeal to my car or eye, and certainly not to my sense of beauty. The theme is crude . . . The words are not

[1] Wherever possible, I have kept the words *good*, *not good*, etc., in my extracts, to show which side the writer came down on, and to serve as a gloss on vague ambiguous comment. Cuttings apart, everything is given *verbatim*, including misspellings and errors of punctuation. These, we may note, are *not* typical of the more incompetent readers, though haste *may* explain their frequency in intelligent comments.

beautiful, they are clumsy and some of the thoughts are not too well expressed.

1C a highly beautiful poem in its language. 'A lonely impulse of delight' is a line which is quite impossible to paraphrase and seems a good example of the poem's technique from beginning to end.

1D dull and pointless . . . no beauty.

It is not enough to side against either of these paired contestants: if one's business is teaching, it is necessary to ask how these views came into being. The next group supports the verdict that the lines are lacking in beauty and offers reasons:

2A cannot be compared with Tennyson's 'Lotus-Eaters' or Wordsworth's 'Ode' . . . nor Coleridge's 'Ancient Mariner'. They have all something wonderful in them, music, romance, or some sublime thought or dream. . . . No – this is not a good poem.

2B Good poetry should come from the heart and not from the brain, as does this poem. . . . Not imaginative or clever in any way, it is just bear.

The required critical standards of good poetry are fairly clear in these comments, though the second might have inquired whether 'bareness' was so strictly debarred. The same criteria are presumably behind the directer condemnation of 2C and the mental conflict of 2D and 2E:

2C bad. It does not convey anything that poetry should. The metre is not good, neither is the language used. . . .

2D a good piece. For although it is not actually a poem, it is written on that basis and as such is easier to understand. Unlike some poets the author has written . . . because he was urged to do it, not because he had to. It contains his own feelings and his own honest views.

It seems probable that some of the verdicts in Group 1 have behind them either a steady appreciation or a steady distaste for traditional romantic poetry. The following comment, which serves as a gloss on 2D, shows (with a tinge of comical irony) how the study of great literature may give the impression that a poet is a person who talks only in a remote tongue about things very obscure (which, if 2D is right, he probably does not mean):

2E good . . . because written on a modern subject. If compared with the language of *Paradise Lost* this is found to be understood much more easily, though P.L. might be fine.

Others, it would seem, thought the connection with 'real life' made the piece unpoetical. Elsewhere, it was thought to be risky for the poet's fame, even though his verses might be appreciated today:

2F the readers seem to be upon the clouds with him. . . . And that is where a poet or author wants his readers to be, with the hero, as we are with Macbeth. . . . But when reading Wordsworth's or Keats' poetry, we do not want to be taught history at the same time. He . . . had better write about things that will not date.

The reactions listed in Group 2 certainly explain why these lines should be regarded as something less than poetry. The troubles of 2D to 2F supply a useful comment on the Spens Committee's view that 'prescribed books do more to injure the growth of a budding sentiment for literature than to encourage it'.[1] The boy who thinks *Milton might be fine* deserves proper respect: as much for his open-mindedness about the unintelligible as for his frankness. But before considerations of value can be approached, it is necessary to deal with pre-critical difficulties, i.e. the results of the paraphrase, as they showed the reading-process at work. In Group 3 the sense, or statement-value of the words is considered, all the bracketed numbers giving a line-reference to the poem.

### SENSE

The first line occasionally caused trouble, sometimes even derailing the reader at once and controlling all the rest:

3A(1) fate will catch up with me and I shall be gone from this earth.

3B(1) good . . . complete belief in *fate* . . . the outlook of many aviators.

The whole passage from lines 3-8, and particularly 3-4 and 7-8, resulted in a far more important series of confusions, often

[1] *Secondary Education* (1938) p. 175.

as the outcome of not paying enough attention to the word *Irish* in the title. Failure to realize that 'those that I guard' are mainly *English*, and that the airman might conceivably regard them as a different people had some curious effects, for which 'lack of imagination' does not always seem the happy phrase.

3C(3) ... nor does he care for those who are his own people ... a good description of a poor Irish man who loves only to be a pilot, where he is alone with himself, and where death seems beautiful to him.

3D(3) He is indifferent to mankind. ... Brings out the man's utter misery and shows he sees life through a distorted lens, which brings all life's vices to the fore.

The absence of the conventional motives for a military life has led these readers to conclude that the airman's world must be empty; so he comes out as a 'stock-type' – the pessimist. Others met the difficulty with a familiar kind of chop-logic:

3E(3) If he delighted in fighting, I don't think he could love his enemies ... (he) just appears tired of everything.

The statement that he guards those he does not *love* has been twisted into something more familiar, till *not hate* turns into *love*. The reader has been shocked into rejecting the poem with the assistance of verbal jugglery. The motive is quite obscure (Group 6 may offer an explanation); but these blunders will enable us to appreciate the reading of those whose wits take them past these snags.

3F(3) an account by an Irish airman of his reasons for joining the army of a country not his own.

3G(3) If he fought it would not be because he hated the enemy, not because he loved English people, for his country is Kiltartan Cross. ...

This is the first real crux, the airman's character being often deduced (and condemned) from a single misreading. This leads on to questions of feeling; but first the puzzles of lines 7-8 must be explored. The troublesome word is 'end':

3A(7) No death which came by chance would bring them loss. (The 'fate' reading of 3A(1) continued.)

3B(7) His countrymen are poor. They would not loose him if he died.

3C(7) however he dies they will neither feel the loss or be the happier.

3D(7) his people would not lose anything by his death.

These frequent errors demonstrate that the right reading is not as self-evident as it may appear. All lead to misunderstandings of the feeling, the last three offering the youthful reader a side-track towards self-pity ('Nobody wants me!'); so that the airman is called hopeless, bored, weary of life, in love with death, or in utter misery. (See above, 3A-B-C(3).) His feeling of 'indifference' (the word applied to many mental attitudes) has been partly caught, but misrationalized. The reader 'gets the feeling', but only to distort it: substituting some familiar 'romantic' attitude (as of life-weariness, etc.). For those who attend to the words there is no difficulty:

3D(7)b My country is Kiltartan, and whether we win this war or not will not make any difference to my poor countrymen.

This middle passage does so much to determine the rest that there is no need to record misreadings of the latter part of the poem. A few sideslips show the main directions, right or wrong:

3A(11) it was just an impulse of my own which drove me to these battles in the sky.

3B(11) it was not law or duty, etc. . . . which brought me to fight: it was instinct.

3C(11) Perhaps the best lines are 'nor law . . . clouds'. Even these have their weak points, e.g. the reader does not know what is the 'tumult' in the clouds.

Allowing for the difficulty noted by 1C, the first may be called goodish: the word *lonely*, with its emotive bearing on both *impulse* and *delight*, does almost defy paraphrase. The emotional misjudgments caused by the middle passages are often considerable by the time the end is reached:

3A(14) the years to come did not seem worth living . . . compared to the dead (sc. death?) he was going to, which was a new life. (Cf. 3A(3) on death.)

3B(14) The lines about his ideas of death appeal to me very much because I so often feel the same when faced with the monotony of life even though I am only young yet. They are exquisite in their simplicity and deep sincerity.

It may be observed that the last sentence would sound a most appreciative comment if given by itself. Such general verdicts are common in all examination work; yet they may be meaningless, or mere blankets for soft nonsense such as this. The next group, where feeling is under examination, displays more of the failings of the sensitive.

### FEELING

First, the intelligent sentimentalist, caught in the act of beginning to drift away into a private poem:

4A This poem . . . almost cries with pain at being torn from its perfect form and deliberately drawn out into prose. The balance and tranquillity of the delight expressed . . . is ruined by paraphrasing it. It is simple to understand . . . and shows very well that poetry is far more than prose in a pattern. I love the slow movement of clouds and the serenity of the poem. I love its Irishness.

This is admittedly sensitive; but the cloud-movements have been imported and have spread rather too much peacefulness about them. The final (unhappily unexpanded) remark opens quite a new field of inquiry, where the feeling of the poem and the tone in which the reader is addressed are frequently misjudged and the results blamed on to the airman. The verbal blunders of Group 3 are behind many of these injustices to Ireland, though not the first:

4B (2A cont'd). This poem is inclined to be silly, at least this man's ideas of life are very peculiar, but he was Irish. No – this is not a good poem . . . (but) it would be rather clever for an Irishman to write a poem like this.

4C a good poem from the point of view of an Irishman, but a bad one from an Englishman's. I like the thought about the air.

The line-up within the mind of 4C shows some awareness of what is troubling those who bandy the words 'patriotic' and 'unpatriotic' about. This comment may perhaps make 4B less absurdly snubbing than it seems. The conflict between the 'Englishman's' poems is continued below, where most of the emotive forces can be seen at work:

4D seems . . . very unpatriotic when he says he is not guarding those he loves, although he may be guarding some other country and not his own.

4E extremely unpatriotic . . . no love of one's country.

4F The man was tired of life and had not the courage or strength to go on. . . . A man nearly always has something to live for and in this instance might have made it the service of his country. But perhaps he was embittered against England over the Home Rule business.

4G (3E(3) cont'd). . . . his country is Kiltartan Cross . . . his poor countrymen have never been allowed to be happy in the first place.

The impersonal pronoun in 4E has an irony which is only too clearly unintentional. The other sentences would supply good material for answering those who doubt the practical value of poetry and, in particular, its effectiveness in widening one's imaginative sympathies. 4D and 4F just wobble off the edge of understanding; and it is a perilously delicate exercise in discrimination to decide whether 4G does or does not go too far in the other direction (cf. 7A). Even some who fell for the crude question of (irrelevant) patriotism could still see the difficulties of a 'dramatic' interpretation:

4H There is no sense of patriotism in the poem, which does not suggest the motive of the writer. From this point of view the poem is bad . . . (but) good . . . from the point of view of a carefree person.

The airman can, however, be damned for failing to resemble some type-figure of manly virtue: much as Rymer damned Iago:

4I no ambition, no 'guts' to it. It lacks the bravery of an airman and gives a picture of a white-haired old man reading it to his grandchildren. This is because of the lack of speed. Apart from that it is good and extremely patriotic.

What the second means by 'patriotic' is past guessing; but this is unimportant in comparison with the repetition of the struggles of 4C in 4H, and his attempt to decide between a 'propagandist' and a 'dramatic' reading. (The first reading assumes that its effect as stimulant or depressant determines its value: the second that a well-drawn 'bad character' makes a good poem.) These problems are behind the wonderful variety of opinion on the airman's character listed in Group 5, where we are confronted with some of the by-products of the orthodox (Verity, etc.) method of studying Shakespeare – in which 'character points' are from the text and used as pegs for moral approbation or disapproval.[1]

Some of the more fantastic misjudgments depend on assuming that the virtue which the Stoics called ataraxia should be regarded as a vice, which makes the 'indifferent' man as promising for evil as the Elizabethan found the victim of melancholy.

5A explains the lengths to which a person will go who is bored and has no interest in life.

5B written, I should think, by someone inclined to be lazy – so much so that he could not bother to live. (From 1B.)

5C bad. The airman has no sense of duty nor love of his fellow-men and his life seems to be without any purpose whatever but just to die somewhere in the clouds.

There is here a grave misunderstanding of the use of the negatives in the middle lines of the poem. Instead of feeling the immense emphasis given to the 'lonely impulse' which drove him to combat, these readers have felt that all conceivable motives have been negated. Without imperatives or applause they can see nothing to act for; so the airman becomes a 'weak' or 'bad' character, conventionalized and condemned. This process of type-invention was sometimes illustrated by the use of some key word arbitrarily picked out and overworked:

[1] The Spens Report makes no comment on this potent source of moral judgments on human character.

5D The whole poem gives an idea of loneliness.

5E good . . . probably expresses the feelings of many lonely men in the world for whom the future holds nothing . . . (and) . . . so join up in the army . . . they have nothing to lose, and so . . . do not mind taking such a risk, and are not afraid to die.

Here, as in 4I, a conventional figure is being invoked: the self-sufficient airman is vulgarized to a novelette or talkie type, 'the man with nothing to live for'.

It is only a step from this to denunciation, and the usual demands for suppression in the name of morality.

5F he is rather indifferent to all emotions. . . . The actual writing is not bad, but the spirit it is written in is very wrong. Such things should not be written and ought to be destroyed if written.

5G The view expressed here, is surely that of a man who has a grievance against mankind and can find nothing to live for. This outlook is utterly unsuitable for any human being to have in his mind, and so it cannot be good for others to read.

It is vain to search the poem for what these budding censors have found, as for the 'utter misery' and weariness noted in Group 3. These *fears* (for what else are they?) are in the readers, and one of the practical uses of poetry is that by *good* (self-aware) reading they may be understood, and probably exorcised without the help of the psycho-therapist. He too puts in an appearance, in a comment which might serve as a text to teach teachers discretion:

5H The Irishman is complaining of the unfairness of life in modern times. . . . This man probably had an inferiority complex, for it often happens that men who feel small and insignificant believe that if they can climb higher than other men bodily, they will be spiritually better. This is the psychological point of view, and probably many would not believe it or think it possible.

Unfortunately, it is not enough to produce the incredibly true: relevance is required. The rock-climber can reply that this is a by-product of Shakespearean character-sketching, and feel no need to secure his self-respect by tying-on to the burly form of Sir Leslie Stephen. Yet it seems to offer a dismal warning of what is going to happen if traditional methods of Shakespeare-study are retained, while being expounded in terms of psychologies less 'literary' than those of the nineteenth century. On this point it must be frankly admitted that the teacher is in a jam. If the 'wise teacher' is to train his pupils '*to understand, if they can, the mind behind the written word, the man behind the book; and so, in the end, to understand their own emotions and reactions as well as experiencing them*',[1] then analysis of character – if it is essential – must be in terms of a psychology which does not contain too many too-unwarrantable assumptions. The issue is then clear cut: we must decide between accepting the crude-seemingness of much contemporary psychological language (generally called jargon) *in a literary setting*, and the alternative of a critical study of Elizabethan prepsychology. The need of help in 'understanding their own emotions and reactions' is plain enough in the comment of one intelligent and courageous young moralist:

5I It is difficult to know what is the opinion of a young man today on the subject of death in warfare, but this piece does certainly give one type of man's opinion. If I met the man . . . I probably wouldn't like him, but I cannot help feeling that he probably made . . . a better poet than an airman. After all he was fighting only for an impulse, not for his country or against someone he hated – which is rather pointless; . . . if we all did things solely on impulse of delight, regardless of the good or bad, well, life would be a sorry mess. Personally I think he ought to have thought why he had this impulse and act accordingly. . . Actually I rather like the poem and think it good because of the truth there is in the substance.

This is discerning, as well as being a good example of the 'well-drawn bad-character' reading. The dangers of isolating the dramatic figure must be left till later discussion (group 7). The controlling influence of lines 11-12 is made clearer by other successful readings:

5J good . . . a new idea . . . in simple language the spirit of independence and unruled thought.

5K good. . . . The writer expresses so absolutely his feelings. . . . The glorious feeling of recklessness is there, the utter futility of life

[1] *Spens Report*, p. 223.

on earth as lived by ordinary people in a humdrum existence, when he could be flying among the clouds. . . .

Surely this is the reaction we should expect from youth, and should accept as normal, if only the less happy of these readers could see that their inhibitions were beside the point. If 5I is 'unusually mature', what can we call the hag-ridden pseudo-patriots and suckling suppressors, hating even imaginary impulses of delight? Yet even a good 'placing' of the dramatic figure can be strangely cautious:

5L Perhaps the perfect soldier. Anyway the perfect fighter. Only a few who have been in a like position could possibly sympathize with such an outlook.

The opportunities given by the poem for extending the range of the mind's experience are pleasantly suggested by the following paired collisions of opinion, where readings of both feeling and tone cancel out completely:

5M well written . . . a wrong attitude to look upon life, and very dismal.

5N cheerful (unlike most war poems), unusual, refreshing if startling quality.

5O One cannot help feeling that the poet is failing in life – he is neither enjoying it or using it in a way beneficial to anyone. Too vague and undecided. . . .

5P good . . . sets out what it says in clear true language. There is no indecision about it. I think it is true of what many clever men must feel. They do not wish to serve their country . . . they cannot feel they are doing their duty. . . . They are not idealists or religious men, and live in the present, having thought out and analised their feelings.

The last, though it isolates the 'character' makes his life too much of a *pis aller*. The next gives the right turn towards positive feelings:

5Q good . . . because it expresses plainly and simply a plain and simple emotion, without hypocricy. The airman did not try to gain honour and glory by saying he was fighting for an ideal, or duty, or to help his country, but just gives the reason, which was love of flying . . . nothing mattered except the glorious sensation of flying high up in the sky, alone and away from everything.

The importance of lines 11-12 in this balancing-process is obvious here, as in the following incidental comments:

5R (quotes lines 9-10 and 11-12, notes the contrast, and adds:) These 4 lines show the difference between this man and other men.

5S . . . while you read it you have the feeling of his great love for the air and the clouds.

Such representative comments show how very little readjustment of the mind would enable all those between 2A and 2E to appreciate the feeling of the poem; and perhaps to find it not so incompatible with their romantic demands. Occasionally, however, these were of a sort for which the distinguished authors mentioned in Group 2 cannot be held responsible:

5T (2B cont'd). It does not show you the humours of his feeling or the delights of death in the air. He does not make you feel as if you could see that aeroplane flying through the clouds and suddenly coming to grief, and of it falling, falling, falling . . . and of the catastrophe of it all.

The type of reading preferred by this writer is obvious; but it is worth suggesting that the critical *process* (that of damning the piece for not being what it isn't) is no more crude than that employed by 2A and others who use a big name as a Big Stick.

The last considerable misreading of the piece depends on weighting the (wrong) impression given by the incrementum of negatives from outside, this time with special feelings about war. The sixth group may be said to branch away from the place where 5P is just *off* the right track, and 5Q safely *on*:

6A The part where he says that if he fought it would not be because of hate seems to be characteristic of many men today.

6B The lines 'those . . . love' perhaps mean more today than ever before, they seem to sum up three-quarters of the tragedy of all war.

6C . . . shows well the futilities of war by saying that people do not care whether we win or lose, and yet . . . have got to risk their lives.

Good sentiments, and well expressed; but as little to do with the 'lonely impulse of delight' as the jabber about patriotism, to which they supply a sort of converse. The 'all-atoning name' which Dryden attributed to the Patriot has been assumed by the Pacifist, and the poet is again ordered to march in step. A few rejected the poem outright because of such associations:

6D I do not like the thought . . . as it always encircles the thought of invasions and war.

Sometimes the process of wandering away to the whistle of accepted ('advanced') ideas can be watched in growth:

6E good, because it stirs up the reader's imagination as to what may go on in a good many airmen. (It) shows that not every airman fights for his country . . . but simply for his own love of enjoyment, and desire to be above the rest of the people. It tells us that many airmen may choose to risk their lives for their own reasons, not just because they are forced to or wish for honour. This is good in these days of national service when we imagine that everybody is stirred to defend their country by force or law.

This interesting muddle would repay analysis. The 'impulse of delight' has been felt, but emerges snubbed: the writer feels that it is 'wrong' (cf. 5I). At one point the oddities of 5H (the psychoanalyst) seem to be touched; the tone is throughout the effect of the conflict between the implications of 'stirred' and 'by force or law'. The comment should say a lot to the historian, striving to realize the uncertainties of the democratic mind as a particular period, but has little to do with the poem. The Irish airman is surely the last person to say 'We don't want to fight, but we're devils when we're stirred.' We may guess that 6E has caught a glimpse of a magnificent devil and been scared.

### JUDGMENTS

This analysis has shown all the more common ways of misreading the poem, and demonstrated the generation of mistaken verdicts from wrong comparisons, verbal misapprehensions and imported ideas. Before turning to the most successful pieces of writing which the exercise produced, it is worth while to consider the main traps and sidetracks which these readers have contrived to avoid. In this the main analysable components of the mind's experience in reading must be kept closer together than in the preliminary groupings.

Though there is no difficulty with the words, the tone of the first two lines is so dependent on the last four that it will be a lucky hit if we find it before the second reading.

> I know that I shall meet my fate
> Somewhere among the clouds above;

*might* be the index to a great variety of different attitudes, from defiance to passive fortitude, or even self-pity. The last, it may be remarked, need not necessarily be condemned in a 'dramatic' figure which might be a convenient symbol for suggesting the general feeling which we get in Synge's lines: 'And isn't it a pitiful thing there is nothing left of a man who was a great rower and fisher but a bit of an old shirt and a plain stocking?' We can agree that this anticipation of the end, though it is most unlikely to do any particular airman much good, is something which a poet may profitably convey. The firm equanimity of thought and verse-movement in the closing lines, however, makes such a reading impossible. The force with which the repeated *all* leaps from its line, the stress on the word *life*, and the emotional balance of the lines between make it clear that this man has no overpowering sense of regret.

> I balanced *all*, brought *all* to mind,
> The years to come seemed waste of breath,
> A waste of breath the years behind
> In balance with this *life*, this death.

Still less is *this life* to be felt as a sort of death-in-life. The essential lift of the voice on the stressed *all's* descends with a sardonic fall at each *waste of breath*: though death is the price of it, the man who wants abundant *life* has got it, and does not wince or repine at the bargain. The unity of the poem is as evident in these organic connections as in the implied contrast between the self-determined feeling of the end and the negation of other, more popular, appeals in lines 3 to 10. The airman dismisses hatred, public service, subservience to law, the applause of crowds with the contempt of a man accustomed to think for himself and feel for himself *privately*, irrespective of what *public* voices may say.

Though we may stop at the dramatic figure, and be content with 'the perfect fighter' of 5L, such a reading is incomplete: the airman is also a poetic symbol representing the difference between the personal, unmistakable, deeper emotions and the shallower sentiments of the crowd.

Once this is seen, it is clear how wide of the mark are all those verdicts in which 'patriotism' plays a controlling part. In the lines:

Those that I fight I do not hate,
Those that I guard I do not love;

it has to be emotively grasped that *love* is a very strong term (a reaction which the traditional course of poetry may, perhaps, tend to make more difficult). Without this discrimination, the rhythm of the following lines will probably go astray: the two *my's* will not receive their defiant emphasis, and the strictures on sing-song rhythm will seem natural. But when the airman says:

My country is Kiltartan Cross,
My countrymen, Kiltartan's poor,

he is expressing a patriotism (the word means 'love of one's native country', we may remind ourselves) which is genuine, personal, and deep: it justifies the word *love*, and puts him beyond reproach in saying that he has no such feeling for those he guards. Even if we feel very strongly that Ireland is part of the British Empire and that the airman ought to have some feeling for 'one's country' (4E), the distinction between a personal love and a generally expected attitude of loyalty is real. How much more we may read into these lines depends entirely on how we take an Irishman's statement to the effect that 'I do not love the English'. If it has been overlooked (or unparticularly felt) that the man is Irish, he naturally seems 'very peculiar' (4B) or to have 'no sense of patriotism' (4H). The other extreme will as naturally be reached by those who take 'I do not love' as a considerable meiosis, and accordingly make the very most of lines 7 and 8:

No likely end could bring them loss
Or leave them happier than before.

Dreadful as it would seem, there may be those to whom victory and defeat are remote newspaper terms, in comparison with the loves and hates of Kiltartan Cross; and to whom the term *poor* does not exclude some measure of personal happiness. The airman is recognizing this state of affairs, with the same lucid clarity of vision that he brings to bear on himself. Rejecting a false patriotism, he insists the more firmly on the true: the shallow 'thought-up' sentiment ('feeling as it is expected of you') is made to contrast with the personal sentiment which has the depth given by being based on fact, not fiction. He loves his village; he loves the excitement of aerial combat; but the two feelings have no direct connection with one another. The gap between them is the place where we run all the interpretative risks; where, even if we avoid the temptations to bring in irrelevant feelings about 'patriotism' or 'pacifism' (as in 6A to 6E), there is still the difficult matter of arriving at a right estimate of his 'Irishness', and the right degree of response to his sharp demarcation of the contrasted spheres of interest. By stressing the word *poor*, after giving the strongest sense to *I do not love*, it is easy to arrive at a reading of lines 7-8 which *will* make the airman the type and symbol of his distressful country, as in 4F and 4G. Such an interpretation may be justified by a consideration of the writer's work as a whole; but on the evidence of these verses only, the following makes too much of what is at most a part of the poem:

7A characterizes the airman with a full unguarded beauty. What so many people would condemn as lack of the finer qualities of mankind is here presented in a warm, kind, pitiful glow that pricks the world's conscience for this hopeless isolated man and country. The beauty is the beauty of resignation and not despair, sadness and not hate, dispassionate reasoning and not flaming passion. It shows pain that has caused a philosophy and grief that has overthrown care. I like it.

We can assume that 'the finer qualities of mankind' refers to 'duty' (or general fraternal love, perhaps?) than to responding to the demands of law, public men or cheers. But it is still clear that 'resignations' is too passive a word, too little has been made of the virile hardness of the airman's 'delight', and too much of Kiltartan's poor: the general effect of the poem has been softened in a mist of Irishry – too much of the orthodox (English) feeling about Irish 'sentiment'. But to go firmly beyond this we need to know that the same poet wrote the following lines:

No longer in Lethean foliage caught
Begin the preparation for your death
And from the fortieth winter by that thought
Test every work of intellect and faith,
And everything that your own hands have wrought,
And call those works extravagance of breath
That are not suited for such men as come
Proud open-eyed and laughing to the tomb.

The tough-minded quality in the crowning line represents something which 7A has missed entirely. The quotation is given only to show how the airman's attitude matters to this poet, quite apart from wars and national loyalties. It enables the analyst or examiner to see the weakness of the impressively controlled writing 7A, as well as the shortcomings here:

7B by Yeats . . . an expression of hopelessness . . . (but) . . . something not entirely negative in the thought. If there is precision in the thinking, there is also a perfect structure. . . . Its form and structure I find one of its chief delights.

The first sentence can only be given the benefit of the doubt, such generalities being (by now) suspect. But it is exactly the 'precision in the thinking', the perfect cool control of the mind's experience through the steady and balanced words which makes the piece so remarkable – and which accounts, perhaps, for the various evasions and rejections of those to whom the metaphysicals and Swift are names, and not recollections of impassioned thought. It is this 'precision', mistaken for coldness or 'indifference', which prompts the derogative comparisons with the great romantics noted in Groups 1 and 2. Only by keeping all these considerations in mind can full tribute be paid to the final exhibit: a piece of writing which assuredly deserves the name of criticism:

7C by the late W. B. Yeats . . . in my opinion a 'good' piece of writing. At first . . . gives a sense of unemotionalism, as if the writer had no feeling left for anything. This, however, is immediately outweighed by the tremendous urgency behind the words,

A lonely impulse of delight
Drove to this tumult in the clouds.

'Tumult' – that is not unfeeling. On the contrary, it is charged with it, and it is the key to the whole piece. Life and death had become one in the airman's mind. He has little thought for them; but (?by) his almost sulky

> My country is Kiltartan Cross,
> My countrymen Kiltartan's poor

– so there, you fool of an Englishman! he hurls feelings of the deepest substance full in the face of the 'others' who have 'joined up' for the reasons which he scorns. The poem is more than 'good'. It is of the class which is called great, for the sheer simplicity of its construction.

A practised critic might feel something approximating to humility on being sent in to bat after this. A note might be added on the energy of the word *drove*, though 'tremendous urgency' probably implies it. The absence of any references to war – as distinct from motives for joining up – and the deft handling of the 'Irish problem' mark, in the light of other reactions, a triumphantly good reading. But when the question of the poem's 'greatness' comes up (one, we may remember, which T. S. Eliot holds to be quite probably beyond the reach of undergraduates), we may offer other grounds than simplicity of construction, without diminishing the excellence of this comment. (We must reflect, too, that the last phrase *may* refer to the ordinance of the thought and feeling, the precision and directness mentioned by 7B.) Now that the poem has been formally attributed to its author (a fact suppressed in 4A since the writer derived nothing useful from knowing it) we can go further, and say that this is not a 'war poem' at all, unless the reader feels a strong urge to regard it as one. Should evidence for this view be required, the volume called *The Wild Swans at Coole* (1919) may be searched for Yeats' reactions to the last world-conflict; when, among better things, this will be found[1]:

ON BEING ASKED FOR A WAR POEM

> I think it better that in times like these
> A poet's mouth be silent, for in truth
> We have no gift to set a statesman right;

[1] *Collected Poems*, p. 175.

He has had enough of meddling who can please
A young girl in the indolence of her youth,
Or an old man upon a winter's night.

The 'Irish Airman' is in this same volume; and we may search the next (1941) and more besides, without finding Yeats go back on his word.[1] The peculiar position of an Irish fighter in 1914-18 has provided him with 'an image': a symbol representative of the poet's sharp discrimination between feelings that may be called 'sincere' and those, we must, by contrast, call 'factitious'. The 'lonely impulse' is, as it were, a *sample* of genuine experience, attributed to a figure (perhaps idealized, perhaps imaginary) which need not be pursued beyond the gesture of acceptance. The man *may* be socially undesirable (as 5I suggests): the experience of the alarming sincerity he conveys is not. And this sincerity of the active man is unlikely to be vocal.

[1] Cf. *Politics in Last Poems and Plays*, p. 82.

# VIII

# *FUNDAMENTALS AND RETROSPECT*

THE journal *The Use of English* has always been concerned to answer the question: what is English teaching *for*? Though its space has been largely given over to classroom reports, direct tips and suggestions for teachers, and to genuine reviewing, all this has rested on a common sense of aims. From time to time there have been attempts to restate the purpose and place of English studies, as teachers have felt ever more keenly the importance and present vulnerability of this particular lifeline of continuing civilization.

# *The Place of English Literature in a Liberal Education*[1]

L. C. KNIGHTS

We are here not to consider specifically literary questions or the nature of literary activity and enjoyment, but to try to clear up our minds about the part played by the discipline of 'English' in the wider processes of education. In what ways does it contribute to the development of that maturity of judgment, that capacity for seeing things in a truly human way, which we have in mind when we try to say what we mean by 'a liberal education'? Our question is not What is poetry? or What is literary criticism? but What is the *use* of literary study? – though naturally we cannot attempt an answer to that question without having in mind a working conception of poetry and literature and of profitable ways of tackling literature.

What I have to say will fall under three heads and a postscript. First I want to say something about English as basic training in the use of the mother tongue – the humblest but most essential level. This is not the concern of the English teacher alone, though naturally he will feel a special responsibility. Then I shall dwell on and try to justify the great claim for English literature as an instrument of education, namely that it offers an education of the imagination: this *is* the English teacher's special concern. And thirdly I want to deal with the relation of English to other studies within a humane general education; and here again the English teacher joins hands with his colleagues. Clearly the second of these is central, and I shall spend most of my time on it; but I want to suggest how it is related to and depends on the first, the basic training, just as the 'use' of literature for the purpose of social or political or historical

[1] A talk given to English teachers at a one-day conference arranged by the Manchester University Institute of Education in October 1956, and at a similar Conference arranged by the Bristol University Institute of Education in March 1957.

understanding depends in its turn on imaginative grasp. Having dealt with these matters in this order, I shall return to the second and central one and try to suggest something of its relation to quite fundamental concerns.

## I

The question of basic training in the use of the English language may seem at first sight to lie rather outside the scope of a paper on the place of English *literature* in a liberal education. It is there, however, that I want to start, partly because the question is in itself of such importance, and partly because it is in this way that we can best begin to establish a connection between literary studies and the life of the individual in its whole range of interests.

Learning to say what we mean and to understand what we read go together. There does seem reason to believe that in our vast 'literate' population basic skills in expression and in understanding are left at a dangerously rudimentary stage. How many of those who have had a secondary education can write simply and effectively, can say a plain thing in a plain way? I cannot give a precise answer to that large question, but I am told that at Cambridge there is concern about the inability of research scientists to write up the results of their research. And I know that in an Honours School of English (with students selected largely on good marks in two Advanced Subjects in G.C.E.) we have great difficulty in getting common orderliness, exactness and clarity in so-called literary essays. And sometimes we find failure not only to achieve these qualities but even to see that they are important. Reading student essays I sometimes feel like Fluellen in conversation with Pistol: 'Aunchient Pistol, I do not partly understand your meaning.' To which, you may remember, Pistol replies, 'Why then, rejoice therefore.' It is very much a hit-or-miss affair. The attitude of the writer tends to be, 'Well, you see what I mean, don't you?' – and it is impossible not to connect this attitude with the widespread indifference to the absence of clarity and forthrightness in the commoner forms of reading matter. The first job of the English teacher, indeed of all teachers, is to counter haziness of expression,[1] to foster a lively respect for the living language.

I take it we are all agreed about this, and there is no need to urge it further here. What I want to insist is that in this elementary matter of respect for clarity and exactness – for the life of speech – not only are we dealing with the foundation of literary taste, and our ability to read Shakespeare depends on it, we are taking the necessary first step in any argument designed to bring out the place of English literature in a liberal education. Let me dwell on this point for a moment.

I suppose if any of us were asked today to write a 'defence' of poetry, we should feel unable to use the rather exalted terms with which Shelley ended his *Defence of Poetry* (in which, by the way, he says some very good things about the significance of imaginative literature):

> Poets are the hierophants of an unapprehended inspiration; the mirrors of the gigantic shadows which futurity casts upon the present. . . . Poets are the unacknowledged legislators of the world.

Which is certainly not meaningless and may be true, but it is not precisely the ground on which we should meet an enquiring scientist or sociologist who came to us wanting to know what end our study of literature served. For that purpose we should do better to start with some words written by Ezra Pound a quarter of a century ago. Answering his own question, 'Has literature a function in the state?' he says:

> It has to do with the clarity and vigour of 'any and every' thought and opinion. It has to do with maintaining the very cleanliness of the tools, the health of the very matter of thought itself. . . . [Words are indispensable agents of communication] and the solidity and validity of these words is in the care of the damned and despised *literati*. When their work goes rotten . . . i.e. becomes slushy and inexact, or excessive or bloated, the whole machinery of social and individual thought and order goes to pot. (*How to Read*.)

[1] By 'haziness of expression' Professor Knights means only the inability to express simple ideas in simple prose, and *not* those ambitious moments, to be recognized and welcomed, when the student's spurt of growth carries with it sudden disorders of expression. Consider the ten-year-old boy's 'Free Writing' on page 16 or, at a different level, A. P. Rossiter's comment on the erratic spelling of perceptive children on page 193. – B. J.

Put beside this a phrase used by H. G. Wells to characterize the twentieth century – 'A vast and increasing inattention', and I think we have found our starting-point. The very condition of mental life is *attention* – a steady holding of the interest, a focusing of the mind. There is no need for me to talk in general terms about the indispensable part played by words in making observation possible, even in the physical and material realm: you *see* much more of the forest when you know the names of the trees. And when we come to imponderables and intangibles – moral qualities, human relationships and the like – our capacity for understanding is largely if not entirely dependent on our command of language. The decay of a language means the decay of a civilization. That is why, in Keats' phrase, 'English ought to be kept up'.

## 2

Now attention, of course, is not only the condition of all mental life, it is in a very special sense the foundation of literary criticism. 'What! would you teach boys and girls at school, as well as the branded ware called Honours English students, "literary criticism"?' Yes, indeed – though in such a way (I trust) as not to rob them of spontaneity and unselfconscious enjoyment. For literary criticism is simply the habit of disciplined attention. If we ponder the meaning of this remark we may learn something about that education of the imagination which gives English literature its unique place in a liberal education. And at the same time we shall, I think, find that we can relate imaginative activity to the simpler skills and perceptions whose importance I began by emphasizing.

Now here I find myself at a loss, for what we need is to go together through a nicely graded course of 'practical criticism'. Instead, I must compress, and take a good deal for granted. I can put the matter like this: suppose you have been asked to take a class in literature with 'non-literary' people – engineers for example; how would you set about arousing their interest and convincing them that literature has very much to offer them besides entertainment or 'escape'? One way is to spring on them a significant but difficult poem – a real poem: one of T. S. Eliot's for example – and let it make its own disturbing impact; after which you can answer questions. Another way (not incompatible with this) is to start at the bottom and work up. You can show that, at a very elementary level, when deciding whether any bit of non-imaginative writing is good or bad, all that is necessary is to attend to the simple sense of the words and to weigh them in the scale of common sense: are they clear and straightforward or are they vague, muddled and contradictory? and so on. The need for simple attention once established, you go on to show that literature demands a more complex kind of attention than that given, say, to a news report, a cookery book, or a company prospectus: that you have to listen more intently to overtones and implications and make wider and sometimes more complicated connections; that you need to become sensitive to rhythm and imagery and see how they can contribute to depth and fullness of meaning. All this, and the examples with which it is supported, will be designed to show that literature demands from the reader a collaborative activity, which has the effect of *realising* – making real – whatever is being talked about, in a way quite impossible in non-imaginative discourse. It is the nature of imaginative realisation that I want to dwell on, but first let me invoke a particular example of what it is I am talking about.

In the great pastoral scene in *The Winter's Tale* Florizel praises Perdita:

What you do
Still betters what is done. When you speak, sweet,
I'ld have you do it ever; when you sing,
I'ld have you buy and sell so, so give alms,
Pray so; and, for the ordering your affairs,
To sing them too: when you do dance, I wish you
A wave o' the sea, that you might ever do
Nothing but that; move still, still so,
And own no other function: each your doing,
So singular in each particular,
Crowns what you are doing in the present deeds,
That all your acts are queens.

About such poetry it is difficult to speak, but I think we do it no wrong if we say that what it most conveys is a grace of action felt as effortless, of movement that has the quality of stillness. Without any hint of monotony the lines circle from and return to a few simple words – the five times repeated 'so' – with its insistence on the uniqueness of each action: thus and not otherwise – the four 'do's', reinforced by 'done', 'doing' (twice) and 'deeds'. The simplicity and familiarity of these words is important. 'Do', whether as infinitive or present tense, conveys presentness – for 'What you do Still betters what is done' – and it is the barest possible expression of action, not unlike the phrase Wordsworth was fond of, 'goings on'. When the doing is given specificness it is still in terms of everyday action – to speak, to sing, to buy and sell, to give alms, to pray, to order your affairs, to dance. It is with the clause introduced by 'dance' that we are made aware of how much these everyday activities really imply, of the depths they draw on:

> when you do dance, I wish you
> A wave o' the sea, that you might ever do
> Nothing but that; move still, still so,
> And own no other function.

It isn't merely that the subtle rhythm beautifully suggests the sea, the ripple and wash of it, the pause and fall of the waves: our sense of the sea blends with our sense of the human dancer – the moving moment that seems timeless ('move still, still so'), the personal grace that has behind it a force as deep and impersonal as the sea.

Now literature of course has virtually infinite resources through which the responsive reader is prompted to imaginative realization. I have quoted this one example partly because when we use phrases like 'imaginative realization' it is as well to have in mind at least one instance of what we mean; partly because it has allowed me to suggest how entirely the power of the words depends on the collaborative activity of the reader. As I. A. Richards says, in discussing the effect of a good poem that he has analysed, 'there is a prodigious activity between the words as we read them':

> Following, exploring, realizing, *becoming* that activity is . . . the essential thing in reading the poem. Understanding is not a preparation for reading the poem. It is itself the poem. And it is a constructive, hazardous, free creative process, a process of conception through which a new being is growing in the mind.

I hope that this has at least suggested a meaning for 'imaginative activity' which distinguishes it sharply from day-dreaming or any kind of escape from reality. I know that imagination is sometimes referred to as though it were something quite different from – or even opposed to – those mental processes by which we reach out for truth and try to ground ourselves on things as they are. That is not so. Imagination in the writer is that responsive, creative activity by which he realizes – makes real – a particular bit of experience, and embodies in words his sense of it in its directness and fullness – its implications, and its significance and value to him as a living human being. The activity to which his words prompt the reader is similarly an imaginative activity – responsive, creative and realizing. That realizing activity may demand now the use of the discursive reason, now the play of feeling and sympathy, now the awareness of the senses, but it is more than the sum of thinking plus feeling plus sensing. As Coleridge noted long ago, it is an activity of the whole soul of man.

There is a further claim I want to make – that the imaginative realization to which we are prompted by the poets is a genuine form of knowing. There is a widespread notion – fostered, I believe, by a contemporary trend in linguistic theory – that all language which is not strictly referential is 'merely emotive'. Either you use words as pointers to scientifically verifiable events, or you use them simply to express your emotions and emotional attitudes and to evoke corresponding emotions in others. The American critic, Philip Wheelwright, in a recent book called *The Burning Fountain: a Study in the Language of Symbolism* (Indiana University Press) deals effectively with this linguistic positivism. The problem of poetry, he remarks, does not stand alone:

> For the issue . . . amounts to this: whether there is such a thing as *poetic vision*, or whether the only true vision of things must be ultimately scientific. If you accept the latter alternative – the position of semantic positivism – then the consequences, provided you carry them out vigorously, will be utterly destructive for religion, for metaphysics, and even for ethics as independent disciplines; and that is to say, for the very mainsprings of significant human living (pp. 38-39).

You are, of course, at liberty to take this positivist standpoint, and to leave for poetry, as for religion, only an emotional or affective function; but to do so, Wheelwright remarks, is not strictly scientific, for it quite arbitrarily rules out the alternative possibility, which is that poetry, like religious insights, conveys genuine knowledge. There are two lines of argument here. The first involves an appeal to experience:

A poem affects a mature reader as it does partly because it seems to him, notwithstanding its fantasies and pseudo-statements, to be offering a kind of genuine insight and thereby revealing, however obscurely and elusively, a kind of truth. . . . [*King Lear*] is great because in and through such poetic devices it reveals depth-meaning – it adumbrates truths . . . of high importance about such matters as human nature, old age, false seeming, and self-confrontation through suffering. . . . If the depth-meaning is not at least dimly and subconsciously adumbrated – and perhaps too sharp a focus of it is generally undesirable – the reader's response will hardly be the same. Impoverishment or distortion of the intellectual response will involve some impoverishment or distortion of the emotive. To regard the specifically poetic response as purely emotive, then, is a naive way of psychologizing (pp. 45-46).

The second, related, argument concerns the nature of language. Roughly speaking, the positivist assumption, already glanced at, is that there are two main types of language, the referential and the emotive. Now it is true that one mode of discourse is entirely referential – literal, logical and free from all emotion – and that another mode is purely emotive, with no descriptive function. But, says Wheelwright, what is ignored by those who deny 'truth' to poetry, leaving it only an affective function, is that 'referential' and 'emotive' are not necessarily contraries: there may be, indeed there is, language which is both; and that is expressive or poetic language. 'My thesis,' he says, 'is that truly expressive symbolism – in a poem, for example – means, refers, awakens insight, *in and through* the emotions which it engenders, and that so far as the emotion is not aroused the full insight is correspondingly not awakened' (p. 48).

Shakespeare's Gloucester in *King Lear*, we may recall, speaks of the man 'who will not see because he doth not feel'. The insight or vision that we obtain from poetry, from imaginative literature, is inseparable not only from feeling but from that fullness of realization which I have spoken of as the distinguishing mark of imaginative activity. It is knowledge in this sense – knowledge in depth and fullness, knowledge that involves us as persons and not just as observers – that is made possible by the imaginative, or generative, use of language. And that, in turn, is why an education that fails to cultivate at least some responsiveness to poetic or imaginative language cannot be described as truly liberal or humane education.

## 3[1]

What now of the complementary and related aspect of a literary education – its broadly humanizing power? To frequent great imaginative works – to frequent them, that is, with any inwardness – is itself an education. But to bring the mind to bear on a literature of any scope and variety is to find oneself inevitably drawn on beyond 'literature'; and it is the way in which the literary student is drawn on – to the realm of history, politics, or morals – that constitutes a further excellence of literature as a medium of education. It is difficult to speak here without being misunderstood. To say that an education in letters is an education in so much else besides does *not* mean that other, more specialized, disciplines can be dispensed with. It simply takes for granted the following propositions:

(*a*) That many of the books properly studied in a literary course were not intended as 'literature' in the way in which a modern novelist, for example, is likely to think of his work: they are works of instruction distinguished by exceptional powers of mind, and any serious study of them is the study of how particular imaginative insights illuminate a particular subject matter, whether this is a question of conduct, the working of individual minds, or the behaviour of men in society.

[1] This section is an abbreviation of a part of my article, 'The Claims of English', in *Universities Quarterly*, May 1955. It is reprinted here by kind permission of the Editor of that journal.

(*b*) That many deliberate works of art spring from and embody a concern with contemporary problems, particularly political and social problems, which thus necessarily come within the view of the literary student.

(*c*) That at the more advanced levels individual works are not studied in isolation but in relation to each other within a tradition (this is very different from a study of 'influences'), and in relation to the particular culture of which they form a part. So literary study, at some stage, necessarily raises the question of what we mean by a healthy culture and a living tradition, and of the relation of these to the more obvious day-to-day workings of society.

If considerations such as these are allowed to shape a course in literature there should be no fear of the student despising the other disciplines. (There is, I think, no need to make a sharp distinction between university and sixth-form teaching; if much can only be done at the university there is no reason why a similar approach to more limited material should not be followed in the schools.) Aware of his own ignorance, he will know when he wants the help of the specialist and will have some idea where to run for it. He will not think that he has a ready-made answer to the problems of human existence: indeed, he is likely to distrust the panaceas of the terrible simplifiers. He will, on the other hand, possess certain standards of relevance and cogency. And he will have encountered some central concerns of the adult mind. Thus equipped he will be the less likely to fall a victim to that spirit of abstraction which would reduce complex matters to 'nothing but' a problem in social engineering, or whatever it may be.

There is no need to do more than indicate the bearing of the propositions I have listed on the study of English literature. Many of our great writers were moralists and social critics, and whether they transmute their 'message' into great poetry and imaginative literature (as Langland does in *Piers Plowman*, or Bunyan in *The Pilgrim's Progress*) or preach in simpler ways (as Ruskin does in *Unto this Last*, or Morris in his *Lectures to Working Men*) the value of the 'content' – of the social analysis, of the writer's attitude to his material, of the incitement that he offers to fuller and more genuinely responsive living – is necessarily at the centre of attention; and it must almost necessarily be drawn into relation with the needs of the present. Not that the good teacher will be over-much intent on pointing a twentieth-century moral; some things can simply be left to sink in, to form part of the student's permanent equipment for assessing his world. But certain works falling well within a normal English course illuminate a scene so like our own that to engage with them in any serious sense must mean to apply them to our world. *Culture and Anarchy* – lively and not too difficult for an upper form at school – illustrates by specific examples (today's parallels being ready to hand) what is meant by the play of disinterested intelligence on the contemporary scene. Whilst for the undergraduate *The Statesman's Manual* of Coleridge (read first perhaps because of an interest in Coleridge's criticism) may well be an introduction to the deeply human – indeed the spiritual – roots and implications of 'questions' (political and other) that are distorted and denatured when considered, as they commonly are, out of relation to their deeper significance. (For an example of the special timeliness for us, now, of Coleridge's thought, see the diagnosis of the causes of the French Revolution, *Political Tracts of Wordsworth, Coleridge, Shelley,* edited with an Introduction by R. J. White, pp. 27-8. But it is difficult to imagine a period when Coleridge's thinking about politics will not be timely.) It must also be remembered that political and 'social' interests, however transmuted, enter deeply into the work of some of our major writers (Milton, Dryden, Swift, Blake, Wordsworth . . .). Our first business as students of literature is not with past problems but with what is permanently *made* out of the transitory; yet the writer's contemporary attitudes (Marvell's to Cromwell, Dryden's to Shaftesbury, Wordsworth's to the French Revolution, and Blake's to the new industrial England) are likely to have a direct relevance to *our* contemporary scene. This is a secondary but, it seems to me, inevitable result of the act of literary appreciation: it would be an oddly limited approach to *Absalom and Achitophel* that did not raise the question of the conservative temperament in politics; you can't 'appreciate' *An Horatian Ode upon Cromwell's Return from Ireland* and retain crude notions about the rights and wrongs of a civil war. (For a suggestive contrast see Santayana's essay on 'Shelley: or the Poetic Value of Revolutionary Principles' in *Winds of Doctrine.*) Anything done on the lines suggested here would of course be subordinate, even though closely related, to the central literary education that I tried to define earlier in this paper. But it is precisely because the discipline of English is essentially a training to respond to values as realized and embodied that it can so focus, in terms of the concrete and particular, those wider questions concerning the quality of human living. Indeed, that inwardness of apprehension at which it aims, towards which it is steadily directed, is a necessary condition of valid thinking in the field of liberal studies.

I have spoken so far of what can be done – of windows that can be opened on the world at large – simply as opportunity offers. But any consistent scheme of English study will suggest particular directions of interest in the exploration of the extra-literary relations of literature, of the wider civilization which at any time is so much more than a background to creative achievement. If, for example, the student attempts to get some sense of 'the Shakespearean moment' (and his study of the drama alone must surely prompt him to make the attempt), he will be led to consider the state of the language, and all that implies; the assumptions, interest and habits of mind uniting writers and audience at different levels; the availability of standards acting as a challenge to moral and intellectual inertia, as positive incitement to fuller and more conscious living; and so on.[1] In other words, through works whose continuing vitality is a safeguard against merely abstract and external formulations, he will *begin* to grasp the meaning of a living culture and a living tradition. And he will find that this understanding, even in what he may come to consider its elementary stages, illuminates for him, helps him to think effectively about, the world of Yeats and Eliot – which in any case he has to live in. He is also likely to ask himself some decidedly relevant questions about the nature of the forces that created the modern world, even though it is outside literature that he will look for the answers. Of course there is no question of English providing 'solutions' to the

[1] Patrick Cruttwell's *The Shakespearean Moment* is a valuable introduction to the study of the forces that help to explain the literary fertility of the period. Since space is limited, and it is desirable to be specific, perhaps I may refer to some papers of my own that suggest further lines of inquiry: 'On the Social Background of Metaphysical Poetry' (*Scrutiny*, XIII, 1), 'Reflections on Clarendon's History of the Rebellion' (*Scrutiny*, XV, 2), and *Poetry, Politics and the English Tradition* (Chatto and Windus, 1954).

problems of civilization in our time. All that is claimed is that the study of English literature can set young minds working on matters that anyone alive to his time will recognize as central; that by the very nature of its basic material it keeps the student in touch with standards of effective thinking and imaginative awareness; that it is in the fullest sense a liberal and humanizing study.

## 4

What I have tried to say is that, in a liberal education, English has a three-fold function: there is the basic training in understanding, in clarity of expression and respect for the living language; there is the awakening and education of the imagination; and there is the almost incidental but nevertheless important opening out from literature into questions concerning varied aspects of civilization which – approached from that angle – should be seen in a truly human way, not abstracted and schematized. And now let me add the postscript that I threatened. It shall be brief.

There are various ways of describing what is perhaps the chief danger of our time. We may speak with Gabriel Marcel of the spirit of abstraction, which so easily allies itself with fanaticism and violence. Or we may use the terminology of Martin Buber and speak of the encroachment of the world of 'it' (the world of experiencing, using and manipulating) upon the world of 'thou' (the world of meeting and relationship). However we describe it, what is in question is the substitution of a surface awareness for awareness in depth, the substitution of general notions for a living response to the individual and unique, the obscuring of a whole dimension of consciousness. 'Even for our grandparents', says Rilke, 'a "House", a "Well", a familiar tower, their very dress, their cloak, was infinitely more, infinitely more intimate: almost everything a vessel in which they found and stored humanity. Now there come crowding over from America, empty, indifferent things, pseudo-things, *dummy life*. . . . A house in the American understanding, an American apple or vine, has *nothing* in common with the house, the fruit, the grape into which the hope and meditation of our forefathers had entered.'[1]

[1] *Sonnets to Orpheus*, tr. Leishman, quoted in Introduction, pp. 20-21.

And the impoverishment of spirit that Rilke here describes can spread even more disastrously beyond our relations with things and places, important as these relations are. There is the encroachment of what may be called a newspaper consciousness, made up of a few stereotypes; there is the habit of thinking of men either as masses or in terms of economic functioning; there is, in so many spheres, the loss of inwardness, of relationship, of living significance, which has been a major theme of our greatest writers for the last half-century or more: Henry James called it 'the awful doom of general dishumanisation'. It is, I think, in this context that, ultimately, we have to set our concern for literature and the teaching of literature. By which I do not mean that we should approach our pupils with a sombre missionary zeal, or that we should regard literature as a panacea for the world's ills. Literature is not a substitute for either religion or philosophy; and it may reasonably be said that we do enough if we foster in those we teach a delight in understanding what a few great authors and a handful of lesser ones have to give. But little as we may need to say explicitly about the function of literature, our sense of these wider implications should, I think, underlie and inform our teaching. For the fact remains that literature – and for Englishmen English literature above all – is *one* of the great humanizing agencies: it is a bulwark against arid, 'surface' theorizing; it helps to keep in good heart the soil from which genuinely responsive living may grow. It is because the poet is, as Wordsworth said, 'a rock of defence for human nature' that English literature has its necessary and central place in a liberal education.

# *A Reflection*

## DENYS THOMPSON

THE journal from which this volume is extracted has been in existence for twenty-three years. The fact offers an opportunity for taking stock of the teaching of English.

Two things strike one. First, a development actively hostile to the teaching of English: the degree to which children have become the target of a commercial environment that spends much cash and cunning on persuading them to eat sweets, read comics and spend their shillings in ways profitable to the entertainment industry.

Secondly, thc extent to which the examination system has spread and strengthened its grip. For some subjects this may not matter very much. Most of them have a 'content', and examinations may provide a stimulus to and a gauge of success, so that teachers may be happier with examinations than they would be without. But the best of English teaching cannot be examined. The teacher's aim is to bring to life and develop his pupils' capacity for literature. There are other aims, we know; we need not despise the bread-and-butter tasks of developing the power of communication, but it is one that cannot engage more than a small part of the interest and energy of the teacher and his pupils.

Examinations cannot test what the teacher of English is constantly trying to evokc – a response to literature. They do not pretend to. Instead, according to a common formula, they set out to measure 'a candidate's ability to use and understand the mother tongue'. But how much of this ability can be assessed under conditions in which tens of thousands of candidates take the same questions, to be marked with uniform fairness? Inevitably those questions are set that can be speedily and accurately marked – hit-or-miss comprehension questions, identification and labelling of figures of speech, the correction of synthetic grammatical mistakes, clause analysis, and so on. In short, the candidate has to learn certain tricks with words to pass an examination that certifies his proficiency in such manipulation. The O level Language Paper tells us nothing about a candidate's capacity for expression; it is well known that almost illiterate pupils can be pushed through without any improvement in their illiteracy. Futile as a test, it is disastrous for teaching. Commonly the G.C.E. year at O level is spent (so far as English is concerned) in working through back papers or depressing little manuals designed all too efficiently to look like back papers. And this in what is for most children their last year at school, when the effort should be made to get them to read with zest and enterprise. The dreary business sometimes occupies a good part even of a child's fourth year at the secondary school, and throughout the school time is wasted on working through comprehension booklets that should be spent on real books. The examination system produces a flow of text-books that choke the life out of teaching.

No wonder then that so many young people on leaving school are incompetent writers. No wonder that the universities find that all subjects are suffering from their students' increasing inability to express their meaning clearly and simply. Worse still, they have nothing to express, because they have been fed on a diet of snippets instead of whole books. The universities of Oxford and Cambridge (in the explicit hope that others will follow) have decided to remedy a situation, caused in part by the O level Language Paper, by yet another language paper. Thus the examination stranglehold on the teaching of English in schools is complete, and its life throttled. The two universities cannot seriously have examined the problem that faced them. Had they made the slightest attempt to do so they could not have failed to see that the English Language Paper at O level is much worse than useless. It is a bar to developing literacy, and it is illiteracy from which we and the university entrants suffer. The universities through their examining boards have helped to deaden much of the teaching of English; they now expose their full irresponsibility by imposing a test that can only worsen the plight it is intended to alleviate.

The universities with a touching innocence profess their belief that their new entrance test will not affect Sixth Form work; 'it can be taken in the stride'. What inevitably will happen is that the average Sixth Form will be fed on back papers and the expected manuals. The universities could hardly have done worse if they had gone over to the American system and evolved a paper of multiple-choice questions, electronically marked and processed. Mr George Bruce (Secretary to the London University Examinations Council) in discussing the American questionnaire-type examination has observed:

> If it is argued that this type of question makes for bad teaching and harmful coaching, I would only say that at present we sell about fifteen thousand pounds' worth of past G.C.E. papers each year and the amount of working through these must be enormous and stultifying. Once candidates are familiar with the multiple-choice techniques there is little or no advantage in further practice at old papers.

'Enormous and stultifying.' That very neatly sums up the impact of examinations upon the teaching of English. What the older universities decide and the example they offer will eventually influence secondary schools of all types. This makes it all the more deplorable that it seems never to have occurred to them, in planning their new Language Paper, that the poor English of undergraduates is the consequence of a decline in the study of literature in school and at home. Illiteracy is exactly what the word implies.

For the standards that help to measure good writing we must turn to literature. For instruction in writing, the best guide is literature. And without the ideas, perceptiveness and sensitivity that flow from the study of literature practice in writing is sterile. The good writing sought by the universities on the one hand and by employers on the other can only to a limited extent be taught; and then the best teaching must draw its life from literature. Plenty of good reading and teaching related to it will help writing to come, almost as a by-product. This is not just a pious hope. The 'Ford' report (*Liberal Education in a Technical Age*) noted that the most marked improvement in 'everyday' English occurred in those colleges where the teaching was not restricted by a utilitarian conception. Conversely, in those parts of the English-speaking world where much energy is devoted, with the aid of heavy and exhaustive text-books, to practical English, the results are meagre.

It ought to be a truism that the literature chosen should be the best that children can grasp; and this for the average and below-average child may not be very ambitious. Most of their reading should be whole books – short books, easy books, perhaps abridgements, but books and not collections of extracts. There may be a place for the latter, if they are made with a special purpose. But the mass of collections made for schools are pointless, and seem designed merely to keep the children mildly entertained. Nor for most children should there be much in the way of 'appreciation', some not very elaborate written work being set to make sure that the pupil has read the book. With abler children there is a place for looking closely at the effects of key passages – how they are obtained, and what contribution of background, mood or narrative, they make to the total impact of the work. But not volumes of extracts for comprehension exercises. The output of these is phenomenal, and the results tedium and a distaste for English periods. If children are capable of such exercises, the work should be done in connection with the books, the whole books, that they are reading.

Too many text-books, too much examining. The text-books fence off children from the enjoyment of literature. The examining has produced a generation of tested and graded teachers that accepts the chains because it does not know freedom. But there is still ample room for the teacher of English who sees it as his main concern to bring his pupils into touch with literature; the same anarchy that permits really poor work also provides excellent scope for teaching with life in it. And any teachers-in-training who read this can be certain that almost all children respond at once to teaching with life in it – however bored they may be by grammar and exercises and aids. This volume aims at the goal, and points the direction. A companion volume would offer ways and means.

# IX

## *NOTES AND BIBLIOGRAPHIES*

### I

(The dates refer to the year in which the articles were first published.)

II *'A GATHERING OF VOICES'*

A much fuller anthology well worth careful reading is to be found in *Young Readers, Young Writers* edited by Boris Ford (Hutchinson).

III English and Idiom in the Primary School (1956-7)

The Point of Making Things Up (1953)

A further draft of this essay is to be found in *English for Maturity* by David Holbrook (C.U.P.).

Teaching Writing in the Grammar School (1942)

For further stimulating work in the grammar school see *The Education of the Poetic Spirit* by M. L. Hourd (Heinemann).
The poems discussed by Mr Reeves, together with many others just as useful, can be found in *Collected Poems of D. H. Lawrence* (Heinemann), and *One Hundred and Seventy Poems from the Chinese* by A. Waley (Constable).

IV Grammar, Language and Style (1953)

The Teaching of Formal English Grammar (1955)

For further thought on the teaching of grammar and linguistics, the reader might well turn up:

*Growth and Structure of the English Language* by Otto Jespersen (Blackwell)
*The Story of Language* by Mario Pei (Allen & Unwin)

English and Intelligence (1951)

Some of the books behind this article included:

*Intelligence, Concrete and Abstract* by W. P. Alexander (C.U.P.)
*Northamptonshire Composition Scale* by G. P. Williams (Harrap)
*The Nature of Intelligence* by L. L. Thurstone (Kegan Paul)
*The Psychology of Intelligence* by J. Piaget (Routledge).

V Twelfth Night (1953)

For further reading on *Twelfth Night* see:

*Shakespeare and his Comedies* by J. Russell Brown (Methuen)
*Shakespeare's Festive Comedies* by C. Barber (Princeton U.P.)

An Approach to Nostromo (1959)

For further work on Nostromo see:

*The Great Tradition* by F. R. Leavis (Chatto)
*Introduction to the Novel* by A. Kettle (Hutchinson)

Conrad: The Shadow Line (1947)

For a school edition of *The Shadow Line* see:

*Three Tales from Conrad* by D. Brown (Hutchinson)

Looking at a Poem (1954)

The reader is reminded of the brilliant analysis of Shakespeare's sonnet 129 in:

*A Survey of Modernist Poetry* by L. Riding and R. Graves (Heinemann)

and of the different kinds of local perception in

*Seven Types of Ambiguity* by William Empson (Chatto)

A Plea for Mediaeval Drama (1955)

For seminal discussions of mediaeval drama see:

*English Drama from Early Times to the Elizabethans* by A. P. Rossiter (Hutchinson)
*Mediaeval English Literature: the non-Chaucerian Tradition* by J. Speirs (Faber)

For texts see:

*The Chester Mystery Plays* edited by M. Hussey (Heinemann)
*The York Cycle of Mystery Plays* edited by J. S. Purvis (S.P.C.K.)

The Authorized Version of the Bible (1957)

For further reading see, in whole or in part:

*Records of the English Bible* by A. W. Pollard (Frowde) (esp. the introduction)
*English Literature in the Sixteenth Century* by C. S. Lewis (O.U.P.)
*English Literature in the Earlier Seventeenth Century* by D. Bush (O.U.P.)
*The Work of Tindale* by S. L. Greenslade (Blackie) which contains an
*Essay on Tindale and the English Language* by G. D. Bone
*Man's Unconquerable Mind* by R. W. Chambers (Cape) (for the chapter on More and Tindale)
*On Englishing the Bible* by R. A. Knox (Burns)
*The Making of English* by H. Bradley (Macmillan)

*The English Language* by C. L. Wrenn (Methuen)

*The Bible in its Ancient and English Versions* by H. Wheeler Robinson (O.U.P.) (esp. chapters 5, 6 and 7: this last is the best of all comment on the language, style and influence of the English Bible).

Some suggestions for reading in the Bible itself:

### NARRATIVE

The Wooing of Rebekah. Genesis xxiv
The Life of Joseph. Genesis xxxvii, xxxix-l
The Death of Sisera. Judges iv
Jephthah's Daughter. Judges xi
The Adventures of Samson. Judges xiii-xvi
The Books of Ruth, Esther, Judith, Tobit
The Saga of David. I. Samuel xvi to end of Book
II. Samuel-Kings ii
The Death of Saul. I. Chronicles x
Solomon in all his glory. II. Chronicles ix
Daniel. Daniel i-vi
The Nativity narrative. St. Luke ii
Paul at Ephesus. Acts xix. 21-41
His sea-voyage. Acts xxvii-xxviii, 14

### WISDOM OR GNOMIC LITERATURE

Book of Job
Passages in praise of Wisdom: Proverbs iii, 13-19; Proverbs viii; the Wisdom of Solomon vii, 22-viii, 9
The virtuous woman. Proverbs xxxi, 10 to end
Her opposite. Proverbs vii
The virtuous woman and her opposite. Ecclesiasticus xxv
'Vanity of Vanities'. Ecclesiastes, end of last chapter
The occupations of men. Ecclesiasticus xxxviii, 24 seq
Human misery. Ecclesiasticus xl, 1-10
Natural Beauty. Ecclesiasticus xliii
'Let us now praise famous men.' Ecclesiasticus xliv, 1-15
'Let us crown ourselves with rosebuds.' The Wisdom of Solomon ii
The souls of the righteous. The Wisdom of Solomon iii, 1-9

### SELECTED PSALMS

xviii, xxii, xlv, lxxxviii, xci, cvii, cix, cxxxvii, cxlviii

### SATIRE AND INVECTIVE

Against Idols. Jeremiah x, 1-16; Isaiah xliv, 9-20
The Fall of Tyre. Ezekiel xxvii
False Shepherds. Ezekiel xxxiv, 1-10

### ELEGY

David's Lament over Saul and Jonathan. II. Samuel i, 17-27

### LOVE LYRICS

The Song of Songs (Solomon's Song, Canticles)

### POETIC PASSAGES FROM ISAIAH

The down-to-earth imagery of Ch. i
The lyrical exaltation of xl
The dramatic dialogue of lxiii, 1-14

### PAULINE PROSE

Hymn to Love. I. Corinthians xiii
The Whole Armour of God. Ephesians vi, 10-20
'What shall we then say. . . ?' Romans viii, 31-37
Letter to Philemon

### VISION LITERATURE

The Valley of Dry Bones. Ezekiel xxxvii
Dies Irae. Joel ii, 1-11
Revelation i and xxii.

VI THE MAKING OF TEXT-BOOKS (1951)

THE PRESENT-DAY DEBASEMENT OF THE LANGUAGE (1959)

LET US HAVE NO PRETENCES (1957)

GEORGE STURT (1956)

CALDWELL COOK (1945)

Caldwell Cook's own account of his work is in his book *The Play Way* (Heinemann)

FREE WRITING (1958).

VII MARKING COMPOSITION (1960)

MEASURING THE INNER LIGHT (1950)

An Exercise in Applied Criticism (1944)

The reader might find it worth while to turn back to:

*Principles of Literary Criticism* by I. A. Richards (Routledge)

and for discussion of Yeats' poetry to:

*New Bearings in English Poetry* by F. R. Leavis (Chatto)

*Explorations* by L. C. Knights (Chatto).

VIII The Place of English Literature in a Liberal Education (1958)

A Reflection (1961)

For important, though very different, 'fundamental' writings bearing upon English and its place in education and in society, see:

*Fantasia of the Unconscious* by D. H. Lawrence (Martin Secker)

*English for the English* by G. Sampson (C.U.P.)

*The Problem of Style* by J. M. Murry (O.U.P.)

*Culture and Environment* by F. R. Leavis and D. Thompson (Chatto)

*Education and the University* by F. R. Leavis (Chatto)

The cultural changes in the 21 years spanned so far by the two journals can, perhaps, best be sensed by reading:

*Fiction and the Reading Public* by Q. D. Leavis (Chatto) – 1932

*Culture and Environment* by F. R. Leavis and D. Thompson (Chatto) – 1933

as against –

*The Uses of Literacy* by R. Hoggart (Chatto) – 1957

*Culture and Society* by R. Williams (Chatto) – 1958.

## 2

## A brief bibliography of articles in the back numbers of *The Use of English*

### 1. WORK IN PRIMARY SCHOOLS

| AUTHOR | ARTICLE | VOLUME AND NUMBER |
|---|---|---|
| E. Austen | Writing at 9 years | III. 3 |
| J. C. Ives | Teaching Poetry | VI. 3 |
| I. Michael | Examiner and Junior School | V. 2 |
| F. Stevens | Choice of Poetry | V. 4 & VI. 1 |
| R. M. Towes | Looking to the Grammar School | VII. 3 |
| W. Worthy | English in the Junior School | IV. 1 |

### 2. WORK IN GRAMMAR SCHOOLS

| AUTHOR | ARTICLE | VOLUME AND NUMBER |
|---|---|---|
| D. R. Barnes | Reading in the First Form | X. 4 |
| J. T. Evans | Verse Writing in Class | X. 2 |
| J. Hanratty | The Douglas Tragedy | X. 4 |
| R. B. Kennedy | Chaucer in the Sixth | VII. 2 |
| M. K. Paffard | Free Writing | IX. 1 & 2 |
| B. Reeve | Learning English | I. 4 |
| W. Walsh | Literary Texts | IV. 1 |
| J. Wilks | Writing Free Verse | XI. 3 |

### 3. WORK IN SECONDARY MODERN SCHOOLS

| | | |
|---|---|---|
| E. Blishen | English in the Modern School | X. 4 |
| R. J. Harris | English in the Modern School | X. 2 |
| D. Holbrook | Some Notes on English Song | V. 4 |
| J. H. Walsh | Composition in the Modern School | IV. 3 |

### 4. WORK WITH ADULT STUDENTS

| | | |
|---|---|---|
| G. H. Bantock | English in the Training College | IV. 2 |
| M. Diggle | English in Further Education | V. 1 |
| W. Walsh | Literature in the Training of Teachers | XI. 3 & 4 |
| R. Williams | Literature Teaching in Adult Education | III. 3 |

### 5. TEACHING GRAMMAR

| | | |
|---|---|---|
| E. Baranyai | Learning Grammar | I. 1 |
| H. Diack | A Re-examination of Grammar | VII. 4 |
| D. J. Ritchie | Meaningful Grammar | V. 3 |
| D. M. Skew | Grammar: Dry Bones | XI. 3 |
| S. Tucker | Grammar: Still A Problem | X. 2 |
| F. Whitehead | Modern Linguistics | IX. 1 |

### 6. WORK IN DRAMA

| | | |
|---|---|---|
| T. R. Barnes | Drama and Values | VIII. 2 |
| T. R. Barnes | Producing Shakespeare | III. 3 |
| J. Hanratty | Arden of Feversham | XI. 3 |
| L. Salingar | Shakespeare in School | I. 2 |
| F. Whitehead | Drama in the Classroom | I. 1 |

### 7. WORK ON PARTICULAR TEXTS

| AUTHOR | ARTICLE | VOLUME AND NUMBER |
|---|---|---|
| T. R. Barnes | Julius Caesar | VIII. 4 |
| F. Chapman | Far From the Madding Crowd | XI. 1 |
| F. Chapman | Henry IV. Part One | V. 1 |
| F. Chapman | The Nun's Priest's Tale | VI. 3 |
| M. Emslie | As You Like It | VI. 2 |
| C. Gillie | Samson Agonistes | V. 4 |
| C. Gillie | The Tempest | VII. 1 |
| J. D. Hainsworth | Redgauntlet | IX. 2 |
| J. Hanratty | Hardy in School | VII. 4 |
| M. Hussey | The Horse Dealer's Daughter | V. 2 |
| M. Hussey | Great Expectations | VII. 2 |
| R. O'Malley | Macbeth | VI. 4 |
| J. R. Osgerby | Pride and Prejudice | XII. 2 |
| B. C. Southam | Gibbon's Autobiography | X. 2 |
| B. C. Southam | Sense and Sensibility | XI. 1 |
| J. H. Walsh | History of Mr Polly | V. 2 |
| J. G. Watson | The Unquiet Grave | VII. 1 |

### 8. 'CULTURE AND ENVIRONMENT'

| | | |
|---|---|---|
| R. Hoggart | Towards a Candy Floss World | VIII. 2 & 3 |
| C. Poster and G. Summerfield | Newspaper Projects | X. 1 |
| J. G. Watson | Self Education | IV. 4 |
| R. Williams | Stocktaking – 1 | I. 3 |

### 9. THE ENGLISH LANGUAGE PAPER AT 'O' LEVEL

| | | |
|---|---|---|
| T. R. Barnes | English Language in the G.C.E. | IV. 4 |
| J. Britton | English Language at 'O' level | VI. 3 |
| D. Brown | The Use of English | XII. 2 |
| J. Holloway | Use of English and Use of Literature | XII. 3 |

### 10. A MISCELLANEOUS GROUP OF OTHER THEMES

| | | |
|---|---|---|
| J. R. Baker | English in Scientific Papers | VIII. 1 |
| I. Michael | Text-Books and Teaching | VIII. 1 |
| R. O'Malley | Accumulation and Growth | XI. 1 |
| M. Paffard | Free Writing | IX. 2 & 3 |
| J. Reeves | Counterfeit Poetry | IV. 4 |
| F. Whitehead | English through Exercises | III. 3 |